The Infrastructure We Ride On

Joseph Berechman

The Infrastructure We Ride On

Decision Making in Transportation Investment

palgrave
macmillan

Joseph Berechman
City College of New York
University of New York
New York, NY, USA

ISBN 978-3-030-09034-0 ISBN 978-3-319-74606-7 (eBook)
https://doi.org/10.1007/978-3-319-74606-7

Softcover re-print of the Hardcover 1st edition 2018

Cover Design: Fatima Jamadar

Printed on acid-free paper

This Palgrave Macmillan imprint is published by the registered company Springer International Publishing AG part of Springer Nature.
The registered company address is: Gewerbestrasse 11, 6330 Cham, Switzerland

In memory of my parents

Acknowledgment

I wish to acknowledge the generous financial support for editorial assistance that I have received from Tel Aviv University, Israel. I am also quite grateful to the University Transportation Research Center, Region 2, for their financial support when conducting the basic research for the book. I would like to thank Mrs. Nina Reshef for her painstaking editorial work of the manuscript. Special thanks to Ms. Patrizia Nobbe who did a first-rate job in helping me to build the database, used in this book, and perform statistical tests, which she also used for her dissertation. My research assistant, Mr. Ahmed Elkhouly, did a great job compiling the authors index.

Several of my academic colleagues were kind enough to give me useful comments and suggestions on parts of early drafts of the manuscript. In particular, the following colleagues (in alphabetic order) read chapters of the book and provided me with invaluable insights, which I tried to incorporate into the manuscript. These are Professor David Gillen, The Sauder School of Business, University of British Columbia; Professor Genevieve Giuliano, the Price School of Public Policy, Planning and Development, University of Southern California; and Professor Patricia Mokhtarian, School of Civil and Environmental Engineering, Georgia Institute of Technology. I received other useful comments from faculty and students during seminars I gave on topics discussed in the book. While the contributions of these scholars, undoubtedly, have improved the manuscript, the responsibility for the views, analysis and conclusions expressed in the book is solely mine.

Last but not least I wish to thank profoundly my wife, Professor Iris Geva-May, visiting professor at NYU, for her support and the many discussions we had on issues related to public policy and policy analysis, which are her areas of expertise.

Contents

About the Author

Joseph Berechman earned his BA degree in Economics from The Hebrew University in Jerusalem, and his MBA and PhD from the University of Pennsylvania in Philadelphia. He is an emeritus professor from Tel Aviv University. Presently, he is a Marvin Kristein Chair professor of economics at the City College, The City University of New York. Professor Berechman is the author of numerous articles and six books. His main areas of academic interest are transportation economics and policy.

List of Figures

List of Tables

CHAPTER 1

Introduction

1.1 Rationale

Transportation infrastructure projects, of all types, fall within the domain of public investments that reflect public sector priorities and objectives, non-pecuniary and financial constraints, and decision-making processes. Since infrastructure investments typically affect large populations, extend over large territories and carry substantial opportunity costs, many western democracies have instituted formal procedures for quantitatively appraising their multiple outcomes as aides in choosing optimal projects. These procedures, their underlying rationale, analytical structure and empirical applications are subjects of graduate classes in various fields of academic studies, including economics, public policy, civil engineering, city planning and environmental studies. Governments, at all levels, have engaged numerous professionals and resources in the technical analysis of specific infrastructure projects. These undertakings encompass highly skilled activities ranging from the coding of networks—highways and rail—to estimating travel time and the ensuing cost savings, to assessing the monetary returns on the investment and its alternatives.

Against this background one would expect that the selection and implementation of projects, especially capital-intensive mega-projects, would be rational and optimal relative to their costs and benefits, broadly defined. And yet, numerous studies have revealed that this portrayal of infrastructure project evaluation and choice is largely inaccurate. A significant

J. Berechman, *The Infrastructure We Ride On*,
https://doi.org/10.1007/978-3-319-74606-7_1

proportion of implemented mega-projects have been found to be inferior *ex ante*, with many not delivering the returns they were promised to offer *ex post*. In fact, many projects were not subjected to any type of evaluation, formal or otherwise, and were selected for implementation either on shaky and suspicious grounds or due to funding that, once secured, effectively precluded conducting formal scrutiny of impacts and validation of the project's transportation-economic value. Given the dire state of funding for new transportation infrastructure and the below-standard maintenance of many systems in place, one cannot but wonder how to explain this phenomenon, where huge investments are made in unworthy projects. To be clear, by ***unworthy*** I mean projects with unacceptable *ex-ante* net welfare contributions indicated by, say, insignificant benefits-to-costs ratios, or *ex post* by substantial cost overruns, way off target implementation periods and excessive under-utilization.

The common explanation given to this phenomenon is that politics, however defined, rather than transportation-economic values and criteria, represents the decisive factor in project selection (Altshuler and Luberoff 2003). But is this truly a credible account of how projects are selected? Do other factors enter the choice process? If so, what are they and what are their relative weights? Most crucially, how can the project selection and decision-making be characterized? These questions constitute the rationale for writing—and reading—this book.

The spending of massive financial resources on transportation infrastructure, particularly low-performing mega-projects, represents a public sector puzzle[1]: Why are public funds being wasted? Put differently, why are projects built when their opportunity costs, namely, the returns on alternative projects subsequently not built, are often significant? That is, the wasting of funds implies the generation of insufficient benefits given the costs, meaning that society foregoes returns that could have been realized had the money been invested wisely. Such foregone benefits may include congestion mitigation, improved accessibility and reliability, reduced road fatalities and lower air pollution levels. In social welfare terms, the expenditure of resources whose value exceeds that of the received benefits implies net welfare losses. From the public's perspective, the problem is further confounded when we consider the role of our elected officials as guardians of public funds; hence the importance of studying the process leading to the choice of unworthy projects. Indeed, who will guard the guardians?

1.2 Objectives and Scope

A project's engineering and planning aspects are, obviously, extremely important for its construction and successful utilization. High-yielding projects can turn out to be failures if marred with faulty planning and design, as well as sloppy management. In this book, however, I am mainly concerned with the non-technical factors that underlie the decision-making surrounding project choice and implementation. Chief among these factors are the project's non-engineering transportation-economic attributes, such as the value of improved accessibility, together with its institutional, financial and social impact factors.

In concurrence with a common assumption in the field of political economy, I assume that politicians are incentivized by these factors in light of their goals of garnering voters' support and reducing opposition through policies and resource allocation decisions. The direct objective of this book is, therefore, to analyze the major factors that tend to underlie project decision-making so as to unpack the reasons why projects are so often selected despite their inability to meet acceptable project choice criteria. From my perspective, the analysis of such choices calls for the use of political economy theories and methods, which explains why I have adopted such an approach in this book.

The common approach to the economic analysis of socio-economic phenomena rests on construction of a model for the purpose of *describing* and *explaining* the selected phenomena. Once the model's underlying logic and tenets are elaborated, it can be used to *predict* the consequences of selected policy changes. For example, we can theorize and then build a formal model to explain how users make rational choices between transportation modes for their daily commute given their socio-economic characteristics and each mode's travel time and price attributes. Once the model has been formalized, we can estimate its parameters, which will then be used to predict the impact on future choices once one or more attributes have been modified (e.g., by a policy that shortens travel times by public transit).

Another use of economic modeling is to *critique* economic decisions. In this case, a theory-based model is used to ascertain the appropriateness of the decision-maker's rationale and reasoning (Gilboa et al. 2014). For example, public-finance models based on economic welfare theory suggest that a project's net welfare contribution should be the key criterion for its implementation. A selection decision that fails to meet this criterion is thus open to criticism regarding the reasoning and motivation behind it.

The allocation of societal resources involves judgments of two fundamental types: those of efficiency and those of fairness or equity. Based on accepted economic principles, we distinguish between a *normative* and a *positive* economic analysis. Under the former, the goal is to derive rules capable of indicating the optimal allocation of resources, where optimality refers to efficiency and fairness or to their tradeoffs. An example would be the derivation of an optimal highway congestion toll that should be collected to support highway improvements and/or expansion. In contrast, positive analysis focuses on *what is*, where the goal is to ascertain how economic agents actually behave given the market prices and economic incentives observed. Estimation of the degree to which highway congestion will be reduced following a road capacity expansion project provides an instance of positive analysis, with equity and fairness criteria embedded within.

These two types of economic inquiry are reflected in a third area, namely *policy design*, defined here as the use of normative rules and positive observations to construct a plan aimed at achieving policy objectives. To illustrate, a regional congestion-mitigation plan can combine pricing rules (e.g., optimal tolls) with a new infrastructure investment (e.g., a rail line), using information on how auto users actually behave in similar situations when a new transit facility is built. We should note, however, that a policy-maker, when stating her policy choices, simultaneously reveals her value-based rules for reaching those goals. She may decide to invest in a specific subway line, thus reflecting her aims of reducing congestion (crowdedness) on other lines, but also to stimulate real-estate development in the adjacent areas.

Given these types of economic models and economic inquiry, the focus in this book is on the use of transportation-economic-based criteria to critically examine observed infrastructure investment projects. My examination takes the form of assessments regarding the properties of a sample of projects rooted in public investment policies that presumably were derived from the application of acceptable efficiency and equity rules. For example, from a normative perspective, transportation investments should meet economic efficiency criteria such as benefit-cost ratios above a designated threshold, with benefits and costs, including externalities, equitably distributed among the relevant populations, or ensure that no single socio-economic group disproportionately bears the costs. If an *ex-ante* analysis reveals this not to be the case, for example, the actual benefit-to-cost ratio is below the acceptable level, the project is regarded as inferior or unworthy.

The data presented in this book demonstrate that many transportation mega-projects are veritably unworthy investments. The question asked here is, therefore, why such poor investment decisions were made at all. To begin answering this question, the book hypothesizes that the respective investment decisions were the product of relationships between an array of inputs and interested stakeholders. The book subsequently sets out the kinds of inputs that enter most if not all decision processes, together with the nature of their inter-relationships. These determinants include, among others, the project's history, the institutions affected, the identity of special interest groups, demand and cost projections, and sources of funding.

1.3 The Book's Structure

Following this introductory chapter, the book is divided into three main parts. Part A, entitled "The Conundrum of Mega-Project Provision", sets the scene for the subsequent analysis by reviewing, in Chap. 2, the gap between transportation investment needs and actual funding. Chapter 3 discusses the formal requirements and procedures applied by most Western countries for investment analysis and choice. Then, in light of the universality of these practices, the chapter asks why a significant number of projects are, in fact, inferior or unworthy. Chapter 4, which introduces a paradigm explaining actual investment decision-making, aims at explaining why inferior and unworthy projects are indeed selected.

Part B, "The Political Economy of Mega-Projects", critically examines those factors hypothesized to impact on decision-making and project choice. Chapter 5 examines the nature and role of benefit-cost forecasting. The project's history and its implications for problem framing and public acceptance are discussed in Chap. 6. The roles of opposition and special interest groups are examined in Chap. 7. Chapter 8 analyzes the crucial influence of funding availability in this process. Chapter 9 reviews the role of oversight institutions in project choice. The effects of equity considerations and transportation externalities on decision-making are examined in Chap. 10.

Part C, "Where It All Comes Together", summarizes the previous analysis relative to our chosen sphere, transportation infrastructure investments. Using models and methods of decision-making under risk,

Chap. 11 first reviews what we can learn about infrastructure decision-making in the public sector. The chapter then presents conclusions regarding what actually determined the observed choice of projects. It demonstrates the inevitability of choosing inferior and unworthy projects under current practices. Lastly, the chapter recommends several policy actions that, if adopted, should improve transportation infrastructure investment decision-making.

1.4 A Note on Data

Many sources of information were accessed within the framework of the book's analysis. Most important is the database constructed by Dr. Nobbe and me (Nobbe and Berechman 2014). It contains information on 60 mega-projects, worldwide, relative to 58 key project attributes. A detailed description of the database is provided in Chap. 4, Appendix.

One key shortcoming of our database, and all other data sources for that matter, is that it does not report alternatives to the projects actually selected, relative to their transportation-economic value. Thus, we do not know whether other alternatives were considered and, if so, whether the best one was chosen. Similarly, there is virtually no direct information on the actual decision process and decision criteria used to reach the respective decision. Hence, the best we can do is to treat decision-making as a black box and observe the degree to which the postulated input factors entered and influenced all the selected cases. Concurrently, we analyze the process's outputs, namely, each project's individual attributes. The core of the argument is that this approach—entailing the observation and assessment of inputs and outputs—will explain the fundamentals of transportation infrastructure investment decision-making.

Note

1. To illustrate, New York's Second Avenue Subway (Phase 1 is currently under construction) expenditures have reached $2.25 billion per mile. While this project is on the very expensive side, the costs of most infrastructure projects, especially rail, reach billions of US dollars.

References

Altshuler, A., and D. Luberoff. 2003. *Mega-Projects: The Changing Politics of Urban Public Investment*. Washington, DC: The Brookings Institution.

Gilboa, I., A. Postlewaite, L. Samuelson, and D. Schmeidler. 2014. *A Model of Modeling*. http://itzhakgilboa.weebly.com/uploads/8/3/6/3/8363317/gpss_model_of_modeling.pdf.

Nobbe, P., and J. Berechman. 2014. *The Politics of Infrastructure Investment Decision-Making: Report of the Statistical Analysis of Selected Hypotheses*. University Transportation Research Center Region 2, CCNY, CUNY, Final Report, March.

CHAPTER 2

Infrastructure Needs and Reality

2.1 Introduction

It has long been documented that from transportation-economic as well as social perspectives, a significant number of all transportation infrastructure mega-projects have been either complete failures or unworthy of initiation. Moreover, even among more or less successful projects, a large number were not subjected to comprehensive, or even partial, benefit-cost analysis. Hence, because all projects are the result of decision-making whether by individual decision-makers or by institutions, the fundamental question invited is as follows: What kind of process led to this reality? As stated in Chap. 1, the aim of this book is to investigate the major aspects of transportation investment decision-making in an attempt to respond to this question and thereby explain these phenomena.

As a preliminary to this task, we need to define the basic terms, concepts and tenets that underlie the analysis. I begin with the term *transportation mega-project*, which I define as a large-scale *new* enterprise, with capital outlays of $1 billion or more investment in capacity. Needless to say, this definition of mega-projects is arbitrary; its benefits lie in its handy distinction between large-scale infrastructure projects and other transport investments. In reality, the majority of transportation infrastructure projects involve repair, maintenance and rebuilding investments that are, by and large, of smaller scale than new capacity investments. And so, to be clear, the focus in this book is on the latter type of investment and its attributes.

J. Berechman, *The Infrastructure We Ride On*,
https://doi.org/10.1007/978-3-319-74606-7_2

Transportation projects are also distinguished by their physical characteristics. In this book I focus primarily on surface (land) transportation facilities including roads, bridges, tunnels, light and heavy rail and subways (metro or underground), and delve into the relationships of the respective questions relative to them. For example, the literature shows that rail projects are more prone to failure than are road projects due to the tendency to massively under-estimate their cost (generally referred to as cost overruns) and over-project future passenger loads (Flyvbjerg 2007).

Another distinguishing factor is that between *passenger* and *freight transportation*. While cargo hauling is a crucial component of any national or regional transportation system, in this book I focus almost exclusively on passenger transportation. A key reason for this choice is that many rail freight projects are carried out by private sector firms, where decision-making regarding capital investments differs significantly from the public sector. Although the fact that highway projects serve both types of transportation, freight (trucks) and passenger, complicates this choice (passenger travel constitutes the bulk of highway volume), it remains warranted.

The last major concept requiring definition is *locus of decision-making*. While mega-projects are all too often wholly or partially subsidized by central and state governments, transportation infrastructure projects are, by and large, local or regional in scope. In physical terms, very few extend beyond a metropolitan area or a region even though their impacts can spill over beyond these boundaries. As a result, *local decision-making* often lies at the core of the entire process. It therefore follows that I pay special attention to local (city, region and state) decision-making components.

With some exceptions, this book examines mega-projects already implemented. For each of these, many worthy projects probably never reached the construction stage. Exploration of the reasons for their failure to get beyond the proposal stage could shed light on the vagaries of the decision process underlying these as well as other projects. However, due to the lack of appropriate information, such an analysis cannot be performed, which does not prevent their mention, whenever possible, as examples of selected decision-making dynamics.

It might be argued that the decision-making process behind each mega-project should be viewed as a black box, representing a unique instance relative to key external and internal factors. *External factors* may include transportation and design properties, project location, socio-economic elements, funding availability, and institutional, political and judicial conditions. *Internal factors* may involve implicit decision rules and the identity and political stance of key players. In consequence, the decision-making underlying such projects is idiosyncratic and therefore bereft of the common features necessary for an analytical and/or comparative study. This argument might hold true if we were comparing the real-life decisions made. However, here I ask a different question: What determines transportation mega-project decision-making, and are these factors common, to varying degrees, to all mega-project decision processes? The emphasis here is, therefore, on the factors that affect most mega-project investments as a class of decisions rather than the specific decisions themselves, in full recognition that the last are, to a large extent, contextual in nature.

My main argument is that the key factors shaping mega-project decisions throughout are the project's history, the institutions involved (not least the agencies charged with oversight), support and opposition groups, funding methods and sources, as well as external effects (e.g., job creation, tax revenues and equity). The role and validity of the formal methodological framework employed to compute direct project benefits and costs is also to be considered. While the *importance* and *relevance* of each factor is probably unique per project, I maintain that these determinants affect *all* mega-project decision-making. The study of these determinants and their respective weights is where the book's main focus lies.

Beyond the analytic interest provided, a legitimate question to be asked pertains to the size of the phenomenon under study. A quantitative response requires that we ask the following: What is the overall level of transportation infrastructure investment in the developed world and, it follows, what proportion of these investments involve mega-projects? I deal with these issues next.

2.2 The Provision of Transportation Infrastructure Investment

As per my delineation of the topic, I will answer the previous questions in terms of land transportation mega-projects undertaken in developed countries, primarily highway and rail infrastructure facilities, for example, roads, bridges, tunnels, above- and underground passenger rail.

2.2.1 Extent of Investment

Recent statistical analyses of the data (ITF 2012, 2015) indicate that land transportation investment, as a percent of Gross Domestic Product (GDP), after some fluctuation has been fairly stable over the last two decades in developed countries. Land transportation has seen OECD countries (excluding Japan)[1] allocating about 0.8% of GDP annually[2] during the period 1995–2015 (in 2005 prices), and North American countries (USA, Mexico and Canada) investing about 0.6% of their GDP during the same period. In contrast, developing countries, especially in Eastern Europe,[3] have followed a different path, increasing their investment in land transport from about 0.8% (in 1995) to 1.7% of GDP in 2010.

However, when we consider investment in terms of volume, (1995 base year index = 100), we find diverging trends. OECD countries (excluding Japan) raised the volume of their investments from 1995 = 100 to over 280 in 2008–2009, but have since fallen back to 160 in 2013 (ITF 2015). North American countries, however, stayed at about the same level reached in 1995 despite marked population and travel growth during those years. Japan reduced its volume of investment from 100 projects (in 1995) to about 50 (in 2010). On the other hand, Australia and New Zealand more than doubled their investments during that period, from the same base year index (1995 = 100) to about 260 (in 2010).

A recent OECD report states that in its nine leading economies, which account for more than 60% of global GDP, annual long-term transportation investments in the amount of €14.3 trillion ($18.8 trillion) in real terms will be needed by 2020. And yet, irrespective of these forecasts, the respective countries' long-term investments amounted to only €9 trillion ($11.7 trillion) in 2010 (International Transport Forum 2013).

These trends raise three important questions. First, of all annual land investment, what is the proportion of new capital versus maintenance and renovation outlays? Second, what is the share of rail versus highway in overall land transport investment volume? Based on the resulting figures, we can answer a third question: What proportion of highway and rail investments can be defined as *mega-projects* out of all the new land transport investments made annually?

International Transport Forum (ITF) statistics show that maintenance and upgrading, as a proportion of road expenditures (in constant prices), varies considerably between countries. In 2009, for example, the share of maintenance was less than 20% in Japan, whereas it reached above 50% in Italy. In the USA, the rate was 30% (in 2009), while in the UK it was 40% (in 2010). For most countries, this rate averages about 30% of total road expenditures, with the balance representing new investments. Thus, if the USA's real GDP in 2010 was $13.24 trillion, then $18 billion and $42 billion were spent on maintenance and new land transport investments, respectively.[4] Whether these annual levels of maintenance and investment are sufficient to meet the country's needs is an important question, which I examine shortly (in Sect. 2.4). Here I focus on the proportion of new investment in highway and rail that can be considered to be on the mega-project level.

We should notice, first, that in most developed countries, the distribution of total transport investment between highway and rail is roughly 70% and 30%, respectively (ITF 2012). Using these figures as benchmarks, we estimate that of the $42 billion new transport investment in the USA in 2010, about $30 billion and $12 billion were spent on highway and rail, respectively. Referring to our mega-project database,[5] we further notice that the cost of a typical highway mega-project ranges from $1.3 billion to $5.37 billion ($2.71 billion on average), while that of a typical rail mega-project ranges from $1.0 billion to $16.0 billion ($5.04 billion on average). Using these figures, we can conclude that in the USA there were roughly 6–23 highway mega-projects and 1–15 rail mega-projects initiated in 2010.[6] Next I briefly comment on how the value of infrastructure is measured, a necessary introduction to needs estimation but also mega-project categorization.

2.3 Measuring the Value of Existing Infrastructure Facilities

There are several methods by which infrastructure facilities can be monetarily estimated. One method is to quantify the value of a project's direct benefits, such as time saved, and its indirect benefits, such as tax revenues. For example, consider, the costs incurred by disruption of Port Authority Trans Hudson (PATH) train service in lower Manhattan in the wake of the September 11, 2001, terror attack. The New York Metropolitan Transportation Authority (MTA) estimated that restoring basic PATH service cost $550 million. Due to the loss of PATH service, about 15,000 workers had to travel from locations in New Jersey to lower Manhattan using New Jersey Transit to Penn Station (average trip time: 30 minutes) and then on to their final destinations by subway (another 30 minutes, on average). Thus, the additional time cost is about one hour in each direction per day. If we value the time spent traveling at $25/hour, the added costs amounted to $100 million per year over the five- to six-year restoration period. Total opportunity costs of the PATH train system thus came to over $1.1 billion.

A related method is to compute the performance of the transportation system in place (in terms of travel time and costs) *without* a specific facility. The difference in direct transportation benefits of the system, with and without the facility, represents its economic value. The main problem with this approach is that it implicitly assumes activity locations as given, with no change over time. That is, it assumes that if the facility had not been built, residential and commercial locations would be the same as they are today, an assumption that may be very faulty.

If the facility generates revenues in the form of, let us say tolls or passenger fares, a third approach to computing the transportation facility's value would be to compute its discounted future stream of revenues. In the absence of actual tolls, as is the case with most roads, shadow tolls, namely the tolls that should have been imposed given the observed level of traffic, can be computed.

What undermines these or similar approaches, is the absence of the data needed to perform the computations for each existing transportation facility. Therefore, the most common approach to estimating the value of existing transportation facilities is to use their construction costs, less depreciation, as a reflection of their economic value.

2.4 Infrastructure Supply Versus Needs

The conventional approach for determining transportation infrastructure investment requirements is the so-called *needs-based approach*, which can be applied in two alternative ways. In the first, current travel conditions in an area are assessed against a yardstick of *desired* travel conditions (in units of traffic volume, travel times or costs); the difference is then defined as the area's *travel needs*. In the second, current traffic conditions are extrapolated to some future date; the resulting travel conditions are compared against *desired* travel conditions, with the difference likewise defined as *travel needs*. Within this framework, infrastructure investment is viewed as the supply-side response to these needs.[7] A related approach requires assessment of the engineering quality and Level of Service (LOS) of the transportation facilities in place as a means to determine the extent to which they meet present-day or future needs. The gap between what facilities actually deliver and what they ought to deliver, given their state of repair, determines the level of required new investments.

Several reports have documented required transport infrastructure investments based on these approaches. A celebrated report prepared by the American Society of Civil Engineers (ASCE) concluded that over the last 30 years, vehicle-miles traveled have doubled although total number of highway lanes grew only by 4.4%. The Federal Highway Administration has reported that over half of the vehicle-miles traveled on federal highways took place on roads that are in less than a *state of good repair*. Congestion in urban areas alone has resulted in 4.8 billion hours of traveler delays and consumption of an additional 3.9 billion gallons of fuel in 2009 (ASCE 2009, 2011). Given these *needs*, the same ASCE report called for an estimated $2.2 trillion to be spent over five years to repair the nation's deteriorating infrastructure. When broken down by mode of travel, the ASCE concluded that one-third of America's major roads are in poor or mediocre condition and that 45% of major urban highways are congested. Current (2000) spending of $70.3 billion per year for highway capital improvements is therefore well below the estimated $186 billion needed annually to substantially improve conditions.[8]

Turning to rail, the ASCE (2009, 2011) report stated that growth and changes in demand have created bottlenecks that constrain rail traffic in crucial areas. Freight and passenger rail generally share the same network; a significant potential increase in passenger rail demand will, as a result, intensify the challenges to freight rail capacity. As a consequence, more than $200 billion is needed from 2009 through 2035 to accommodate anticipated growth in both services.

Regarding mass transit, the Federal Transit Administration (FTA) concluded that transit use increased by 25% between 1995 and 2005, faster than any other mode of transportation. However, nearly half of American households do not have access to bus or rail transit, and only 25% have what they consider to be a good transit option. The FTA estimates that $15.8 billion is needed annually to maintain conditions, with another $21.6 billion required to improve conditions. In contrast to these estimates, federal capital outlays for transit were only $9.8 billion in 2008.[9]

2.5 Conclusion

All in all, in terms of funding gaps, surface transportation in the USA will receive only 49% of what will be needed by 2020. Given the relatively small number of mega-projects indicated above, we can readily conclude that the current supply of large-scale transportation infrastructure falls far short of what is necessary, even if we wish to maintain only the current LOS in all modes.[10]

Considering this grim situation, how can we explain the fact that a significant number of the mega-projects built have turned out to be unworthy or inferior in terms of their delivered transportation-economic net benefits? If transportation needs are so immense in comparison to the relatively scanty actual supply, selection of the best welfare-maximizing projects becomes imperative. It is this situation that has prompted the question explored in this book: What kind of decision-making process underlies implementation of mega-projects in general and why does this process culminate in the implementation of such a significant number of projects considered inferior in terms of their transportation-economic performance?

Notes

1. The Organization for Economic Cooperation and Development (OECD), whose members number 34 countries.
2. During the 1990s, Japan followed a different economic path as it used infrastructure investment, mainly in transportation, as a fiscal stimulus to boost its flagging economy. In 1995 it invested 2.8% of its GDP in land transport infrastructure. This high level has since declined steadily, reaching about 1.6% in 2010 (ITF 2012).
3. Includes Albania, Bulgaria, Croatia, Czech Republic, Estonia, Romania, Hungary, Latvia, Lithuania, Poland, Romania, Serbia, Slovakia, Slovenia, and the Soviet federation.
4. In these calculations, we apply the US figures, namely, that the total of land transport investments represented 0.6% of GDP, of which 30% were allocated to maintenance.
5. This database is discussed in Chap. 4.
6. The German Federal Transportation Infrastructure Investment Plan (FTIP) for 1992–2012 provides another indication of the volume of mega-projects. The plan calls for about €225 billion (in 1991 prices) for investment in transportation infrastructure, of which half is to be allocated to rail and inland waterway projects. Three investments that fall into the mega-

project range were begun in Germany in the early 1990s. These amounted to 15%–20% of total investment for the respective 20-year FTIP.

7. An alternative approach, which might be called a *planning-based approach*, considers the desired transportation (including land-use) structure in a metropolitan area; one would then determine the supply level needed to support this desired structure.
8. The report has defined needs as follows: Americans spend 4.2 billion hours a year stuck in traffic at a cost to the economy of $78.2 billion, or $710 per motorist. Poor conditions cost motorists $67 billion a year in repairs and operating costs.
9. According to a report by the Congressional Budget Office (CBO 2011, 2012; Mathur 2011, 2012), the total US government spending between 2008 and 2011 was approximately $200 billion a year on surface transportation infrastructure projects; federal spending was $50 billion per year and local spending reached $150 billion per year. An additional $12 billion in capital expenditures were spent on privately owned railroads by private investors. The report notes that if current funding levels persist, an additional $13 billion per year will be needed to maintain and operate existing highway and transit infrastructure. A further $83 billion per year will be needed to support projects with potential positive returns.
10. Overall, about 10% of the 609,539 bridges in the USA currently are rated as *structurally deficient*, meaning one or more of their main structural components do not meet acceptable structural standards. Another 14% are considered as *functionally obsolete*, meaning they are no longer suited to their current task because of overuse or a lack of safety features; yet they are still in use (see USA Department of Transportation (US DOT) 2010).

References

American Society of Civil Engineers (ASCE). 2009. *Report Card for America's Infrastructure*. http://www.asce.org/reportcard/.

———. 2011. *Economic Report on Surface Transportation*. http://www.asce.org/uploadedFiles/Infrastructure/Failure_to_Act/SCE44%20summary_report_FINAL-hires.pdf.

Congressional Budget Office (CBO). 2011. www.cbo.gov; U.S Department of the Treasury, www.treasurydirect.gov/govt/reports/ir/ir_expense.htm and www.treasurydirect.gov/govt/rates/pd/avg/2011/2011_02.htm.

———. 2012. *Infrastructure Banks and Surface Transportation*. CBO: Non-Partisan Analysis for the US Congress. http://www.cbo.gov/sites/default/files/cbofiles/attachments/07-12-12-InfrastructureBanks.pdf. Accessed April 16, 2013.

Flyvbjerg, B. 2007. Cost Overruns and Demand Shortfalls in Urban Rail and Other Infrastructure. *Transportation Planning and Technology* 30 (1): 9–30.

International Transport Forum (ITF). 2012, 2015. Statistic Brief, Infrastructure Investment. http://www.internationaltransportforum.org/statistics/StatBrief/2012-06.pdf.

———. 2013. Tackling Transport's Funding Dilemma. *Motion Magazine*, 3, 2013.

Mathur, S. 2012. *A Decision-Support Framework for Using Value Capture to Fund Public Transit: Lessons from Project-Specific Analyses.* San Jose, CA: Mineta Transportation Institute, College of Business, San Jose State University.

USA Department of Transportation (US DOT). 2010. *Status of the Nation's Highway, Bridges, and Transit: Conditions and Performance.* Biennial Report to Congress.

CHAPTER 3

The Dubious Status of Formal Project Evaluation Procedures

3.1 Introduction

For the last several decades developed countries have adopted and utilized formal transportation project evaluation schemes whose objective is to "provide an assessment of whether a proposal is worthwhile, and clearly communicate conclusions and recommendations" (UK, *Green Book* 2011). Such project evaluation procedures set the rationale for government intervention, define a project's objectives and alternatives, and examine the direct transportation-economic costs and benefits for each option.[1] Within this framework, Cost-Benefit Analysis (CBA) is the key analytical component because it is meant to appraise the net economic value of each alternative's *direct* transportation benefits, given the required resources, in a way that treats all projects equally and unambiguously (Vickerman 2000). The end result of this process should be prioritization of the suggested options, based on welfare-economic foundations. Other evaluation approaches, such as the UK's New Approach To Appraisal (NATA),[2] require application of supplementary techniques, in addition to CBA, for the purpose of examining and weighing *indirect* costs and benefits—economic development, community cohesion and equity, to name just a few.

One core issue associated with the use of these schemes is their legal and administrative status. That is, does an appraisal's outcome have statutory standing as the principal decision criteria for a project's selection, especially in the case of mega-projects? If it does, should the decision be

J. Berechman, *The Infrastructure We Ride On*,
https://doi.org/10.1007/978-3-319-74606-7_3

accompanied by an appraisal report or its summary, sufficiently detailed regarding the underlying assumptions, data and methods of analysis, to ensure transparency? Alternatively, if the appraisal is legally defined solely as a decision support tool, the issue becomes the extent to which policy- and decision-makers actually base their decisions on its findings. As I argue below, the answers to these questions are rather uncertain. In order to grasp the significance of these questions for our topic, we should first review the fundamental structure of formal appraisal schemes. Figure 3.1, below, schematically depicts the main components of the typical evaluation procedure.

Notice that the evaluation scheme depicted in Fig. 3.1 has three main modules: the project alternatives module (labeled *investment policy*), a CBA module and a *project selection* module. The last module refers to the stage of scoring and ranking project alternatives based on pre-defined weights and selection criteria related to various selected transportation and

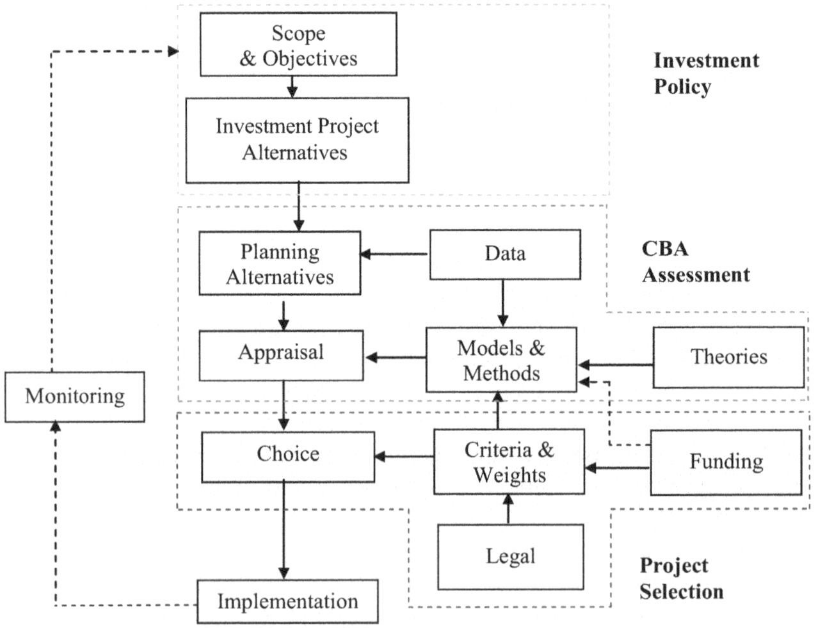

Fig. 3.1 A schematic view of a typical project evaluation procedure. Source: Berechman (2009)

non-transportation effects. On the foundations of this generic scheme, I later refer to some of the diverse formal procedures employed in various countries to appraise new capital investment projects.

As depicted in Fig. 3.1, all formal evaluation procedures contain a CBA component at their core. To familiarize the reader unfamiliar with the principles of welfare economics underlying CBA, I begin by succinctly examining these economic underpinnings of CBA (see Sects. 3.2 and 3.3). Subsequently, in Sect. 3.4, I review and compare several procedures. The question of whether, if at all, these procedures and their results are legally and/or institutionally binding when it comes to choosing a particular project, especially a mega-project, is discussed in Sect. 3.5. Conclusions are presented in Sect. 3.6.

3.2 Welfare-Economic Principles of CBA

A basic assumption guiding project appraisal is that a public investment should improve social welfare. The theoretical principles associated with social welfare as a concept relate to the notion of efficiency in the allocation and use of resources. The objective of the analysis is, then, to ascertain whether a project will produce a positive *net* social welfare gain.

To calculate the net social welfare gain or loss from a proposed transportation project, we must factor in the annual stream of benefits and costs of the resources used to generate these benefits. Selection of the alternative promising the highest net welfare gain lies at the heart of all CBA methodologies.

Based on the above, various complex techniques have been developed to measure the net welfare contribution arising from a given project. Net Present Value (NPV),[3] expressed in monetary value, and Benefit-to-Cost (B/C) ratio are the most common criteria used to rank project alternatives relative to their welfare contributions.[4]

Before proceeding, we should mention that the above exposition is subject to three major *ideal* conditions. First, no distortions appear in the economy, that is, the prices that consumers face, do not diverge from true social marginal costs. For example, car users face travel time and car-use expenses when making trips. However, if these costs fall short of the associated social costs, which include congestion and pollution costs, then travel markets can be regarded as distorted. In reality, the relevant markets (in this case labor, land and travel) are often distorted due to the presence of monopolies, market entry barriers or some externality. If these distortions are severe, the end results might be widely off the theoretically anticipated mark, a situation that demands correction of the welfare gain estimates presented in the original analysis.[5]

The second condition is that we need to consider the welfare gains of independent projects, that is, situations where implementation of one project does not necessitate implementation of either a complementary project or exclusion (and sometimes substitution) of another project. If that is not the case, the measurement of welfare contribution may be faulty. And yet, real projects are often dependent for their completion on subsidiary projects, as in the case of a rail line whose completion may require construction of access roads at considerable costs. If primary projects are dependent on secondary projects, we need to apply the same economic criteria for the *entire* set of projects, viewed as a composite whole.

The third condition is that decision-making entities indeed attempt to optimize social welfare. But what if the agency in charge of the evaluation, selection and implementation of a project operates according to an agenda that disregards, totally or in part, social welfare? I return to this issue in Chap. 7.

3.3 What Are We Measuring?

Travel is normally subject to dis-utilities, the costs incurred by users and operators; it follows that transportation improvements necessarily imply reductions in these costs, both direct and indirect. Hence, when evaluating transportation improvements, cost reductions are usually regarded as the prime direct benefit to trip-makers and to society as a whole. Travel costs to the individual are normally measured in terms of *generalized costs of travel*, especially monetary outlays and travel time. Many studies have shown that for highway commuters, the key cost component is actual door-to-door travel time, followed by auto operating costs and related expenses, such as the costs incurred from highway accidents (Ozbay et al. 2001). For public transit users, wait and mode-transfer time, in addition to in-vehicle travel time and fares, comprise the main travel costs. It therefore should not surprise us that the main benefits from a transportation project are presented as savings in time and mode-related expenses.

A key analysis to be done before conducting a CBA that considers these items is monetization of the range of time-cost savings. This is done in two distinct steps: measurement of the time and costs saved, and only then their transformation into monetary values. Calculation of the time saved by a project is a complicated and laborious activity because the entire network in which the specific project is to be embedded (e.g., a new link of an existing highway network) must be examined. This explains the importance of traffic network analysis (or *network assignment* in professional parlance) in the respective project assessments.

The second step, conversion of time saved into monetary values, is carried out with the use of Value of Time (VOT) parameters, defined in units of dollars per hour (or in local currency per hour). There is a voluminous literature on the theoretical foundations of VOT, covering econometric estimation and variations among classes of trip-makers and trip types (see Berechman 2009, Chap. 4, for a detailed analysis). Some countries actually mandate precise VOT values for each type of trip-maker (e.g., professional vs. non-professional drivers), mode (e.g., trucks vs. private cars) and trip type (e.g., home-to-work vs. leisure). To illustrate, the US government recommends the use of percentages of hourly wage rates for the quantification of VOT (Berechman 2009, Chap. 4), as shown in Table 3.1.

As Table 3.1 clearly shows, higher values are assigned for out-of-vehicle time than for in-vehicle time, a recommendation reflecting the finding that travelers perceive time spent waiting, walking or changing modes to be more onerous than time spent in a moving vehicle.[6] The values given in

Table 3.1 US VOT savings as a percentage of hourly wage rate (2000)

Trip type	*Surface modes*[a,b]	*Truck drivers*
Local travel		
In-vehicle time—personal trips	35%–60% (50%)[c]	
In-vehicle time—business trips	80%–120% (100%)[c]	100%
Out-of-vehicle time—personal trips (wait, walk, transfer)	100%	
Out-of-vehicle time—business trips (wait, walk, transfer)	100%	
Inter-city		
In-vehicle time—personal trips	60%–90% (70%)[c]	
In-vehicle time—business trips	80%–120% (100%)[c]	100%

Source: US DOT (2001)

[a]Applies to all combinations of in-vehicle and other transit time

[b]Walk, wait and transfer times should be evaluated at 100% of the wage rate when improvements affect only these elements of transit time

[c]Percentages in brackets are recommended values

that table provide the basis for the following US-recommended VOT parameters, specified in dollars per average hour of work (Table 3.2).

For comparison, see Table 3.3 for the VOT figures, by trip type, employed in France.

Given that the figures in Tables 3.2 and 3.3 reflect national economic differences as well as the proclivity of governments to treat various components of travel time differently, the two tables are not amenable to direct comparison. Irrespective of these national differences, because the estimated benefits from a project directly result from the travel times saved and their respective VOT values, even a small change in VOT can decisively affect the overall net welfare value of the project that affects hun-

Table 3.2 US-recommended VOT in $ per average hour of work (2000 prices)

Trip type	*Surface modes*	*Truck drivers*
Local travel		
Personal trips	$7.40–$12.70 ($10.60)[a]	
Business trips	$17.00–$25.40 ($21.20)[a]	$18.10
All purposes	$7.90–$13.40 ($11.20)[a]	
Inter-city		
Personal	$12.70–$19.00 ($14.80)[a]	
Business	$17.00–$25.40 ($21.20)[a]	$18.10
All purposes	$13.20–$19.80 ($15.60)[a]	

Source: US DOT (2001)
[a]Figures in brackets are recommended values

Table 3.3 French VOT by trip type (1998 prices in €)

Trip purpose[a]	*Percent of gross salary*[b]	*Percent of wage costs*[c]	*France (€)*	*Ile de France (Paris region) (€)*[d]
Business	85%	61%	10.5	13.0
Home-to-work	77%	55%	9.5	11.6
Non-work[e]	42%	30%	5.2	6.4
Mean value if trip purpose is unknown	59%	42%	7.2	8.8

Source: Boiteux (2000); Quinet and Vickerman (2004)
[a]Assuming that 10% of all trips are business trips, 35% home-to-work trips and 55% trips for all other purposes
[b]Based on 1998 average gross monthly salary, assuming a 39-hour work week
[c]On average, wage costs equal about 70% of gross salary
[d]In Ile de France, salaries were about 23% above the national average
[e] Shopping, leisure, and so on

dreds of thousands of users. Not surprisingly, variables such as VOT are often called ***policy variables*** as they can be used by decision-makers to influence a project's CBA result.[7] I will return to this issue when discussing actual project decision-making in Chap. 11.

3.4 Evaluation Methods in Various Countries

As mentioned, not all countries use the same procedures to appraise transportation infrastructure projects although the most common procedures remain CBA and Multi-Criteria Analysis (MCA). The latter approach compensates for traditional CBA limitations by adding other elements, such as environmental externalities, equity and land use to the assessments produced. At the final stage of the MCA, a weight is assigned to each element to come up with the project's total welfare value (Harberger 1978; Berechman 2009, Chap. 14). Table 3.4 lists the methods used in various countries along with the common lifetime or evaluation period (another crucial assessment variable) assigned to all projects of a given type (primarily highways).

Table 3.4 Evaluation methods in various countries (1995)

Country	*Main evaluation method*	*Evaluation period (years)*
Belgium	MCA, CBA (NPV)	Project's lifetime
Denmark	CBA (first year rate of return)	30
Finland	CBA (B/C ratio)	30
France	CBA (first year rate of return), MCA	N/A
Germany	CBA (B/C ratio)	30
Ireland	CBA (B/C ratio)	30
Israel	CBA (NPV) with externalities	15
Italy	CBA (B/C ratio)	N/A
Japan	MCA (no weights), CBA	
Netherlands	MCA, CBA (NPV)	30
Norway	CBA (B/C ratio)	25
Portugal	CBA (NPV)	20
Spain	CBA (B/C ratio)	30
Sweden	CBA (B/C ratio)	40
United Kingdom	CBA (B/C ratio)	30
Australia	CBA (B/C ratio)	30
Canada	CBA (NPV)	30
New Zealand	CBA (B/C ratio)	25
South Africa	CBA (B/C ratio)	30
United States	CBA (B/C ratio), ISTEA[a] criteria	40

Source: Berechman (2009, Chap. 6); Assembled from EURET/385/94, 2001
[a]Intermodal Surface Transportation Efficiency Act

Several detailed reviews of the appraisal methodologies applied internationally are available in the literature. Based on this literature, Table 3.5 compares the key properties of the methods used in the selected countries.[8]

As Table 3.5 shows, travel time and cost reductions are almost universally regarded as the main sources of the social welfare benefits to be gained from transportation investment projects. CBA criteria like NPV and B/C ratios are the most common measures used when ranking projects. As the table also shows, each of the surveyed countries employs a formal procedure (often available today in the form of a computerized package) meant to dictate the steps analysts must follow when conducting the evaluation that include, as observed earlier, pre-specified parameters (labeled above as *policy variables*), among other things. The mandatory appraisal of environmental externalities is, however, often carried out prior to (sometimes by years) the appraisal's conduct. At times, this more-limited analysis may substitute for a comprehensive CBA, a practice that frequently leads to decisions based on partial or outdated estimates.

3.5 The Regulatory Status of Formal Evaluation Schemes

As Fig. 3.1 shows, in addition to the actual assessment module (labeled *CBA Assessment*), the evaluation process contains two additional modules: *Investment Policy* and *Project Selection*. Given the welfare-maximizing principles underlying CBAs, the operational requirements of the entire evaluation scheme's implementation need elucidation. In general, we expect the entire scheme's procedures to be based on five principles: (1) *clarity*, meaning the clear specification of investment goals, performance measures, data needs and appraisal outcomes; (2) *integrity*, or the truthful presentation of underlying assumptions, data and data sources, process structure and findings; (3) *rationality*, meaning logical and systematic analysis leading to findings, reached with the aid of corroborated data; (4) *transparency*, with the data, the conduct of the analysis, the results and conclusions freely visible to the public; and (5) *accountability*, which demands that the analysts who perform the evaluation accept the responsibility of adherence to professional standards just as decision-makers are assumed to be answerable to the public.

But how well do these evaluators actually adhere to these five principles? Provision of an accurate response to this question is difficult mainly for the lack of full and proper information. *Integrity*, *transparency* and *accountability*, particularly the last two, are not universally considered to

Table 3.5 Key properties of appraisal methodologies used in selected countries (2000)

Property	*UK (NATA)*	*France*	*Japan (Benefit Index Table)*	*USA*[a]	*Germany (Federal Transport Infrastructure Plan)*	*Israel (Transport Project Appraisal)*
Main benefits	Time saved; accident reduction	Travel time and costs savings	Time and costs savings; safety; environment impacts; regional development; equity	Time and costs savings; safety; induced demand; environment impacts; funding	Travel time and cost reduction; infrastructure costs; safety; environmental impacts	Travel time and cost savings; safety; environmental impacts; agglomeration
Approach or criteria for project's choice	Financial viability, given the budget	Pre-determined weights for MCA	Benefit incidence table (BIT) of qualitative and quantitative impacts	CBA criteria (mainly NPV and B/C ratio)	CBA criteria (mainly NPV and B/C ratio)	CBA criteria (mainly NPV, B/C ratio and project risk)
Additional criteria	Environmental impacts and economic impacts	Safety; air and noise pollution; land use	Living standards and emergencies	Economic development and land use	Environmental impacts and competitiveness of railroads	Environmental impacts and equity
Formal evaluation package	Design manual for roads and bridges	Plans de Deplacement Urbaine;[b] inter-city road appraisal	Manuals for road, rail, airports and seaports	User benefit analysis of highways and bus transit improvements[c]	Federal Transport Infrastructure Plan (BVWP)	Transportation projects procedure (*Nohal Prat*)

(*continued*)

Table 3.5 (continued)

Property	*UK (NATA)*	*France*	*Japan (Benefit Index Table)*	*USA*[a]	*Germany (Federal Transport Infrastructure Plan)*	*Israel (Transport Project Appraisal)*
Next phase	NATA; use of appraisal summary table (AST) on key criteria; multi-modal	Setting specific goals for transport benefits[b]; use of unique criterion like Internal Rate of Return (IRR)	Ascertain availability of public transit; regional benefits	Setting a common basis for comparing projects	Include regional and network impacts	Include funding network-wide impacts in assessment process
Regulatory status[d]	Not specified or unclear	Not specified or unclear	Not specified or unclear	Not specified or unclear	Not specified or unclear	Not specified or unclear

Source: Based on Hayashi and Morisugi (2000)

[a]See Appendix for two procedures used in the USA

[b]Under the new PDU (Plans de Deplacement Urbaine) procedure (urban displacement plans)

[c]AASHTO (2010)

[d]Indicates how binding are, in terms of project choice, the application of the mentioned project evaluation process and its results. See below in text

be integral to the evaluation process, nor are they always specifically mentioned in the published documents. A key reason for this situation is the *regulatory status* defined in the last row of Table 3.5, which indicates just how binding are project evaluation and its results on project choice. For the sake of clarity, I should note that I refer here to the *entire* project evaluation process and *not* just to environmental impact statements, which are mandatory for the approval of transportation mega-projects in most countries.

The regulatory status of evaluation in transportation project approval implies five elements. First, all capital investment projects, regardless of mode, location or reasonable magnitude, must undergo a project evaluation procedure. Second, the proposal chosen must comply with the outcomes of a comprehensive evaluation. That is, if a project is shown to be inferior relative to other alternatives, it cannot be accepted for implementation. Third, all aspects of the project must be reviewed within the boundaries of the evaluation scheme. Such attentiveness avoids situations where impacts (e.g., effects on specific groups or on economic development) neglected in the analysis are later used as key criterion in justifying an otherwise inferior project. Fourth, the methods, criteria and results of the appraisal process must be transparent and made public within a reasonable period after the evaluation's completion. Fifth, if sufficient time (say five years) has elapsed between the appraisal's completion and the project's implementation, a new evaluation must be conducted to allow for possible changes in underlying conditions (e.g., economic, financial, demographic, social, institutional, technological, environmental and legal variables).

Table 3.5 likewise shows that the regulatory status of project appraisal schemes is not unambiguously defined or mandated in every country.[9] As a consequence, formal evaluation procedures do not, by and large, require proper exposition of their underlying assumptions, data collection, methods of analysis and results. The process and its outcomes thus remain cloaked, that is, they lack transparency, which supports the absence of professional and political accountability.

To illustrate this state of non-uniformity, the quotation cited at the outset, taken from the UK's *Green Book*, states that all projects *should* be subject to formal project assessment. Yet, no evaluation results were reported for the UK's own M6 toll road project. Similarly, no assessment, if one was indeed conducted, was reported for the Randstad Rail in the Netherlands. The same applies to the Denver FasTracks and the Portland-Milwaukee Light Rail projects in the USA. Should these instances lead us to conclude that the results of these projects' assessments were either not binding or, for the lack of transparency, they were not publicized to avoid embarrassing questions, especially if the project's CBA produced a poor score? The answer is inconclusive.

In the USA, capital investment grants for construction of a new fixed guideway system or extension of an existing system,[10] costing $75 million or more in Federal New Starts funds, may be allocated only if the transportation secretary determines that the proposed project is[11]:

1. based on the results of an alternative options analysis and a preliminary engineering study;
2. justified by the results of a comprehensive review of the project's mobility improvements, environmental benefits, cost effectiveness, operating efficiencies, economic development effects and public transportation-supporting land-use policies, together with future transit patterns; and
3. supported by an acceptable degree of local financial commitment (including stable, dependable sources of funding) to construct, maintain and operate the system without requiring any reduction in existing public transportation services or level of service.

While these conditions may be seen as stringent, they nevertheless do not amount to a comprehensive CBA or MCA, nor do they demand that the net welfare gain from the project's transportation benefits be demonstrated and made transparent. Crucially, these guidelines do not make clear what conditions meet the transportation secretary's requirements.

We should, however, consider the Nobbe and Berechman (2014a) findings indicating that project transparency is statistically unrelated to project success, a conclusion that challenges some of the theoretical explanations of project efficiency (e.g., Flyvbjerg et al. 2003). And yet, Nobbe and Berechman also found that the wealthier a country is, the greater the transparency of its formal project evaluation process, a finding that has important implications for sound public policy. Finally, the same study also found that in countries governed by a federal system, such as the USA, the regulatory status of evaluation schemes, irrespective of their legislative status, is even more blurred.

In the same vein, at the local and state level, a 2011 survey of transportation investments in the USA found considerable differences among the 50 states and the District of Columbia.[12] Just 13 states were observed to actively promote stipulation of the goals, performance measures and data that decision-makers were to use when selecting cost-effective policy options, instituted in order to ensure the likelihood of strong returns for taxpayers. This study appeared at a time when most states were entering their fourth continuous year of budgetary crisis, after already closing gaps valued at more than $400 billion in 2008. Furthermore, the study appeared just as policy and business leaders across the country began to acknowledge that state transportation systems were essential supports for short- and long-term economic growth.

3.6 Conclusions

In this chapter we reviewed the formal schemes developed for the evaluation of transportation investment projects. We also questioned the regulatory status of these schemes and noted that this issue is rather ambiguous. Complicating resolution of the issue is the government's federal political and administrative structure, which makes it difficult to coherently decide which agency or department is responsible for evaluating projects. For instance, projects proposed by states and localities, especially if funded with federal money, require federal approval. Notwithstanding these strictures, poor evaluation outcomes have rarely motivated rejection of a project (Lee 2000). Hence, the key observation relayed in this chapter is that while most countries have instituted some formal project evaluation scheme, as far as one can judge by the significant number of approved projects not subjected to any CBA, these same countries have *not* chosen to make evaluation mandatory in practice. We can therefore conclude that relative to their use and timing, the legal status of these schemes is quite blurred.

Appendix: Appraisal Schemes Commonly Used in the USA

STEAM

The Surface Transportation Efficiency Analysis Model (STEAM) is a CBA decision-making tool developed by the Federal Highway Administration (FHWA) in the 1990s. STEAM is used to compare the benefits and costs of alternative multi-modal transportation projects. It uses information produced from a travel demand model to compute the net value of mobility and safety benefits attributable to the respective projects. STEAM is composed of four modules: (1) the *user interface module* specifies inputs and reads the outputs produced at the end of the analysis; (2) the *network analysis module* reads highway traffic volumes, segment lengths, capacities and other link data to produce travel times and travel distances based on minimum time assignments; (3) the *trip table analysis module* estimates user benefits based on a comparison of the base scenario (no changes) against the improvement scenario, with multi-modal investment based on comparison of trip travel times and out-of-pocket costs; (4) the *evaluation summary module* calculates net present worth and a B/C ratio for the multi-modal investment under consideration.

Website: http://www.fhwa.dot.gov/steam/

AASHTO Red Book

The American Association of State Highway and Transportation Officials (AASHTO) *Red Book* is a manual that provides guidelines for performing user benefit analyses of highway improvements. The manual includes instructions for performing a CBA and provides information and explanations of the scheme's various aspects. In enumerating benefits and costs, several factors are considered, including vehicle operation factors, road variables, vehicle operating costs, travel time saved, VOT and accident costs. The original manual was published in 1977, followed by a major update in 2003 with respect to the theory, methodologies, procedures and practices for assessing user benefits. The 2010 update includes software for conducting the analyses in accordance with the manual's guidelines. A supplement dedicated to providing guidance on estimating non-user benefits, entitled *Non-User Benefit Analysis for Highways: A Supplement to AASHTO's User Benefit Analysis for Highways*, has been published (2007). This update responded to calls for extending the comprehensiveness of highway improvement impact assessment by considering non-user benefits (AASHTO 2010).

User and Non-User Benefit Analysis for Highways: https://bookstore.transportation.org/imageview.aspx?id=884&DB=3

Congressional Budget Office (CBO), 2012, *Infrastructure Banks and Surface Transportation, Congressional: Non-Partisan Analysis for the US Congress.* http://www.cbo.gov/sites/default/files/cbofiles/attachments/07-12-12-InfrastructureBanks.pdf

Notes

1. By *direct effects* we mean those elements that directly relate to the project's construction and operation, such as capital and upkeep costs, as well as savings, such as changes in traffic flow and composition, travel time and monetary savings and safety improvements.
2. *Green Book.*

3. NPV is defined as the value of the discounted streams of the monetized future benefits and costs emanating from the project (Berechman 2009).
4. For a detailed discussion see Small and Verhoef (2007) and Berechman (2009).
5. For a detailed analysis see Venables and Gasiorek (1999).
6. Some research findings indicate that the differentials between in-vehicle and out-of-vehicle travel times are changing and becoming much smaller than previously thought, sometimes to the point of negligibility (Mokhtarian and Salomon 2001; Lyons and Urry 2005).
7. Another important policy variable is the mandated rate used when discounting future streams of benefits and costs (also known as the *discount factor*).
8. See, in particular, the special issue of *Transport Policy*, 2000.
9. Interestingly, the US Federal Office of Information and Regulatory Affairs has issued a document on Regulatory Impact Analyses (RIAs) that obligates all agencies to meet a given set of requirements in their RIAs, relative to the anticipated consequences of economically significant regulatory actions regarding prices and market entry, among other factors.
10. Ranging from heavy to light rail transit (LRT) to bus rapid transit (BRT).
11. As per 49 USC 5309(d), http://www.greenlineextension.org/documents/FTA_NewStarts/FY08_Entire_NS_Report.pdf.
12. The Rockefeller Foundation and the Pew Center on the States (2011).

References

American Association of State Highway and Transportation Officials (AASHTO). 2010. *A Manual on User Benefit Analysis of Highway and Bus Transit Improvements*. Washington, DC: American Association of State Highway and Transportation Officials.

Berechman, J. 2009. *The Evaluation of Transportation Investment Projects*. London: Routledge.

Boiteux, M. 2000. *Transports: choix des investissements et prise en compte des nuisances*. Commissariat General du Plan, Paris: La Documentation Francaise.

EURET. 1994. Cost Benefit and Multi-criteria Analysis for New Road Construction: Final Report. *Report to the Commission of the European Communities, Directorate General for Transport*, Doc. EURET/385/94, Brussels: EURET.

———. 2001. Transport RTD Programme Homepage. *Transport RTD Programme*. http://cordis.europa.eu/transport/.

FHWA. 2013. *Appendix A: Traffic Analysis Tools by Category*. http://www.fhwa.dot.gov/steam/.

Flyvbjerg, B., M.K.S. Holm, and S.L. Buhl. 2003. How Common and How Large Are Cost Overruns in Transport Infrastructure Projects? *Transport Reviews* 23: 71–88.

Harberger, A. 1978. On the Use of Distributional Weights in Social Cost-Benefit Analysis. *Journal of Political Economy* 86 (2): 87–120.

Hayashi, Y., and H. Morisugi. 2000. International Comparison of Background Concept and Methodology of Transportation Project Appraisal. *Transport Policy* 7: 73–88.

HM Treasury. 2011. *The Green Book, Appraisal and Evaluation in Central Government*. London: The Crown. https://www.gov.uk/government/publications/the-green-book-appraisal-and-evaluation-in-central-governent.

Lee, D.B. 2000. Methods for Evaluation of Transportation Projects in the USA. *Transport Reviews* 7: 41–50.

Lyons, G., and J. Urry. 2005. Travel Time Use in the Information Age. *Transportation Research A* 39: 257–276.

Mokhtarian, P., and I. Salomon. 2001. How Derived Is the Demand for Travel? Some Conceptual and Measurement Considerations. *Transportation Research A* 35: 695–719.

Nobbe, P., and J. Berechman. 2014a. *The Politics of Infrastructure Investment Decision-Making: Report of the Statistical Analysis of Selected Hypotheses*. University Transportation Research Center Region 2, CCNY, CUNY, Final Report.

———. 2014b. *A Technical Report*. New York: University Transportation Research Center Region 2, the City College of New York.

Ozbay, K., B. Bartin, and J. Berechman. 2001. Estimation and Evaluation of Full Marginal Costs of Highway Transportation in New Jersey. *Journal of Transportation and Statistics* 4 (1): 81–104.

Quinet, E., and R. Vickerman. 2004. *Principles of Transport Economics*. Northhampton, MA: Edward Elgar.

Rockefeller Foundation and the Pew Center on the States, Lack of Performance Measures to Assess "Success" or "Failure" of Projects Ex Ante and Ex Post, 2011. http://www.pewcenteronthestates.org/initiatives_detail.aspx?initiativeID=85899358927.

Small, K., and E. Verhoef. 2007. *The Economics of Urban Transportation*. London: Routledge.

US Department of Transportation (DOT). 2001. *The Value of Travel Time: Departmental Guidance for Conducting Economic Evaluations*. Washington, DC: US Government Printing Office.

Venables, A.J., and M. Gasiorek. 1999. *The Welfare Implications of Transport Improvements in the Presence of Market Failure, Report to Standing Committee on Trunk Road Assessment (SACTRA)*. London: Department of Environment, Transport and Regions.

Vickerman, R. 2000. Evaluation Methodologies for Transport Projects in the United Kingdom. *Transport Policy* 7: 7–16.

CHAPTER 4

Inferior *and* Unworthy Transportation Mega-Projects

4.1 Introduction

In the previous chapters we saw that many countries, especially in the developed world, have adopted formal project appraisal and selection procedures. While not always mandatory, we might assume that their availability does facilitate the making of rational choices with respect to which projects are worthy among the proposed investment alternatives. And yet, this assumption has been proven wrong in many cases. Various surveys of mega-projects worldwide have revealed that a significant number of the projects selected are inferior to other investment alternatives or even totally unworthy (e.g., see Pickrell 1990, 1992; Flyvbjerg 2007, 2009). Why does this happen?

While I use the terms *inferior* and *unworthy* investment projects interchangeably in this chapter, from an economic policy perspective they are not the same. A publicly funded project is *worthy* when its net contribution to social welfare is positive. Social welfare in this case is defined as the value of the primary transportation benefits (e.g., travel time and costs savings), minus the costs of construction, the value of negative externalities (e.g., pollution), plus the value of positive externalities (e.g., economic development). Any economic damage (or loss) incurred from a project with a negative welfare contribution is reflected in the foregone positive returns that might have been earned had public capital been invested differently. A project that engenders such a negative contribution, as determined by bona fide Cost-Benefit Analysis (CBA), is thus an *unworthy*

J. Berechman, *The Infrastructure We Ride On*,
https://doi.org/10.1007/978-3-319-74606-7_4

project.[1] But even if a CBA indicates a positive welfare contribution, the welfare contribution of a project's investment alternatives might be superior. Should this occur, the project under study is regarded as *inferior* one, relative to those alternatives. As the focus in this book is on the decision-making process that underlies project choice and implementation, we ask the following question: Why are unworthy or inferior projects selected in the first place? Hence the interchangeable use of these terms throughout this chapter and elsewhere in the book.

What if a CBA was not performed *ex ante*, as is often the case (see below)? To compensate for its absence, we could use performance indicators to assess the project's net contribution *ex post*. Those indicators may include actual output (e.g., added capacity and increased service frequency), actual demand (e.g., peak-hour traffic volume or number of passengers) and actual costs (capital and operating). We should nevertheless bear in mind that the results of these analyses largely depend on the point of time at which they are made. An examination of such indicators, 5 as opposed to 20 years after the project's commencement, is likely to produce substantially different results due to long-run trends in land-use and labor markets. A case in a point is the *ex-post* assessment of the San Francisco Bay Area Rapid Transit (BART) system, which was labeled "a planning disaster" (Hall 1980) and considered an inferior project just a few years after its opening in 1972 (Webber 1976). And yet, a significantly different assessment was delivered 20 years later (Cervero and Landis 1997).[2] This does not contradict the conclusion that given the irreversible nature of transportation mega-projects, a project's *ex-post* assessment may be useful for understanding what went wrong (or right) in its planning and evaluation but an *ex-ante* assessment remains the correct approach for identifying a project's worthiness.

Among the most commonly employed methods to appraise project value is Multiple Criteria Analysis (MCA), where the criteria, properly weighted, include decision factors such as direct transportation-economic benefits, community impacts and environmental effects. Within MCA terms, an inferior project is one that was selected even though its weighted score for these criteria was not the highest relative to its alternatives. Needless to say, if a project does not receive a *passing* total weighted score but is nevertheless selected, it is, ipso facto, unworthy. An example of such a project is the Buffalo, NY, Light Rail Transit (LRT) system, which opened in 1982. The system consists of a single, 6.4 mile (10.3 km) subway line running from the University of Buffalo's campus to the city's downtown area. It runs under the city's Main Street for 5.2 miles. Although an early multi-criteria evaluation showed it to be unworthy, the project was built nevertheless. In 1996, annual ridership was about 7 million passengers; 15 years later it was down to a little over 6 million (Federal Transit Administration's National Transit Database, 1996–2011). Reduced ridership was attributed to the decline in Buffalo's population, a trend recognized years before the project's construction had begun (Berechman and Paaswell 1983).[3]

Another class of projects regarded as unworthy are those that did not undergo any CBA at all or, in the same vein, projects that while subjected to a CBA, scored below an acceptable threshold. An example of the latter is the Trans-European Networks (TEN-T) 22 networks. A study (Proost et al. 2010) concluded that only 12 of the project's units provide a yearly rate of return acceptable to the EU, that is, 5% or more. Even after considering spillover and European cohesion effects, a substantial number of projects have been shown to be unworthy (Brocker et al. 2010). A database compiled of 60 transportation mega-projects worldwide (see Appendix) shows that about half of the projects surveyed had received an unacceptable assessment score, while about one-third had not reported their evaluation results at all even though other key information was made public.[4]

How can this sorry state of affairs exist in the face of such scarce transportation infrastructure investment funds and the implied waste of billions in public funds? The mix of answers to this question ranges from shoddy adherence to appraisal procedures to funding realities, to the claim that policy is almost never based on, or even influenced by, impartial empirical analyses and evidence, to dishonesty and fraud.

While all those answers may be valid, I would like to advance a different explanation, namely, unworthy and inferior projects are selected primarily because the various actors involved are not motivated by the same incentives. Let me elaborate. Political decision-makers mainly respond to incentives such as achieving a political consensus, maintaining favorable public opinion, creating positive economic conditions, or even exploiting the symbolic value of a mega-project for their own benefit. Institutions, on the other hand, tend to respond to bureaucratic incentives such as ensuring its own survival, expansion of its mandate, and acquisition of additional resources.[5] Other actors, such as interest groups, are most interested in the costs and benefits emanating from the project, those that accrue in specific functional domains or neighborhoods.

While a project might be chosen *under coercion*,[6] a necessary (but insufficient) condition for the choice of any project, worthy or not, is synchronization of the objectives and incentives of these different actors. The end result of this process is not choice of the *best* project in the normative sense[7] but, rather, a compromise, a project that somehow responds to the needs and motivations of these often antagonistic actors.

Unfortunately, it appears that unworthy and inferior projects are those most often meeting this criterion. In other words, in the real world of mega-project selection, what counts is economic and political feasibility but *not* identification of the best investment. As Manski (2013) states, "[i]t is the rhetoric of advocacy, not science, which carries the day". In light of his observation, what factors do affect project choice and how do they interact?

The aim of this chapter is, therefore, to offer a tentative paradigm of the factors that determine how mega-projects are selected and the way in which they interface. In Part B of the book, I empirically examine the weight of these factors and their impact on decision-making. To that end I make use of a database compiled of information on 60 mega-projects worldwide (Nobbe and Berechman 2014), described in the Appendix. Next I discuss the main determinants of project decision-making, followed by an exposition of the decision-making paradigm.

4.2 Suppositions on Key Determinants of Project Decision-Making

Underlying the approach delineated here is the conjecture that transportation infrastructure mega-projects are, to a large extent, governed and influenced by a common set of factors having varying degrees of impact. I argue that this set includes the following components:

1. demand and cost forecasts
2. project history
3. special interest groups, pro and con
4. funding
5. institutions
6. equity and distribution criteria
7. externalities: negative but mainly positive (e.g., jobs creation)
8. decision-making procedures

Note that this list does not include an environmental component. In all Western countries, a pre-condition for a project's consideration is preparation of an assessment regarding its environmental impacts, known as an Environmental Impact Statement, or Study (EIS). As a result, project selection and choice pre-supposes preparation of an EIS and validation of its favorable environmental effects. Similarly, the above list does not include a specific CBA component. As argued repeatedly throughout, a significant proportion of all the mega-projects selected for the database did not undergo a comprehensive CBA while many others were subjected to only a partial and inconclusive CBA.

4.3 Interface Between Actors, Institutions, Funding and Politics

The aforementioned factors are deemed staples of transportation project-related decision-making irrespective of project type and country. But how do these factors interact? Do some components carry greater weight than others? Is there some causal chain, with some components pre-requisites for others? Do these vary by case? Prior to answering, it would be useful to familiarize ourselves with the structure of their relationships, which is sketched in Fig. 4.1, within the book's framework.

The highly stylized description found in Fig. 4.1 is meant to convey the intricate interplay between the diverse components. While devoid of any attempt to dictate hierarchy, directionality or functionality, this scheme posits that the process begins with an idea or event (e.g., the tearing down of the elevated rail on New York's 2nd Avenue in the early 1940s), but also a recognized need (e.g., easy access to the international airport as in the case of Vancouver's Canada Line). Once voiced, a short—or long—chain of events ensue that I term, for brevity, the project's ***history***. Among the events comprising this history are the efforts made by interest groups to arouse support or opposition according to their respective agendas. As stated, these groups can include institutions as well as informal factors (e.g., public opinion). Once a decision is made to address the idea, a technical analysis is initiated. And yet, despite the inherent logic of this sequence, data show (see Chap. 5) that such analyses quite frequently do not take place (save for EISs) or are carried out years before a final decision is made, a fact that relegates the results to the realm of the irrelevant.

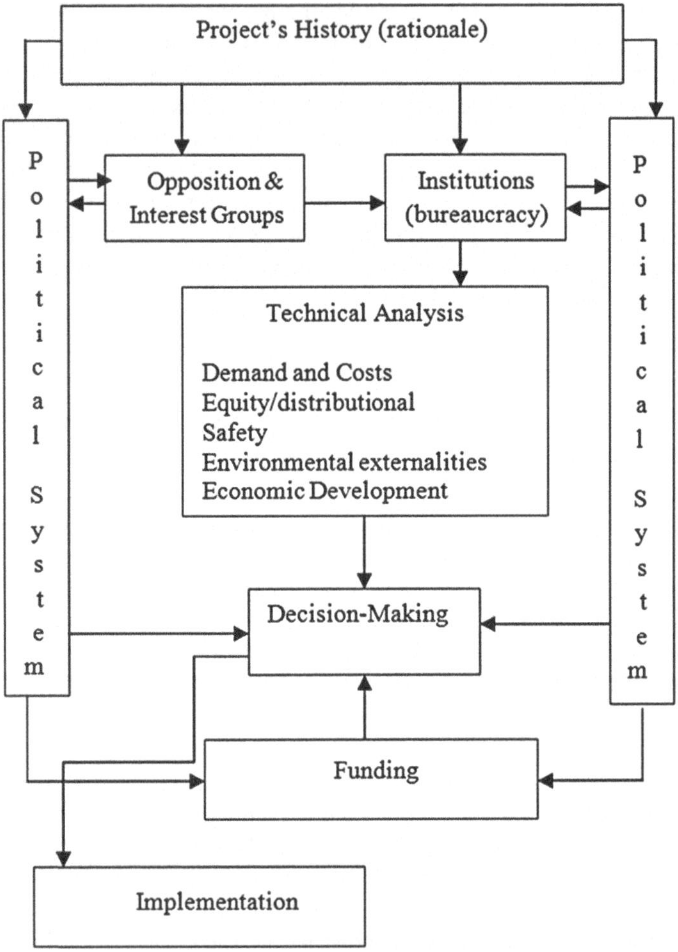

Fig. 4.1 Transportation mega-project decision-making structure

One obvious and crucial decision-making element is project funding, which tends to be heavily influenced by the political system. As the above paradigm shows, the political system interfaces with other factors and the actions of other key players throughout the process. This interaction has received some attention in the public economic literature (Alesina and Tabellini 2008; Greif 2008), which has shown that despite their public mandate, politicians can enact policies only through institutions (the administrative bureaucracy), a situation that induces interdependence and reciprocity. Politicians appoint the bureaucracy's top administrators but also approve the policies formulated by the latter. By the nature of the system and the law, politicians effectively delegate power to the public administration, whose mandate lies in the area of project design and implementation. The latter are thus able to impose constraints on politicians by attempting to (re)define opportunities and feasibilities through, for example, their own planning, technical analysis and organizational capacities.

4.4 Inferior or Unworthy Projects: Funding

How is it that a decision-making process such as the one proposed leads to the choice of inferior or unworthy capital investment projects? The answer lies in the interfaces and interactions of its components, an analysis left to subsequent chapters. Here I briefly dwell on the relationship between decision-making and funding. As detailed in Chap. 8, funding is *the necessary* condition for project choice and implementation. Often, however, should funding become available at some unspecified point in the process, it turns into a *sufficient* condition as well. That is, because funding is intensely tied to political processes, it can be secured despite the absence or fragmentary state of a technical analysis (e.g., pork-barrel or entitlement projects[8]). Politicians, being receptive to the prospects of job creation and accelerated economic growth on the one hand, and pragmatic about the uncertainties surrounding public monetary allocations, on the other, tend to eagerly promote projects regardless of their transportation-economic value. Complicating this issue is the fact that in some countries, such as the USA, mega-projects are often financed wholly or partially from the national government's tax receipts; this availability provides, in turn, added incentives to local (state and municipal) politicians to support a project irrespective of its true contribution to public welfare.[9] While other factors can also affect project choice, this relationship represents the dominant factor influencing selection of a significant number of inferior or unworthy mega-projects without discounting the effect of other intervening factors such as the very structure of government and each level's respective transportation policies and administrative politics, an analysis of which I leave to others.

4.5 Summary

This chapter has delved into why inferior or unworthy transportation mega-projects are too often selected for implementation. As a preliminary to the analysis, I offered a paradigmatic sketch of the interplay between the key elements affecting choice. While not meant to show functionality or directionality, this paradigm implies that the mechanisms by which projects are selected do not ensure that worthy projects will be chosen and may even undermine appropriate choices. This is especially true when we consider the source and timing of funding. In Part B of the book, I examine in detail each of the elements indicated in Fig. 4.1.

Appendix: The Database Used in This Book

Nobbe and Berechman (2014) have assembled a database comprising 60 transportation mega-projects worldwide, projects that were arbitrarily defined as demanding capital investment costs in excess of $1 billion. Discussions and analyses throughout the book make use of this database, described below.

The database spans over 22 countries, with its 60 projects comprised of bridges, tunnels, highway, rail, as well as multi-modal investment projects. A majority of these projects were built in the United States, Europe and Asia during the 1990s and 2000s. A few are still under construction. At the time of their completion, the projects constituted a significant portion of total public transportation investment in their respective countries, 13.5% on average. The following projects are included:

1. Argentine/Rosario-Victoria Bridge; Nuestra Señora del Rosario (Our Lady of Rosario); Puente Rosario-Victoria
2. Australia/City Link
3. Australia/South West Corridor Railway: Mandurah Line New MetroRail; (Mandurah Line); South West Corridor Railway
4. Australia/Sydney Cross City Tunnel
5. Australia/Sydney Harbour Tunnel
6. Canada/Canada Line
7. China (Hong Kong)/High-speed Airport Express Line (AEL), excludes Tung Chung
8. China (Hong Kong)/KCRC West Rail (Kowloon-Canton Railway Corporation)

9. China (Hong Kong)/Western Harbour Crossing
10. Denmark/Copenhagen Metro
11. Denmark/Great Belt Fixed Link; Great Belt Fixed Link Rail and Road Project
12. Denmark/Oeresund Link; Øresundsbroen
13. France/Météor; Paris Météor
14. France/Millau Viaduc
15. France/LGV Méditerranée; TGV Med
16. France/LGV Est-Européenne; TGV Est
17. France/TGV Nord; LGV Nord
18. Germany/BAB 20 Motorway; Bundesautobahn 20; German Unity Transport Project 10; Verkehrsproject Deutsche Einheit 10/VDE10; Baltic Sea Highway; Ostseeautobahn
19. Germany/ICE; Intercity Express (ICE) line Cologne-Rhine/Main; (Neubaustrecke (NBS) Koeln-Rhein-Main)
20. Germany/Tiergartentunnel, Tunnel Tiergarten Spreebogen; larger project
21. Greece/Attiki Odos Athen's toll motorway
22. Greece/Athens Metro; Attiko Metro
23. Greece/Rion Antirion Bridge
24. Israel/Tel Aviv Light Rail
25. Italy/Frejus Road Tunnel
26. Japan/Kyushu Shinkansen
27. Japan/OEDO Line (Loop Section)
28. Japan/Linimo Aichi; Aichi High-Speed Transit Tobu Kyuryo Line
29. Japan/Yamate Tunnel; Metropolitan Expressway Central Circular C2—Shinjuku Route (Shuto Expressway)
30. Korea/KTX-1 Train Express; Gyeongbu High Speed Rail
31. Netherlands/HSL-Zuid; (Hogesnelheidslijn) Zuid
32. Netherlands/Randstad Rail
33. Netherlands/Beneluxlijn
34. Russia/Severo-Murskiy Tunnel
35. Sweden/Arlanda Air-Rail Link; Arlandabanan (the Arlanda Rail Link)
36. Sweden (and Denmark) Oeresund; Öresundsförbindelsen
37. Sweden/Southern Link; Södra länken
38. Thailand/Bangkok/Metro Blue Line; Mass Rapid Transit (MRT) system; officially known as Chaloem Ratchamongkhon
39. Thailand/Bangkok/BTS Skytrain;
40. United Kingdom/CTRL; Channel Tunnel Rail Link, CTRL; now High Speed 1

41. United Kingdom/Jubilee Extension; London Underground Jubilee Line Extension (JLE)
42. United Kingdom/M6 Toll Road
43. United States/Second Avenue Subway—Phase 1
44. United States/AirTrain JFK
45. United States/Alameda Corridor
46. United States/Big Dig; Central Artery/Tunnel Project (CA/T); sometimes Central Artery/Third Tunnel Project
47. United States/Big Dig (Tunnel); Ted Williams Tunnel
48. United States/Big Dig (Road); Big Dig Central Artery
49. United States/Honolulu Rail
50. United States/Denver FasTracks
51. United States/Portland-Milwaukie Light Rail
52. USA/Access to the Region Core (ARC) Tunnel
53. USA/Florida High Speed Rail
54. Turkey/Istanbul-Ankara HSR
55. Turkey/Marmaray
56. Panama/Panama Metro
57. Israel/Yitzhak Rabin Trans-Israel Highway 6
58. Thailand/Bangkok/Elevated Road and Train System
59. Germany/Maglev
60. Portugal/Lisboa-Madrid High-speed Rail

Data on the 60 separate variables were collected or constructed for each of these mega-projects. Although some overlap exists, the data are divided into three basic sets.[10] The first includes the project's technical and cost characteristics: e.g., mode, physical dimensions, costs, construction times, project history and whether the project is a new facility or a network extension. The second set includes data related to project decision-making, including type and source of funding, administrative decision-making level, environmental considerations, transparency and jurisdictions. We also collected a third dataset containing contextual information such as party systems, national GDP and population size. Following is the list of variables for which data were collected:

1. Project name
2. Country
3. Continent
4. National population

5. GDP per capita
6. GDP in Purchasing Power Parity (PPP) per capita (2010)
7. GDP per capita (2000)
8. GDP per capita (1990)
9. Political system: centralized, federalist, unitary
10. Legislative structure
11. Location (inner-city, city, metropolitan, regional, national)
12. Project type (highway, rail, tunnel, other)
13. International border crossing (yes, no)
14. Length
15. Lane miles
16. Public, PPP, Private
17. Concession type
18. Description (e.g., new project, improvement, part of existing project)
19. Project stimulus (e.g., long-term public effort, special interest, crisis)
20. Project status (e.g., completed, partially completed, under planning)
21. Years in planning stage
22. Year of inception
23. Years to completion
24. Dummy for years to completion (e.g., less than ten, more than ten)
25. Construction time
26. Project history (in years, since inception to final approval)
27. Project support (backers and promoters)
28. Project opposition by category (e.g., political, financial or issue-oriented)
29. Initially estimated total costs (at time of approval)
30. Actual costs (at project completion)
31. Capital costs
32. Cost overrun ratio I (not adjusted for inflation)
33. Cost overrun ratio II (inflation adjusted)
34. Cost per mile or km.
35. Source of funding (e.g., local, provincial, national)
36. Type of funding (e.g., grant, debt, loan)
37. Financial obligation data (e.g., interest rate, first loan period, secondary loan period)
38. Estimated level of utilization (e.g., passengers per hour, vehicles per hour)
39. Actual level of utilization
40. Utilization ratio

41. Cost-Benefit Analysis—CBA (completed, partial, none)
42. Year of CBA
43. CBA value
44. Risk analysis (completed, none)
45. Year of risk analysis
46. Environmental Impact Study—EIS (completed, none)
47. Year of EIS
48. Economic development analysis (completed, none)
49. Type of economic development
50. Project transparency (scale of 1–4)
51. Stakeholders (e.g., local, state, agency, other)
52. Decision-makers (e.g., local, state, agency, other)
53. Number of funding sources
54. Political context (support or opposition)
55. Party system (two parties, multiple parties)
56. National voting system (e.g., proportional, plurality, mixed)
57. Dummy for utilization ratio
58. Decade initiated (1970s, 1980s, 1990s, 2000s)
59. Western countries (dummy)
60. Presidential or parliamentary system

The sources of this information—such as a project's website, newspaper/journal articles and public databases—are found primarily in the public domain.[11] For the statistical analyses we used a range of tests to assess data representativeness, theory-led correlation tests and non-parametric tests (e.g., Mann-Whitney U). To test for causality we used linear, multivariate and binary regressions as well as discrete-choice models.

A key issue determining the validity of any statistical analysis is the sample's representativeness. In general, it is difficult to find published systematic data on the proportions of transportation mega-projects out of the total projects under way in a given country within a given time period. To obtain an inkling about the representativeness of the database for each of the surveyed countries, I calculated (using EU data) what percentage of the respective country's gross infrastructure investment was represented by the mega-project investments in the database. The figures in the table below show the gross amount of investment spending (in euros) on road and rail infrastructure in each of the selected countries between 1992 and 2010 (see Table 4.1).[12] After obtaining this figure, I calculated the percentage of that sum in terms of entire infrastructure investment spending over the same period of time. Table 4.1 shows the results of these calculations.

As can be seen from this table, the percentage of investment in mega-projects out of total national investment in road and rail varies considerably, from a low of 2% in Canada to a high of 54% in Denmark, with the majority lying in the range of 5%–12%. After considering all of the necessary statistical qualifications, the figures estimated are quite representative of most countries' gross investments in road and rail.

Table 4.1 Infrastructure database: gross investment by country

	Rail, 1992–2010 (€ million)	*Road, 1992–2010 (€ million)*	*Sum (€ billion)*	*Database: mega-project investment volume, 2010 (€ billion)*	*As a percentage of total national investment*
Argentina				0.052	
Australia	20,100	94,672	114.7	6.64	0.057
Canada	8600	102,380	111.1	2.13	0.019
Hong Kong & China				11.12	
Denmark	10,300	11,078	21.4	11.75	0.54
France	68,000	207,810	275.8	22.46	0.081
Germany	102,000	210,085	312.1	23.05	0.073
Greece	6,100[a]	13,224[a]	19.3	11.28	0.058
Israel				4.3	
Italy	82,700	114,630	197.3		
Japan	150,400	1,593,226	1,743.6	24.97	0.166
South Korea				15.96	
Netherlands	n.a.	n.a.		12.32	
Russia	n.a.	n.a.		0.65	
Panama				1.4	
Portugal	6900	22,400	29.4	7.8	0.265
Sweden	17,500	19,900[a]	37.4	6.5	0.173
Thailand				6.7	
Turkey	5100	19,200	24.4	4.28	0.175
United Kingdom	99,100	109,800	208.9	18.14	0.086
USA	61,500[a]	935,600[a]	997.1	70.33	0.070

Source: http://www.oecd.org/statistics/, Accessed January 10, 2014

LOOK AT: https://stats.oecd.org/Index.aspx?DataSetCode=ITF_INV-MTN_DATA

[a]Data missing for some years

Notes

1. For an analytical review of this subject, see Berechman (2009, Chap. 3).
2. Still, one might argue that had another worthy project been built instead of BART, society could have benefited more from its positive returns throughout those 20 years.
3. Even if demand eventually picks up, Buffalo Light Rail was regarded as an unworthy project for many years, with potential benefits from other investment alternatives lost throughout the entire period.
4. Proost et al. (2010) report that over half of all TEN-T systems (a set comprised of 30 road, rail, air and water transport networks licensed by the EU) failed the CBA test.
5. Altshuler and Luberoff (2003), in their study of transportation infrastructure investments in the USA, reveal the crucial role of institutions in project decision-making (see Chap. 7).
6. This is the case when the project is favored by one powerful actor but not by others.
7. Lewis and Williams (1999) offer one normative approach to public transit decision-making.
8. See Grossman and Helpman (2008) for a study of the impact of political parties and party discipline on the supply of pork-barrel projects.
9. See Knight (2002) on the issue of central government provision of local public goods such as transportation.
10. Note that some data were not recorded due to their unavailability.
11. For instance, the OMEGA Research Centre at the University College London contains detailed information on 30 projects (http://www.omegacentre.bartlett.ucl.ac.uk/studies/index.php).
12. Where appropriate, the US dollar figure was converted into euros.

References

Alesina, A., and T. Tabellini. 2008. Bureaucrats or Politicians? *Journal of Public Economics* 92 (3–4): 426–447.

Altshuler, A., and D. Luberoff. 2003. *Mega-Projects: The Changing Politics of Urban Public Investment.* Washington, DC: The Brookings Institution.

Berechman, J. 2009. *The Evaluation of Transportation Investment Projects.* New York: Routledge.

Berechman, J., and R. Paaswell. 1983. Rail Rapid Transit Investment and CBD Revitalization: Methodology and Results. *Urban Studies* 20 (4): 471–486.

Brocker, J., A. Korzhenevych, and C. Carsten Schurmann. 2010. Assessing Spatial Equity and Efficiency Impacts of Transport Infrastructure Projects. *Transportation Research B* 44: 795–811.

Cervero, R., and J. Landis. 1997. Twenty Years of the Bay Area Rapid Transit System: Land Use and Development Impacts. *Transportation Research Part A* 31 (4): 309–333.

Flyvbjerg, B. 2007. Cost Overruns and Demand Shortfalls in Urban Rail and Other Infrastructure. *Transportation Planning and Technology* 30 (1): 9–30.

———. 2009. Survival of the Un-fittest: Why the Worst Infrastructure Gets Built and What We Can Do About It. *Oxford Review Economic Policy* 25 (3): 344–367.

Greif, A. 2008. The Impact of Administrative Power on Political and Economic Development. In *Institutions and Economic Performance*, ed. E. Helpman. Cambridge, MA: Harvard University Press.

Grossman, G., and E. Helpman. 2008. Party Discipline and Pork-Barrel Politics. In *Institutions and Economic Performance*, ed. E. Helpman. Cambridge, MA: Harvard University Press.

Hall, P. 1980. *Great Planning Disasters*. Oakland, CA: University of California Press.

Knight, B. 2002. *Parochial Interests and the Centralized Provision of Local Public Goods: Evidence from Congressional Voting on Transportation Projects*. Providence, RI: Brown University Press. http://www.econ.brown.edu/fac/Brian_Knight/parochial.pdf.

Lewis, D., and F. Williams. 1999. *Policy and Planning as Public Choice: Mass Transit in the United States*. Farnham: Ashgate.

Manski, C. 2013. *Public Policy in an Uncertain World: Analysis and Decisions*. Cambridge, MA: Harvard University Press.

Nobbe, P., and J. Berechman. 2014. *The Politics of Infrastructure Investment Decision-Making: Report of the Statistical Analysis of Selected Hypotheses, Final Report*. City College of New York: University Transportation Research Center Region 2.

Pickrell, D. 1992. A Desire Named Streetcar—Fantasy and Fact in Rail Transit Planning. *Journal of American Planning Association* 58: 158–176.

Proost, S., F. Dunkerley, S. Van der Loo, N. Adler, J. Brocker, and A. Korzhenevyc. 2010. *Do the Selected Trans European Transport Investments Pass the Cost Benefit Test?* CES Discussion Paper 10.02, Brussels, EU.

Webber, M. 1976. *The BART Experience-What Have We Learned?* Transportation Studies Monograph (26), Berkeley, CA: University of California, Institute of Urban and Regional Development.

CHAPTER 5

Inaccuracies in Cost and Demand Forecasts

5.1 Introduction

Decisions regarding transport infrastructure investments should rest, at least in theory, on *ex-ante* cost and demand projections. These serve to determine the size and capacity of the new facility, its design attributes (e.g., number of lanes), the extent of support facilities (e.g., access roads and intersections), as well as expected operational and maintenance costs and revenues (e.g., farebox or tolls). The associated social costs and benefits should likewise be based on empirical estimation. This chapter focuses on how cost and demand projections are to be made and why significant biases commonly enter into the forecasting process.[1] We subsequently ask how these projections are used in reality. We leave a discussion of other external impacts from investments, such as environmental degradation costs and economic development benefits, to Chap. 10.

Evidence collected over the last two decades shows that erroneous cost and demand estimates are made quite often. This reality raises several important questions directly relating to the main subject of this book. First, what evidence do we have to substantiate the claim that these estimates are indeed so frequently inaccurate and biased? Second, if so, what explains the respective flaws? Although faulty models and technical analyses seem obvious culprits, others include deliberate manipulation of data and results, and project mismanagement. Third,

J. Berechman, *The Infrastructure We Ride On*,
https://doi.org/10.1007/978-3-319-74606-7_5

does it really matter? That is, in reality, to what extent do cost and demand estimates matter for project choice and decision-making? We answer these questions in Sects. 5.2–5.8, with conclusions presented in Sect. 5.9.

5.2 The Methodological Foundations of Cost and Demand Projections

Reduction of travel times and costs, together with changing traffic volume either in terms of passengers or vehicles, coupled with increased safety, constitute, by and large, the core direct objectives to be achieved by building new transportation infrastructure facilities or adding more capacity to existing networks. These variables, expressed in monetary values, comprise the key measures for estimating the direct benefits from an investment. A rich literature on the theoretical foundations of this measure is readily available; for this reason, only the main arguments are presented here in a rather succinct form.[2]

A key phase in computing a transportation project's direct benefits is estimation of the stream of future volumes of passengers and/or vehicles, together with the associated travel times and cost reductions. Once estimated, these variables are monetized by means of the Value of Time (VOT) parameters that express the monetary value to users of an hour saved (see Berechman 2009, Chap. 4). Overseeing authorities (e.g., ministry of transportation) quite often prescribe use of VOTs in terms of trip types (e.g., home-work, home-leisure) and trip-makers (e.g., professional vs. regular drivers). Based on these values, and applying a pre-specified discount rate, the project's appraiser computes the Present Value (PV) of the stream of future direct benefits from the proposed project. Various models are used for the analysis of these benefits, which are collectively known as *travel demand models.*

A similar process is employed to estimate the PV of the future stream of project costs (e.g., capital, maintenance, operating and upgrading costs) with dedicated models. Normally, these models combine engineering and economic tools (e.g., engineering specifications of required labor, material and energy quantities, and the project's life), along with economic assessments of fixed and rolling stock depreciation rates as well as prices of major inputs (e.g., labor, capital, land and structures).

The main product of such cost and demand models are the streams of future costs and benefits anticipated over the project's life span. An assessment of the investment's value is then obtained by computing measures such as the project's Net Present Value (NPV), defined as the difference between the PV of the project's transportation benefits and the PV of its costs. Beyond these basic figures, many appraisal schemes require calculation of additional evaluation criteria, most notably Benefit-to-Cost ratios, the investment's rate of return, the project's Internal Rate of Return (IRR), its payback period and more (see Berechman 2009, Chap. 6). Once completed, the appraisal process is used to determine first, whether or not the investment is economically worthy, and second, the ranks of the investment alternatives relative to their transportation-economic value.

It should be evident from this brief review that if only from a technical perspective, travel demand forecasts are crucial policy- and decision-making inputs because they feed directly into the Cost-Benefit Analysis (CBA) appraisal process. Other procedures, most importantly Environmental Impact Statement (EIS), also list these projections among their key inputs. When considered against their contributions to decision-making, we can appreciate the sensitivity of appraisal criteria to manipulation and bias. However, before examining the nature of the respective intrinsic biases, I would like to present some evidence on the prevalence, magnitude and significance of biased projections.

5.3 The Evidence

Biases can be introduced along different routes. Here I define *projection inaccuracy* as the actual deviation between the predicted and observed cost and demand values. While predicted values are computed *ex ante* prior to the project's CBA, observed values become known only *ex post*, following the project's completion. When the distribution of deviations between the *ex-post* and the *ex-ante* estimates are symmetric (e.g., normally distributed), they imply similar probabilities of under- and over-estimation, suggesting that the inaccuracies are due mainly to innate uncertainties about future events. However, if the distribution is asymmetric, as in the case when demand is systematically over-estimated and costs systematically under-estimated, for example, we can claim the presence of faulty estimation practices and/or deliberate manipulation. This raises the issue of the type of evidence necessary to substantiate assertions of inherent as opposed to intended inaccuracies.

Regretfully, this question is addressed, by and large, primarily in the academic and professional literature; out in the field, *ex-post* project assessment studies are seldom carried out, mainly for lack of interest on the part of the authorities and decision-makers. And yet, more and more evidence on bias in project demand and cost estimation has been coming to light in recent years, especially with regard to mega-projects (Flyvbjerg 2005, 2007; Nobbe and Berechman 2014).[3]

Cost overruns, which express the magnitude by which *ex-post* costs have exceeded *ex-ante* estimates, serve as key indicators of biased cost projections. Jahren and Ashe (1990), using a sample of 1576 projects, found the distribution of cost overruns to be skewed to the right, indicating systematic bias in *ex-ante* cost estimates (i.e., unrealistically low estimates). Flyvbjerg et al. (2004) found a similar phenomenon in a study of 256 mega-projects, while Berechman and Chen (2011) reported a skewed distribution of cost-overrun ratios (CORs), in the same direction, for a sample of 163 road and bridge projects.[4] Similar results have been reported for even smaller samples (e.g., Pickrell's 1990 study of rail projects).

What might the magnitude of these cost overruns be? Odeck (2004) reports a study by the Swedish Auditor General of 15 road and rail projects that shows average cost overruns of 86% for roads and 17% for rail (Algers and Beser 2002). Data taken from the Nobbe and Berechman (2014) database (see Chap. 4, Appendix) indicate average cost overruns of 50% for all projects. Of the 60 projects in this database, 20% had a COR of 1.2, and about 40% had a COR between 1.2 and 2.0 (20% to 100%). An extreme example of such overruns is the Boston Big Dig (the entire highway and tunnel project), which had an inflation-adjusted COR of close to 300%, as did Greece's Attiki Odos rail project, with its inflation-adjusted COR of about 230%.

Turning to demand estimation, Table 5.1 displays findings on demand over-estimation as reported in several selected studies.

Table 5.1 Demand over-estimation

Study	*Range or average over-estimation*	*Mode (no. of cases)*
Trujillo et al. (2002)	20%–60%	All modes (???)
Flyvbjerg et al. (2005)	20%–60%	All modes (???)
Federal transit authority (FTA) (2009)	25%	Rail (18)
Nobbe and Berechman (2014)	20%–40%	All modes (60)
Bain (2011)	40%–60%	Toll roads (7)

Nobbe and Berechman (2014), using the ratio of actual demand divided by the *ex-ante* estimated demand, found that for 60% of all the transportation projects reviewed, the overrun ratio was 1.2–2.0, implying that demand was over-estimated by 120% to 200%. A case in point is the Sydney, Australia, Cross City Tunnel. *Ex-ante* projections indicated demand of 69,600 vehicles per day, while *ex-post* counts showed that only 30,000 vehicles actually used the facility on a daily basis once it was completed; this points to an over-estimate in traffic of about 100%. This level is undoubtedly far beyond what might reasonably be expected from a scrupulous demand projection.

To be sure, biases also occur in the other direction, with costs over-estimated and demand under-estimated. An extreme historical example of this direction of bias is the 60-mile-long Panama Canal linking the Atlantic and Pacific Oceans, the single most-expensive construction project undertaken in US history prior to 1914, the year of completion. The project's actual cost turned out to be below the original estimate: the final 1914 figure was about $23 million below the 1907 estimate of $375 million.[5] The Canada Line, an under- and above-ground light rail rapid transit project linking Vancouver's waterfront with its international airport, received an original demand estimate of 100,000 boarding per day by 2013. By 2011, however, actual boarding exceeded that estimate by 35%. Still another example is Europe's Channel Tunnel Rail Link. Annual passenger estimates for the year 1998 were 6.7 million while the actual number of users reached 22 million, indicating that demand was under-estimated by 328%.

These and similar cases notwithstanding, here we are concerned with negative biases, namely, events where large-scale capital-intensive projects actually cost much more than originally estimated, or when demand for services are significantly below the original projections. The key conclusion from this short survey is that as a rule, the distribution of *ex-post* versus *ex-ante* demand (actual utilization level) tends to be significantly skewed to the left, implying systematic over-estimation inaccuracies (Quinet 1998; Odeck 2013), and the deviation in costs skewed to the right.

Cost and demand forecast inaccuracies continue to remain problematic for road, rail and toll bridge projects alike, although their causes have not been universally agreed upon. Key studies of cost and demand projections tend to be fairly consistent in their overall findings that the figures are biased in the direction of under-estimation of costs and over-estimation of demand, and that the size of these biases vary by travel mode (Flyvbjerg 2005; Pickrell 1990; van Wee 2007). Apart from the observed biases in demand forecasts, the level of accuracy is itself problematic. The cited studies report standard deviations in accuracy above 30%, while half of the rail projects in these studies report standard deviations above 50%.[6]

One key standard explanation for these biases has to do with the intricacies of the methodologies used to generate estimates. However, before examining this issue I should mention some factors, external to the estimation process, which might also explain projection biases. Failure to perform risk analysis is one such factor, with project mismanagement another. Risk analysis has been discussed widely in the literature and is further examined in subsequent chapters. Yet, little is found in the germane literature on project mismanagement as a factor explaining deviations between the *ex-post* cost and demand and their *ex-ante* projections. One organizational factor explaining this lapse, as noted in Chap. 7, is the fact that the agencies overseeing project evaluation and choice tend to be the same ones managing the selected project's construction. Quality of management is an open question as a variable, with little empirical evidence available to enable us to derive concrete conclusions.

One anecdotal example hints at what we might find should an empirical study of project management be undertaken. The head of the New York Metropolitan Transportation Authority (MTA) Capital Construction division, who is also in charge of constructing the Second Avenue Subway (SAS), once stated in an interview that an early cost projection for the SAS was \$3.8 billion, with a 2014 completion date. At present, however, cost estimates have risen to \$4.451 billion, with a 2016 end date. He added, "Estimates put forth way back were estimates that lacked the precision required. As the project started to mature, we started to get much better bids." In his comment he neglected to say how well this project was managed and whether a risk analysis was performed at the time of the cost estimation, factors that could possibly account for a proportion of the substantial cost overruns. Would the project still be built would the true cost figure be known in advance?

5.4 Travel Demand Forecasting and Inaccuracies

One of the main causes for biased demand estimates are the models used in forecasting. For this reason, I begin by reviewing the structure of commonly used demand forecasting modeling process.

Before entering into a detailed discussion, it would be worthwhile taking a look at the schematic layout of the conceptual foundations of a conventional travel demand modeling in Fig. 5.1, such as those employed in many countries.

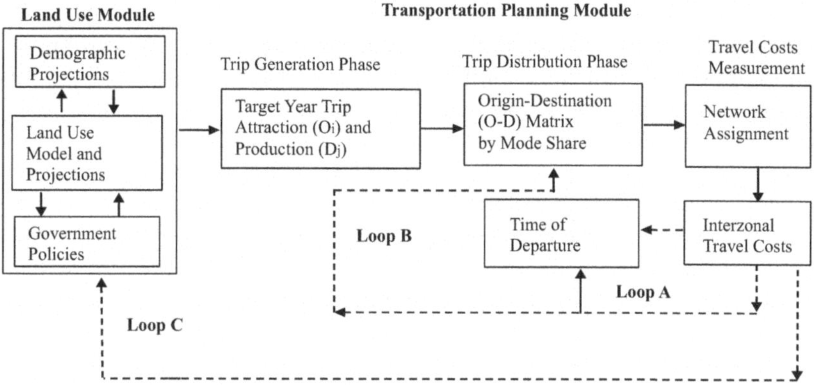

Fig. 5.1 Travel Demand Modeling: The Joint Land-Use-Transportation Modeling Framework. Source: Berechman (2009)

This figure shows what is known as the "joint land-use-transportation modeling framework", which underlies most empirical travel demand forecasting models. It contains two major modules, labeled *land use* and *transportation* (McNally 2000). The latter module incorporates the so-called, four-step transportation planning process, which begins with projections of regional demographic trends, land-use patterns and related public policies (e.g., zoning). These trends, considered external to travel demand projections, serve two key functions: first, at the trip-generation phase, travel volumes originating at specific locations are derived from demographic and land-use data. Second, these same trends serve as upper bounds on estimated future travel demand volumes because the amount of observed and projected travel noted in the plan must not exceed these quantities. For example, the number of future regional passenger-trips is derived from regional demographic trends (e.g., age cohorts and household formation rates) as well as from anticipated numbers of households and commercial enterprises at specific locations. In terms of the travel demand model itself, analysts are prohibited from estimating more trip-makers than the anticipated number of eligible driving-age adults living and working in the specified locations. These constraints can negatively affect the reliability of the derived demand estimates if the future trip functions are mis-specified and/or the external demographic and location data are imprecise. These inaccuracies reduce the forecast's validity and, as a direct consequence, the validity of the derived travel demand estimates, especially for extended horizons (20–40 years).[7]

We should also stress that the assessment of future demographic trends, land-use patterns and technological changes are subject to substantial amounts of risk and uncertainty. Hence, the crucial issues relate to the associated errors, whether systematic or random. Poorly estimated and therefore incorrect coefficients, such as trip rates per 1000 persons, introduce systematic biases into the model. The use of incorrect conversion coefficients from passenger-trips to vehicle-trips matrices, assumed to be uniform over space and constant over time, also generate systematic errors. In contrast, external shocks, such as the introduction of new passenger information technology, result in random forecasting errors.[8] As already noted, only seldom do risk and uncertainty factors enter forecasting models (Trujillo et al. 2002). This problem is exacerbated when, as often happens, multiple actors, such as private consultants and local agencies, perform different segments of the estimation, often under conditions of faulty coordination.[9]

As shown in Fig. 5.1, once trip-generation (travel from origin and destination locations) vectors are estimated, they are distributed among travel zones in order to derive trip matrices (also known as *trip distribution matrices*), that depict trips patterns between locations i and j in the modeled region. These matrices provide the figures for inter-zonal demand functions, constructed according to trip purpose and mode. Many models are used for this purpose, a notable one being the so-called gravity model.[10] However, whatever the model employed, it needs to be calibrated relative to its parameters. Calibration is frequently haphazard in practice, with analysts tending to *borrow* parameters from other studies conducted for other regions during diverse periods. Once an error occurs in the estimated parameter values, it is carried over to succeeding phases of the process.[11]

The next step in the analysis is calculation of inter-zonal travel costs (or prices), which consist mainly of monetized travel times and car-use costs. To that end, *traffic assignment models* are used to load previously estimated inter-zonal travel demand matrices onto a network model constructed specifically for highway, or rail. Different types of assignment models are available, including static, dynamic and microscopic models.[12] All aim at obtaining inter-zonal travel costs once the travel demand volumes are assigned to the network's links, each coded in terms of its capacity and other attributes (e.g., traffic lights, number of lanes, etc.). At this stage, the non-availability of quality network-coded data has been found to be a main source of estimation bias. This bias deepens when large-scale networks, typical to large metropolitan areas having thousands of links and intersections, need to be coded. Still other biases emanate from misspecification of the volume-capacity functions used to derive travel times on capacitated links at assigned traffic volumes. The technical literature provides a variety of such functions, differentiated by their structural parameters, whose appropriateness for the modeled region is not always ascertained in advance.

Figure 5.1 also exhibits three loops, labeled A, B and C, denoting actual market equilibrium estimation processes. Loop A indicates that inter-zonal travel times and costs, once modified in response to capacity-improving infrastructure investments, trigger adjustments in trip-makers' behavior, most notably in departure times. These, in turn, affect travel volumes at peak hours and, in consequence, travel times and costs. Theoretically, this equilibrium-oriented behavior continues until further cost incentives are incapable of persuading trip-makers to adjust their departure times. Loop B indicates the equilibrium obtained between revised inter-zonal travel times and costs and the distribution of trips originating and ending at locations within the respective region. That is, we anticipate that in response to the decline in travel costs and times following capacity improvements, travelers will find it advantageous to adjust their activities (e.g., shopping) in the chosen origins and destinations; generalized travel costs will thus be affected. This process terminates when the impacts of the selected cost-reduction incentives are exhausted. Finally, loop C implies the possibility of reaching a global equilibrium between activity locations and travel costs. Thus, even in the short but certainly in the medium and long run, we posit that households and businesses respond to lower travel costs by relocating to sites where the combination of lower rents and travel costs maximizes their utility. Existing travel patterns are consequently altered. This implies that in the wake of capacity expansion, we often observe new traffic in the upgraded system, with this traffic representing trip-makers who, prior to the expansion, chose not to travel at all[13] or were diverted to other facilities. In brief, loop C captures the (in)compatibility between land uses and transportation systems.

In the real world, market inefficiencies and government policies (e.g., zoning) may restrict realization of these equilibria and thus affect travel demand estimation. Correct travel demand estimation thus requires that these three equilibria be modeled and computed at the mega-project's assessment stage in order to provide a reliable framework for deriving quality predictions. Unfortunately, this step is rarely taken, the outcome of which is distorted travel demand forecasts (Naess et al. 2012).

Finally, demand (like cost) forecasting calls for the use of reference points or benchmarks (also known as the *zero* or *do-nothing* planning alternative) against which parameters are to be calculated. That is, the extrapolation of present conditions, such as congestion levels, to a future date allows creation of a reference point for comparing prospective travel conditions with and without the project. However, as research has shown, these benchmarks are regularly most inaccurate and exaggerated because of the failure to account for general equilibrium effects (Nicolaisen and Naess 2015). Hence, accuracy in forecasting per se is not the issue. Perhaps more importantly is the deviation of these forecasts from the benchmarks that often serve as the pivotal criteria for project valuation and choice.

There are, however, alternatives to the modeling approaches just mentioned. Activity-Based Models (ABMs), for example, begin with observations of the daily activity patterns of individuals, which are aggregated to produce the combined trip generation, modal split and trip distribution forecasts shown in Fig. 5.1. And yet, ABM models still require inter-zonal travel costs as inputs (Recker 2001).[14] The well-reputed Discrete Choice Model (known also as the *random utility model*) treats individual trip-makers as utility maximizers and solves for their travel preferences while considering their socio-economic characteristics (e.g., income) and the attributes (e.g., travel times and costs) of their trip alternatives (Ben-Akiva and Lerman 1985). Forecasts of these travel attributes nonetheless require population and cost estimates, which are determined external to the model itself.

In sum, whatever the modeling approach, travel demand forecasting inaccuracies originate in a range of analytical and computational issues. These may include the flawed prediction of demographic, mainly population trends, employment trends, land-use patterns, and future policies. To this we should add mis-specification of parameters, failure to conduct equilibrium analysis, failure to take account of technological, economic and financial risks and uncertainties, as well as use of unrealistic behavioral assumptions.

As we shall soon see, some researchers (e.g., Trujillo et al. 2002; Flyvbjerg et al. 2005) argue that deliberate manipulation is the primary source of demand estimation bias. A milder version of this argument states that advocacy, often disguised as science, underlies such behavior. Based on my research, I would conclude that the demand estimation biases appearing in a significant proportion of all projects are due mainly to the flawed modeling practices mentioned and *not* to intentional manipulation.

On the other hand, the desire of decision-makers for simple and unequivocal analyses encourages their propensity to blindly accept biased estimates (Manski 2013).

As already noted, the main objective of travel demand forecasting is to provide estimates of future volumes of trips measured in units of car-trips, passenger-trips, vehicle-km, passenger-km, trip rates, trip frequency, destination choices and mode shares, mainly at peak hours. All demand forecasting models, whether implicitly or explicitly, assume that the relevant travel markets are efficient and that individuals optimize their travel choices relative to the market conditions (e.g., location, mode availability, trip objective and route) they face. These assumptions obviously have a direct impact on the structure of the models and thus on the quality of the forecasts. Ironically, as Manski (2013) notes, the stronger the assumptions, the less credible the predictions obtained. Next, I briefly examine some basic assumptions that modelers adopt, implicitly or explicitly, that bear serious impacts on demand estimation accuracy.

With respect to efficiency, markets, especially land-use markets, are far from efficient in practice. Recognition of this fact has spawned a growing body of literature dealing with market imperfections together with their impact on location decisions and transportation behavior (Venables 2007). Yet, by and large, demand forecasting models have failed to reflect these realities. The same can be said for the assumption that individuals optimize their choices, an assumption shown to be questionable by numerous studies in behavioral economics.[15] Until this situation is corrected, the forecasting trip-makers' future choices will continue to veer toward erroneous and thus lead to inaccurate forecasts.

As to prices, the failure to estimate their effect on travel decisions can have particularly grave consequences for demand forecasts. If road tolls are used to finance the project, the level of toll collection will affect car traffic volumes as well as the demand for mass transit. Likewise, if the project is funded, even partially, through farebox revenues, fare structure and level will likewise affect complementary mode demand.

Lastly, disregard for the impacts of complementary transport systems has been noted as another cause of inaccurate demand forecasting (Pickrell 1990; Quinet 1998).[16] But whatever the direct cause, what really matters in forecasting is not any one single factor; rather it is the accumulated effect of all the factors that lead to the colossal biases and inaccuracies in demand forecasts we have observed, especially for mega-projects.[17]

5.5 Cost Estimation and Inaccuracies

As already stated, the literature provides ample evidence of inaccurate cost estimation, mainly in the form of cost overruns (Berechman and Chen 2011; Flyvbjerg 2007; Flyvbjerg et al. 2004; Odeck 2013; Pickrell 1990; Siemiatycki 2009). Yet, save for the reporting of intentional inaccuracies, surprisingly little has been written on the methodological factors contributing to their bias. Here I advance several major causes:

1. Delays in planning, construction and implementation
2. Computation and financing of capital costs
3. Bidding and bidders' behavior, including post-contract renegotiations
4. Use of outdated relationships between past and current construction prices
5. Disregard or inappropriate treatment of risk factors
6. Timing of project's commissioning and forecasting
7. Faulty comparison of costs under state financing and public-private partnerships

The dataset referred to in Chap. 4 provides distributions of planning, construction and implementation times for 60 international mega-projects. Here, *planning time* is defined as the span of time between the onsets of a project's planning to the year of its inception, when the project is formally approved by decision-makers. *Construction time* covers the time between the beginnings to the end of construction. Notice that these two time categories can overlap as some planning is conducted after construction has actually begun. *Implementation time* refers to the time span from the year of the project's inception to its completion. It thus includes duration of construction as well as delays due to external causes such as funding issues. Figure 5.2 displays the distribution of these project phases by time intervals.

Note that Fig. 5.2 does not compare time categories. It simply shows what proportion of projects experience each type of categories. For example, less than 20% of the projects in the database were implemented within 0–5 years. Within this period, about 35% of all projects were planned and constructed. In contrast, about 30% of all projects were implemented within 10–15 years while only 10%–12% were planned and constructed. It thus appears that at 10–15 years and beyond, the proportion of projects implemented is greater than the proportion of projects

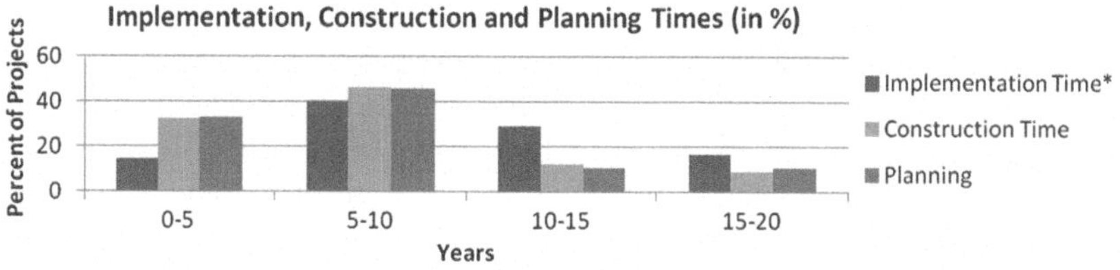

Fig. 5.2 Percent Distribution of Implementation, Construction and Planning Times by Project Time Span. Source: Nobbe and Berechman (2014)

constructed. The importance of this distribution lies in the observation that longer implementation times are associated with larger cost overruns (Flyvbjerg et al. 2004). Construction delays, which affect implementation duration and thereby increase the likelihood of inflated costs, explain this phenomenon. In general, planning and implementation are interrelated in that as planning continues and changes are introduced, early construction estimates decline in their relevance.

Computation of a *project's capital costs* is the second methodological factor explaining overruns. Architectural and engineering design phases, by project type (e.g., surface vs. underground rail), must consider several weighty cost components requiring estimation from an engineering point of view. These include quantities and input factors, mainly labor, material, energy, machinery and land. The prices of some factors, most notably land, are rather speculative. Costs of eminent domain and easement are highly uncertain. Furthermore, even if the land is currently publicly owned, its opportunity costs should be factored in.[18] As to rail projects, these entail substantial rolling stock acquisition, whose cost levels at the time of their estimation is likewise often subject to uncertainty.

Given this range of factors affecting costs, the derivation of estimates is often accomplished by using the unit cost values of comparable past projects or the prices noted in contracts. For *standard* projects, for example, road construction, this practice might be reasonable. Yet, for *non-standard* projects, such as a new subway line, these values are often inadequately adjusted for local conditions, fluctuations in unit prices and current market conditions, including inflation. Such adjustments also apply to actual construction costs incurred for excavation, tunneling, foundations, structures (e.g., stations) and supporting hardware (e.g., electrical systems). Depending on topography (hilly vs. flat terrain), these can vary considerably.

Related to these sources of inaccuracies in unit cost computations are issues connected with bidding, required before public authorities purchase services from private contractors. Bidding, which generally is mandatory, can contribute to cost overruns in two major ways. First, bidders frequently rely on inadequately amended historical unit cost data.[19] Second, the pervasive *design and build* bidding mechanism rests primarily on the lowest bid, commonly required by public agencies. As a result, private-sector bidders are incentivized to under-estimate their costs, mainly by incorporating the mentioned unadjusted cost data.

Reviewing this list of causes, it is reasonable to claim that capital cost assessment unavoidably entails inaccuracies and estimation biases, even if properly executed. As argued previously, it stands to reason that project cost biases (*ex-post* minus *ex-ante* estimates) should be symmetrically distributed, with over- and under-estimations occurring in equal probabilities. The evidence cited above nonetheless refutes this assumption: capital cost biases across samples of projects were found to skew to the right, creating asymmetrical distributions that imply greater under- (than over-) estimation biases. This leaves us to search other factors that might explain this phenomenon.

Risk analysis is one of the major factors to be considered when computing capital costs; it entails estimation of the probability that actual costs will exceed predicted costs by a specific proportion. Statistically, this probability is represented by the right-hand side of the distribution of project cost overruns. With agencies' built-in tendency to exhaust their allotted investment budget (see Chap. 7), the likelihood of post-project cost underruns is rather small relative to the likelihood of overruns. Hence, the asymmetric bias in observed capital costs estimation. Given that all too often the project's CBA, if performed at all, does not involve risk analysis, the right-hand side of the cost distribution remains largely unaccounted for. To be sure, we are not claiming here that the failure to perform risk analysis per se induces capital cost estimation inaccuracies. Rather, it is the lack of risk analysis that demands of us to take biases into account.

However, there is still another factor that can explain the asymmetric distribution of cost estimates: the *timing of forecast commissioning*. This bias is reflected in the combination of two phases: first, when forecasts are actually commissioned and carried out; second, when they are used as input into the project's approval process. A capital cost forecast is generally commissioned as part of the preliminary feasibility study, years before a decision is made to actually implement the project. As decision-making time arrives, these estimates tend to be neither revised nor updated, mainly regarding changes in the input quantities and prices that transpired in the interim. Hence, the disproportionate increase in the cost overruns. I take up the related question of who actually performs the forecast later.

We can now ask whether it is possible to determine the main reason for mega-project costs overruns. All of the factors reviewed certainly contribute to this phenomenon. However, the difference between implementation and construction times, which imply delayed project initiation and thus construction, appears to be pivotal. But that is not all: these delays can be attributed in turn to inadequate institutional approaches and regimes, a constellation that supports changing project objectives in mid-course, to which we must add ineffective decision-making, a lack of managerial responsibility and efficacy, and funding instability (Nijkamp and Ubbels 1999; Bruzelius et al. 2002).

5.6 Manipulation of Cost and Demand Forecasts and Project Mismanagement

The reader may ask why are infrastructure investment projects, particular in transportation, so expensive?[20] Here, however, I focus on what accounts for enormous differences in unit costs as shown in a comparison of mega-projects worldwide. To illustrate the scale of these disparities, consider the SAS in New York, which cost \$4.45 billion, *bought* roughly 3.2 km (2 miles) of new tunnels and three new stations. Then consider the Canada Line project in Vancouver (opened in 2009), a combination of underground and above-ground rail roughly 23.2 km (about 14.5 miles) long and including new 16 stations, which cost \$2.1 billion, half the price of the other project. I wish to offer two kinds of explanations for the difference: institutional and inherent conflicts as well as perverse incentives.

Under the rubric of *institutional factors*, I explore the following four elements:

1. *Labor costs*: For all transportation infrastructure projects, labor costs (the product of labor force size and price) constitute a significant proportion of total costs. In the USA, public projects are required to employ local unionized labor. While this requirement is not necessarily counter-productive a priori, union contracts and labor regulations result in on-site work crews being too large for the task. For similar reasons, the price per unit of unionized labor is much higher than its non-unionized equivalent.[21] While similar rules prevail in other countries, the USA stands out in the high level of these costs.[22]

2. *Buy domestic regulations*: For various political and economic reasons, many countries require that inputs for infrastructure projects be procured only from domestic manufacturers even when local prices are far higher than prices of similar inputs produced elsewhere. For example, the *Buy America* ruling[23] obligates government agencies to buy steel manufactured in the USA even if it is much more expensive than similar grade steel produced overseas. In capital-intensive projects like tunnels and bridges, where steel is a major input, costs consequently skyrocket.[24]
3. *Contracting-out rules*: By and large, bidders for public sector projects compete on price, not quality. These rules create built-in incentives to cut costs by lowering construction standards. Should this practice be constrained by quality inspection practices, bidders will often enter into post-contract renegotiations in order to up the value of their contracts. The number of very expensive legal disputes that have followed proves just how prevalent this practice is (e.g., see Estache et al. 2009).
4. *Lack of in-house expert skills*: Due to the lack of in-house staff with the necessary expertise, public agencies generally contract-out a project's analysis, design and management to private companies. These companies have little incentive to reduce costs or the length of planning or construction schedules. At the procurement stage, the lack of expert knowledge regularly manifests itself in the acquisition of overly expensive material and services. Moreover, public agencies often lack the skills to design bids and contracts including the appropriate workable enforcement mechanisms. Private sector contractors know this, and act accordingly.

In the field of transportation, deliberate manipulation and misrepresentation of data are often cited as the main causes of cost under-estimation and benefit over-estimation, especially of ridership (Flyvbjerg et al. 2002). In consequence, the projects looking best on paper may, in reality, be the very same projects that amass the highest cost overruns and benefit shortfalls. As a result, Wachs (1989, 1990) claims that the analysts who conduct CBAs often find themselves in inherently conflictual positions. Although they serve as the *technical experts* mandated to provide the best possible estimates of project alternatives, they may simultaneously act as *advocates* of the projects favored by their employers or clients. Because project decisions are meant to be supported by facts and figures, planners succumbing to their advocacy role tend to produce biased estimates. In a similar fashion, Flyvbjerg (2009) claims that self-serving incentives, offered by promoters of particular projects, encourage analysts to under-estimate costs and over-estimate benefits, steps thought necessary to improve the likelihood of favored projects being selected. Hartgen (2013) goes further by arguing that forecasts are often deliberately designed to put some projects in a favorable light and others in the shadows.

Several other scholars are less prone to blame forecast manipulation as the cause of biased estimates; instead, they attribute projection bias to the normal tension abounding between professional modelers on the one hand and bureaucrats and decision-makers on the other. Parthasarathi and Levinson (2010), for example, conclude that policy-makers' anti-modeling sentiments are due to their miscomprehension of the estimation process. Pickrell (1992), writing in this vein, attributes projection biases to misinterpretation of the numerical forecasts produced by technical models as early as the planning process.

In all fairness, there is a strong element of truth in these assertions of forecast manipulation. Analysts, especially if hired by agencies to conduct technical evaluations of projects, are often caught between their sense of professional ethics and honesty on the one hand, and loyalty to their clients on the other. It is indeed difficult to deny that those interested in promoting a project all too often use groundless figures to advance their cause.[25] Such a tactic obviously leads to estimates that are products of faulty professional ethics and intentional deceit.[26] But, in light of the inherent complexities, number of assumptions and misspecification of model functions previously discussed, we should expect some estimation bias to enter the process even when professional standards are fully enforced.

In sum, we can readily conclude that the enormous costs of megaprojects are not simply the outcome of magnitude; they are also due to various built-in factors. Proper management and the revision of labor and purchasing rules would clearly serve to decrease costs. This reality shifts the locus of our questions to how these inaccuracies, whether technical or intentional, enter project evaluation. As I have asserted, the conduct of risk analysis and the updating of estimates can reduce inaccuracies whatever their source. An additional step would be to emphasize transparency throughout the process.

5.7 Forecast Commissioning, Transparency and Accountability

In many countries, the stipulation of formal evaluation procedures (see Chap. 3) has been accompanied by entrusting oversight agencies with the preparation of the respective projections: direct transportation benefits (travel times, cost savings, travel volumes and safety) and costs (capital, operating and maintenance). As I argue in Chap. 7, these agencies are not innocent of organizational considerations, inter-agency rivalry and funding concerns, not to mention political meddling. Several studies have pointed out agency tendencies to conceal or delay transmitting forecasts that either do not chime with or undermine their objectives. Flyvbjerg et al. (2006), among the dominant proponents of this view, claim that manipulation of information is the key source of forecast bias, especially for rail projects. They attribute this trend to agency desires to secure political support for capital-intensive projects; this means that biases are often pre-meditated and politically oriented (in this case, in the sphere of institutional politics). We therefore now turn to a discussion of just how these trends are realized in practice.

As we have pointed out, agencies tend to commission benefit and cost forecasts long before they are actually needed. This tendency is supported by the lack of built-in and binding updating mechanisms, a reality that, by itself, can introduce forecast bias. When searching for why no updating mechanisms are mandatory, direct experience indicates a link between who prepares the forecasts and forecast quality. Unfortunately, these issues are more or less absent from the germane scholarly research agenda.

As noted above, transportation agencies, due to their lack of in-house expertise, commission consulting firms that specialize in cost but especially demand forecasting. What makes this issue so sensitive are the terms under which these firms are contracted. On the one hand, they can be asked to conduct a totally genuine and professional analysis; on the other, they can be given a target or total demand estimate, such as the expected number of passengers in a future year, and asked to provide an analysis that corroborates these figures. These objectives are rarely spelled out in a written contract; they are communicated during informal meetings, during which tacit understandings are reached. At the same time, these consulting firms must consider their long-term business interests, interests which may interfere with accurate forecasting. Intensifying this problem is the lack of verification reviews conducted by external, independent consultants with respect to the forecasts' adequacy and quality. We should therefore not be surprised at the frequency of forecasts eventually proven to be off the mark.

It might be argued that the growing demand for forecast transparency would have ensured the revelation of their underlying assumptions, data quality, methodology and computations. But has this vision been realized? The obvious question is, therefore, just how transparent are demand and cost forecasts in the real world of project decision-making?

Based on a statistical analysis of their database, Nobbe and Berechman (2014) have shown that mega-project demand and costs forecasts are, by and large, not transparent. Yet, within the group of all projects, rail projects are statistically more transparent than highway projects. After digging deeper, an additional statistical analysis showed that transparency is associated primarily with factors technically external to the project itself, particularly opposition to the project's implementation and the state of national wealth.

We begin with *project opposition*. The statistical results show that transparency is significantly associated most often with political and ideological opposition. The nature of this causal link is not entirely clear because transparency can arouse opposition, at least potentially, by making the public and interest groups more aware of the project's attributes. Alternatively, opposition can force a project to become more transparent by requiring its promoters to make the germane information public (see Chap. 7 for a detailed review).

Again, statistically, project transparency is more prevalent and more comprehensive in the industrial world's wealthy countries. We would suggest a convergence of factors to promote this result. First, wealthier countries tend to be more democratic and enjoy a longer tradition of public awareness and public sector openness. Second, wealthier countries tend to conduct more benefit-cost analyses that are also better documented. Third, the decision-making leading to highway and railway project approval also tends to be better documented. Finally, the status of a project as new rather than an extension to an existing network adds to the likelihood that the forecast will be transparent because new projects are more likely to be subjected to comprehensive CBAs. As to mega-projects, these are, in general, new projects. However, the above results notwithstanding, mega-projects cannot, as a rule, be assumed to be transparent. The same data show that a significant number of projects, highway and rail, lack transparency or are only somewhat transparent. This observation can therefore partially explain the skewed distribution of projects evidencing cost overruns and demand under-utilization.

Travel demand and traffic models, like those mentioned above, mainly focus on the prediction of future demand and traffic volumes, given the current or projected state of the network. The responsible authorities, whether federal, state and even local, statutorily or as a matter of policy, nonetheless introduce additional major requirements for the forecasts they request. Most noticeable are the prediction of car emissions from future traffic, emerging land-use patterns and impacts on social equity. These issues are largely dealt with at the post-modeling stage and thus incorporate the errors already embedded in the travel forecasts. Since the final choice of an investment, especially a mega-project, is also predicated on these projections, the magnitude of the forecasting error tends to balloon while remaining largely unknown or mis-recognized.

Furthermore, the geographic span of large-scale transportation investments tends to be large, covering multiple jurisdictions and authorities often having quite dissimilar populations, travel needs and objectives, pricing and land-use policies. For instance, central city accessibility is viewed differently by suburban jurisdictions than by city residents. In this situation, the use of a limited forecasting model, similar to that shown in Fig. 5.1, will be inadequate as well as produce substantial errors, which often remain unrecognized or ignored. It may also result in plans being deferred. A review of 23 long-range plans for large-scale US regions showed that they all had similar content, including items designed to meet federal government guidelines on travel and emissions, but targeted primarily to ensure continuous federal funding. For the reason just cited, these plans were by and large left on the shelf, with most deferred to a future funding cycle (Hartgen et al. 2008).

Still another source of inaccuracy in forecasting is the poor treatment of differences in freight and passenger transportation features that vary throughout the network. Currently used forecasting models, mainly through assumptions of vehicle size and use of road capacity, attempt to distinguish between traffic types but too often neglect to capture crucial dissimilarities, such as the distribution of traffic volumes by time of day, parking and loading/unloading space needs, noxious emissions, wear and tear of road surface, pricing schemes and so forth. Another factor often disregarded is the impact of regional existing freight transportation facilities (e.g., ports) that are expected to experience changing volumes as new technologies make possible a growth in the number of super containers ships, for example, docking in outdated ports.

Technological progress is likely to be another source of inaccuracy and error. New travel-related technologies such as driverless vehicles, specialized information technology aimed at providing real-time information to trip-makers, or data mining by large manufacturers and retail establishments are increasingly being used to affect sales. The models presently used cannot respond to technology's impacts on travel behavior. The failure of current forecasting tools to incorporate the same emerging technologies has become a major and unanticipated source of error.[27]

5.8 Does It at All Matter? Implications of Forecasts for CBAs and Choice

Demand and cost estimates are at the heart of CBA procedures. Assuming that forecasts will never be totally accurate and that biases will always enter, the issue shifts to the level of forecasting bias considered tolerable for the modeler as well as for their consumers. For example, assume inaccuracy of 5% in daily traffic turnout, with the true number being 20,000 vehicles. This means that 1000 vehicles daily have been unaccounted for. Is this inaccuracy serious in terms of the forecast's results and the project planned? Naess et al. (2012) found that as *little* as 5% additional demand could result in a loss of more than one-third of expected project benefits. And yet, while such a level of inaccuracy may affect the results of CBA studies, does it at all matter for actual project decision-making? If they do matter, what is their place in the hierarchy of decision variables?

To obtain a reasonable answer we must first qualify the question by adding, "matters to whom"? At the professional level, it certainly does matter, at least to economists, transportation and land-use planners. These professionals may disagree on the weight to be assigned to CBAs in project decision-making but not on the basic need to perform an accurate analysis (Mouter et al. 2013). Turning to political decision-makers, a different response is obtained. Nobbe and Berechman (2014) found that out of the 60 projects in their database, 35% had undergone a complete CBA, 18% only a partial or incomplete CBA, while 47% none at all. To the degree to which this sample is representative of mega-projects (see discussion in Chap. 4), the analysis implies that even if all projects undergo demand and cost estimation, the lack of a CBA when making project choices reduce if not eliminate the value of those estimates.

Some authors assert that decision-making regarding transport infrastructure investments relies more extensively on various types of impact analyses rather than on CBA results (e.g., Nicolaisen and Driscoll 2014). Still others have suggested that the transportation-economic performance of projects is hardly ever a decisive political priority (e.g., Sager and Ravlum 2005). The authors of these studies examined and for the most part confirmed the hypothesis that political decision-makers do gather information but do not use it. They may ask for details and then ignore them. This information, including demand and cost estimates, is used at best for planning items such as service frequency design and required rolling stock. But, as researchers have argued, decision-makers generally make decisions first and look for relevant information afterwards. As a result, a great deal of information is often collected and processed despite its marginal or non-existent impact on final decisions.

A different set of factors undermining the relevance of CBAs is described in Chap. 10, which explores the role of a project's external effects—mainly equity and economic development—on choice. Here we note only that some researchers have proposed that conventional evaluation methods omit many consequential although indirect economic benefits of investment in transportation infrastructure (Banister and Berechman 2000; Banister and Thurstain-Goodwin 2011). They maintain that external rather than the direct transport benefits are increasingly becoming more important in the analysis and choice of advanced transportation networks. These external benefits include regional network effects, output and productivity, agglomeration economies and job creation. As I shall argue in subsequent chapters, environmental concerns, the spatial incidence of benefits and costs, and real-estate development in urban areas have become key priorities, replacing more-traditional objectives.

5.9 Conclusions

The renowned Danish physicist Niels Bohr famously declared that "prediction is very difficult, especially about the future". Irrespective of its current status as a cliché, the statement has not lost its validity when it comes to estimating transportation costs as well as distant demand patterns. This chapter has focused on the factors that make Bohr's comments so relevant.

The evidence presented in this chapter has also confirmed yet another cliché that, by and large, transportation demand and cost projections are inaccurate and biased. If these inaccuracies were random, one would expect demand under- and over-estimates and cost underruns and overruns to be rather normally distributed. Yet, as the data show, the distributions are highly skewed, indicating systematic bias for both parameters.

Several causes were proposed to explain the prevalence of the flawed and skewed results. First, we cited faulty models that overlook equilibrium solutions and often use outdated data for factors external to transportation per se. Key among these are demographic, socio-economic and land-use trends. In addition, the choice of arbitrary benchmarks is another contributing factor. These benchmarks typically portray dismal future travel conditions while disregarding the counter-effects of household behavior (e.g., relocation) as well as urban zoning and parking policies. Alternatively, the commonly used demand forecasting models do not account for radical changes in technology and climate (e.g., introduction of driverless cars or increasingly extreme weather conditions), events that can significantly change future travel patterns in unexpected ways.

Another explanation given in the literature for the inaccuracies typifying mega-project demand and cost estimates is the deliberate manipulation of data and results, including the perverse incentives built into infrastructure decision-making and funding mechanisms. As will be explained in Chap. 9, the multiplicity and rivalry among transportation oversight institutions, especially when funding is low, stimulates a built-in tendency to select preferred projects, with this bias usually infiltrating the entire political system (see Fig. 3.1, Chap. 3). These culminate in the generation of demand and cost projections that convey positive estimates of the preferred project's benefits. While, difficult to prove empirically, such practices no-doubt prevail throughout the project decision-making structure.

Project mismanagement is another major factor explaining biased estimates. That is, even if the estimates are correct, a transportation agency's internal inefficiency can affect the results *ex post*, resulting in sometime very large deviations from the original estimates. Evidence of such inefficiency, while not readily available but perhaps hidden in agency files, is frequently cited by the media.

Finally, there seems to be a wide gap between the messages transmitted by technical analysts and the messages consumers want to hear. By and large, methodological research is poorly disseminated to the public at large, causing the latter to perceive modeling results as too technical and far removed from their *real* transportation and economic needs. This misconception may significantly contribute to the low weight attached by publicly elected officials to the accuracy of forecasts. Yet, the fact that constituents may be uninterested in the projections does not preclude the need to carry them out competently by using the best available tools.

How does all this affect project decision-making? The data available suggest that about half of all mega-projects implemented worldwide did not undergo a comprehensive benefit-cost analysis. Furthermore, a substantial proportion of the other half were subject to only partial CBAs. Hence, demand and cost estimates, whether flawless or inaccurate, did not play a central role in project decision-making and choice. In reality, other criteria seem to have been decisive in a project's choice. Subsequent chapters will delve still further into these factors. On the optimistic side, "a reasonably sophisticated and relatively unbiased report on factual matters in dispute could have important impacts on the portion of the public that has not yet taken a side in the controversy, but whose interests are at stake" (Mazur 1981), meaning that the public could be educated to understand and thus affect transportation decision-making. On the negative side, again quoting Mazur (1981), "[m]any technical controversies are primarily disputes over political goals and only secondarily concerned with the veracity of scientific issues which are related to these goals."

Notes

1. I use the term *bias* in a statistical rather than normative sense.
2. The interested reader is referred to Berechman (2009, Chaps. 3–5) and Small and Verhoef (2007, Chap. 5) for detailed analyses.
3. For evidence of projection inaccuracies in road transport projects in the UK, see the report issued by the Department of Transport (2013). For the EU, see a study by the European Court of Auditors (2013), and for Australia, see Li and Hensher (2010). For the Dutch case see Cantarelli et al. (2012).
4. The COR is defined as the ratio of the *ex-post* values to the *ex-ante* estimate (Berechman and Chen 2011).
5. The Canal's low cost does not reflect its enormous cost in human lives, a factor rarely if ever included in a project's cost estimation. Hospital records indicate that 5609 lives were lost from disease and accidents during the period when the USA was responsible for construction. Deaths during the period of French responsibility reached about 20,000 according to estimates by the project's chief medical officer.
6. In a survey on demand forecasting model accuracy conducted among professionals, the results for anticipated accuracy, for all project types, were as follows: ±9%–10% for calibration (a standard deviation of 6%); ±11% for one year after opening (SD = 7%); ±15% for five years after opening (SD = 7%); ±24% (SD = 13) for 20 years after opening (Hartgen 2014). These results are generally consistent with those obtained by Bain in his survey of 46 demand modelers (Bain 2011).

7. Data used to project these external trends are usually obtained from sources that collect nation-wide, state, regional or sectoral data. In Israel, nation-wide surveys are conducted by the Census Bureau of Statistics (CBS) every 10 years. Special CBS surveys are conducted more frequently for the purpose of eliciting specific travel behavior features, such as home-to-work trip patterns and mode choice, but are based on relatively smaller samples and, at times, representative samples. Regrettably, analysts often make projections based on CBS data collected quite some time ago. Consider the original estimates of 400,000 daily passengers (for the target year 2020) using the $3.5 billion Tel Aviv Light Rail project (currently under construction). These estimates, made in early 2000 and used for the project's (partial) CBA, were based on relatively outdated CBS travel behavior counts, collected in 1996–1997. Updated CBS data and special surveys (carried out in 2008–2012) showed the original estimates to be about 25% larger than they should have been.
8. For studies of inaccuracies in road traffic forecasts, see Bain (2009), Flyvbjerg et al. (2006) and Odeck (2013).
9. See, for example, the historical review of the Tappan Zee Bridge (in New York State) planning and modeling activities, which were performed by different parties for over two decades (Plotch 2015).
10. On the analytical and empirical foundations of these models, see Ort'uzar and Willumsen (2011, Chap. 5).
11. An additional technical complexity is found in the fact that trip distribution matrices represent fixed rather than the actual down-sloping demand curves. This undermines the accuracy of the estimated volumes a priori.
12. While dynamic assignment models are regarded as more accurate, many agencies and consultants still use static models, mainly because the software is available and their computation is relative easy. For a general review see Ort'uzar and Willumsen (2011, Chap. 10); for a review of dynamic models see Peeta and Ziliaskopoulos (2001).
13. Known in the literature as the *induced demand* phenomenon.
14. Donnelly et al. (2010) review the potential sources of inaccuracy in these types of models.
15. See the insightful study by Tversky and Kahneman (1983) where they demonstrate how individuals tend to violate the basic rules of rational decision-making.
16. As an illustration, consider the case of the Bayonne Bridge, rising 151 feet above the Kill Van Kull waterway in the port of New York-New Jersey. The existing bridge is no longer high enough to handle the passage of the large container ships (6000 to 9000 containers) calling at the ports of Staten Island and New Jersey. The $1.3 billion project is aimed at raising the bridge's roadway by 64 feet, to a height of 215 feet above water, thus enabling the bridge passage of container traffic being hauled to inland destinations. And yet, given the area's limited in-land rail capacity, freight

from the port is transported mostly by trucks. Following the project's completion, more truck traffic is expected, which will further congest the already highly clogged road network. It is not clear to what degree, if any, the effect on the road system entered the bridge's CBA by means of the demand forecast previously computed.

17. The estimation of 720,000 passengers per day for the Bangkok (Thailand) Metro Blue Line was never realized, with actual utilization reaching only 140,000 passengers. The gap was due mainly to inadequate demand modeling as well as deficient data quality and poor data analysis.
18. There is considerable debate in the urban economics literature on the correct price of land to be used for public purposes (e.g., costs of exercising eminent domain). For more on this subject see Berechman and Pines (1991) and Small (1999).
19. Based on analysis of 36 highway construction projects in Slovenia, Makovsek (2014) contends that the dominant bidding mechanism is based on the use of historic cost data and that the reliance on such data explains about half of the variance of project cost performance.
20. It might be argued that in terms of costs, each project is unique relative to local travel conditions, technical features, terrain, engineering design and specification, and a host of economic, legal, institutional and financial factors. International comparisons can nevertheless provide useful information on the factors underlying cost differences between projects.
21. Passage of the 1931 Davis-Bacon Act, which requires construction funded by the US federal government in sums exceeding $2000 to comply with *prevailing wage rates*, typically union rates, has resulted in swelled labor costs due to the associated costs such as benefits (e.g., over-time salaries) and the size of work crews.
22. A senior administrator at New York's MTA is quoted as saying: "The MTA is required to overstaff projects so that the same [tunnel boring machine] work, for instance, that can be done in Spain with 9 workers must be done in (New York City) with 25 workers" (Cooper 2014).
23. *Buy America* provisions ensure that transportation infrastructure projects are built with American-made products. Their aim is to ensure that the US Federal Department of Transportation investments will support an entire network of American companies and their employees (http://www.dot.gov/highlights/buyamerica).
24. The head of a US Federal department or agency may waive this rule if the inclusion of steel produced in the USA will increase the overall cost of the project by more than 25%. However, for billion-dollar mega-projects, 25% translates into substantial funds.
25. Consider the following case. Politicians representing the East Side of Manhattan, New York, which includes two of the largest federally financed transportation projects in the nation—the SAS and the East Side Access

network—presented a report indicating that the first segment of the SAS project (capital costs of $4.47 billion) has created 16,000 jobs, generated $842 million in wages and produced $2.87 billion in economic activity. They also claimed that the East Side Access, a $12.275 billion infrastructure project (currently under construction), has created 22,000 jobs, generated $1.176 billion in wages and produced $4 billion in economic activity. No independent study has yet to confirm any of these figures.

26. In New York, a toll road company was sued for fraud over a scheme to purchase public infrastructure at high premiums. It presented deliberately biased and incorrect forecasts of traffic and toll revenues, (presumably) prepared by independent consultants who, in fact, were dependent on the fees they received from the toll road company, based on each project (toll road) approved thanks to their forecasts (AASHTO July 16, 2013).
27. For attempts to deal with some of these issues see, for example, Chow et al. (2012) and Boyce and Williams (2013).

References

AASHTO. 2013. NY Court: Fraud Lawsuit to Proceed Against Toll Road Firm, July 19. https://www.tsp2.org/2013/07/22/n-y-court-fraud-lawsuit-to-proceeds-against-toll-road-firm.

Algers, S., and M. Beser. 2002. SAMPERS – The New Swedish National Demand Forecasting Tool. In *National Transport Models: Recent Developments and Prospects*, ed. S. Lundquist and L.G. Mattsson. New York: Springer.

Bain, R. 2009. Error and Optimism Bias in Toll Road Traffic Forecasts. *Transportation* 36 (5): 469–482.

———. 2011. On the Reasonableness of Traffic Forecasts: A Survey of Predictive Capability. *Traffic Engineering, and Control* 52 (5): 213–217.

Banister, D., and J. Berechman. 2000. *Transportation Investment and Economic Development*. London: University College London Press.

Banister, D., and M. Thurstain-Goodwin. 2011. Quantification of the Non-transport Benefits Resulting from Rail Investment. *Journal of Transport Geography* 19 (2): 212–223.

Ben-Akiva, M., and S. Lerman. 1985. *Discrete Choice Analysis: Theory and Application, to Travel Demand*. Cambridge, MA: The MIT Press.

Berechman, J. 2009. *The Evaluation of Transportation Investment Projects*. London and New York: Routledge.

Berechman, J., and L. Chen. 2011. Incorporating Risk of Cost Overruns Into Transportation Capital Projects Decision-Making. *Journal of Transport Economics and Policy* 45: 83–104.

Berechman, J., and D. Pines. 1991. Financing Road Capacity and Returns to Scale Under Marginal Cost Pricing. *Journal of Transport Economics and Policy* 25 (2): 177–181.

Boyce, D., and H.C.W.L. Williams. 2013. *Forecasting Urban Travel – Past, Present and Future*. Cheltenham: Edward Elgar.
Bruzelius, N., B. Flyvbjerg, and W. Rothengatter. 2002. Big Decision, Big Risks—Improving Accountability in Mega Projects. *Transport Policy* 9: 143–154.
Cantarelli, C., E. Molin, B. van Wee, and B. Flyvbjerg. 2012. Characteristics of Cost Overruns for Dutch Transport Infrastructure Projects and the Importance of the Decision to Build and Project Phases. *Transport Policy* 22: 49–56.
Chow, J., R. Jayakrishnan, and H. Mahmassani. 2012. Is Transport Modeling Education Too Multi-Disciplinary? A Manifesto on the Search of for Its Evolving Identity. In *Travel Behavior Research: Current Foundations, Future Prospects*, ed. E. Miller and M. Roorda. Raleigh, NC: Lulu Press. www.lulu.com.
Cooper, R. 2014. Why Is it so Expensive to Build a Bridge in America? *The Week*, March 10. http://theweek.com/article/index/257684/why-is-it-so-expensive-to-build-a-bridge-in-america.
Department for Transport (UK). 2013. *Transportation Analysis Guidance: Treatment of Uncertainty in Model Forecasting*. Section 3.15.5. http://www.dft.gov.uk/webtag/index.php.
Donnelly, R., et al. 2010. *Advanced Practices in Travel Forecasting: A Synthesis of Highway Practice. National Cooperative Highway Research Program Synthesis 406*. Washington, DC: Transportation Research Board. www.trb.org.
Estache, A., J. Guasch, A. Iimi, and Trujillo Lm. 2009. Multidimensionality and Renegotiation: Evidence from Transport-Sector Public-Private-Partnership Transactions in Latin America. *Review of Industrial Organization* 35: 41.
European Court of Auditors. 2013. *Are EU Cohesion Policy Funds Well Spent on Roads?* Special Report No. 5, Luxembourg: European Court of Auditors. http://eca.europa.eu.
Federal Transit Administration. 2009, 2015. *Travel Forecasting for New Starts Proposals*. Workshop PowerPoint Presentations, a Conference Paper (Review of Transit Modeling with Respect to FTA Guidance). Tampa, FL: Cambridge Systematic, Inc., http://www.fta.dot.gov/12304_9547.html.
Flyvbjerg, B. 2005. Measuring Inaccuracy in Travel Demand Forecasting: Methodological Considerations Regarding Ramp Up and Sampling. *Transportation Research Part A* 39 (6): 522–530.
———. 2007. Cost Overruns and Demand Shortfalls in Urban Rail and Other Infrastructure. *Transportation Planning and Technology* 30 (1): 9–30.
———. 2009. Survival of the Unfittest: Why the Worst Infrastructure Gets Built and What We Can Do About It. *Oxford Review of Economic Policy* 25 (3): 307–326.
Flyvbjerg, B., M.K. Skamris Holm, and S.L. Buhl. 2002. Underestimating Cost of Public Works Projects: Error or Lie? *Journal of the American Planning Association* 68 (3): 279–295.
———. 2004. What Causes Cost Overrun in Transport Infrastructure Projects? *Transport Reviews* 24: 3–18.

———. 2005. How (In)Accurate Are Demand Forecasts in Public Works Projects? The Case of Transportation. *Journal of the American Planning Association* 71: 131–146.

———. 2006. Inaccuracy in Traffic Forecasts. *Transport Reviews* 26 (1): 1–24.

Hartgen, D. 2013. Hubris or Humility? Accuracy Issues for the Next 50 Years of Travel Demand Modeling. *Transportation* 40 (6): 1133–1157.

———. 2014. The Next 50 Years in Travel Analysis: What We Need to Know. *Internet Survey*, January 14–March 17, and TRB Workshop 151, January 2014.

Hartgen, D., G. Fields, and C. Chadwick 2008. *Are They Ready? Mega-regions Growth and Transportation Investment: A Report to the Urban Land Institute.* Concord, NC: The Hartgen Group. http://www.hartgengroup.net/Projects/ULI_Final_Report_2008-03-07.pdf.

Jahren, T., and M. Ashe. 1990. Predictors of Cost Overruns Rates. *Journal of Construction Engineering and Management* 116 (3): 548–552.

Li, Z., and D. Hensher. 2010. Toll Roads in Australia: An Overview of Characteristics and Accuracy of Demand Forecasts. *Transport Review* 30 (5): 541–569.

Makovsek, D. 2014. Systematic Construction Risk, Cost Estimation Mechanism and Unit Price Movement. *Transport Policy* 35: 135–145.

Manski, C. 2013. *Public Policy in an Uncertain World: Analysis and Decisions.* Cambridge, MA: Harvard University Press.

Mazur, A. 1981. *The Dynamics of Technical Controversy.* Washington, DC: Communications Press.

McNally, M. 2000. The Four-Step Model. In *Handbook of Transport Modeling*, ed. D. Hensher and K. Button. New York: Pergamon.

Mouter, N., J. Annema, and B. Van Wee. 2013. Attitudes Towards the Role of Cost-Benefit Analysis in the Decision-Making Process for Spatial Infrastructure Projects: A Dutch Case Study. *Transportation Research A* 58: 1–14.

Naess, P., M. Nicolaisen, and A. Strand. 2012. Traffic Forecasts Ignoring Induced Demand: A Shaky Fundament for Cost-Benefit Analyses. *European Journal of Transport and Infrastructure Research* 12 (3): 291–309.

Nicolaisen, M.S., and P.A. Driscoll. 2014. Ex-post Evaluations of Demand Forecast Accuracy: A Literature Review. *Transport Reviews* 34 (4): 540–557.

Nicolaisen, M.S., and P. Naess. 2015. Roads to Nowhere: The Accuracy of Travel Demand Forecasts for Do-Nothing Alternatives. *Transport Policy* 37: 57–63.

Nijkamp, P., and B. Ubbels. 1999. How Reliable Are Estimates of Infrastructure Costs? A Comparative Analysis. *International Journal of Transport Economics* 26: 23–53.

Nobbe, P., and J. Berechman. 2014. *A Technical Report.* New York: University Transportation Research Center Region 2, The City College of New York.

Odeck, J. 2004. Cost Overruns in Road Construction: What Are Their Sizes and Determinants? *Transport Policy* 11: 43–53.

———. 2013. How Accurate Are National Road Traffic Growth-Rate Forecasts? The Case of Norway. *Transport Policy* 27: 102–111.
Ort'uzar, J., and L. Willumsen. 2011. *Modelling Transport*. 4th ed. Chichester: John Wiley.
Parthasarathi, P., and D. Levinson. 2010. Post Construction Evaluation of Traffic Forecast Accuracy. *Transport Policy* 12 (6): 428–443.
Peeta, S., and A. Ziliaskopoulos. 2001. Foundations of Dynamic Traffic Assignment: The Past, the Present and the Future. *Network and Spatial Economics* 1: 233–265.
Pickrell, D. 1990. *Urban Rail Transit Projects: Forecast Versus Actual Ridership and Cost*. Washington, DC: Urban Mass Transportation Administration, US Dept. of Transportation.
———. 1992. A Desire Named Streetcar – Fantasy and Fact in Rail Transit Planning. *Journal of American Planning Association* 58: 158–176.
Plotch, P. 2015. *Politics Across the Hudson: The Tappan Zee Megaproject*. New Brunswick, NJ: Rutgers University Press.
Quinet, E. 1998. *Principes d'économie des transport*. Paris: Economica.
Recker, W.W. 2001. A Bridge Between Travel Demand Modeling and Activity-Based Travel Analysis. *Transportation Research Part B* 35 (5): 481–506.
Sager, T., and I. Ravlum. 2005. The Political Relevance of Planners' Analysis, the Case of a Parliamentary Standing Committee. *Planning Theory* 4 (1): 33–65.
Siemiatycki, M. 2009. Academics and Auditors: Comparing Perspectives on Transportation Project Cost Overruns. *Journal of Planning Education and Research* 29 (2): 142–156.
Small, K. 1999. Economies of Scale and Self-Financing Rules with Non-competitive Markets. *Journal of Public Economics* 74: 431–450.
Small, K., and E. Verhoef. 2007. *The Economics of Urban Transportation*. London and New York: Routledge.
Trujillo, L., E. Quinet, and A. Estache. 2002. Dealing with Demand Forecasting Games in Transport Privatization. *Transport Policy* 9: 325–334.
Tversky, A., and D. Kahneman. 1983. Extensional vs. Intuitive Reasoning: The Conjunction Fallacy in Probability Judgment. *Psychological Review* 90: 293–315.
Van Wee, B. 2007. Large Infrastructure Projects: A Review of Quality of Demand Forecast and Cost Estimation. *Environment and Planning B* 34: 611–625.
Venables, A. 2007. Evaluating Urban Transport Improvements: Cost-Benefits Analysis in the Presence of Agglomeration and Income Taxation. *Journal of Transport Economics and Policy* 41 (2): 173–188.
Wachs, M. 1989. When Planners Lie with Numbers. *Journal of the American Planning Association* 55: 476–479.
———. 1990. Ethics and Advocacy in Forecasting for Public Policy. *Business and Professional Ethics Journal* 9 (1–2): 141–157.

CHAPTER 6

Mega-Project History and Decision-Making

6.1 Introduction

Economic historians have long surmised that history plays a consequential role in the determination of economic growth patterns and levels of development.[1] While this argument has been shown to be valid for entire national economies, can the same be said for projects, especially regarding the probabilities and trials attached to their implementation? A review of mega-projects worldwide reveals that in many cases significant amounts of time elapsed between the moment when the idea of a project first emerged and its initiation. A case in point is the Eurotunnel. The original idea of a cross-channel fixed link, which in modern times culminated in the Channel Tunnel rail project, was first conceived over two centuries ago, in 1802. Diverse geopolitical factors (e.g., British-French relations) and evolving economic realities hindered its construction until 1988. Especially relevant to this observation is the fact that an idea's origination was often rooted in a single or a series of historical events. Consider the development of the plans for the airport hub constructed in Frankfurt, Germany, in the early 1950s; these plans can be traced to the need to relocate the hub from its original site in Berlin, which stemmed in turn from Germany's division after World War II. Germany's unification in 1990 did not, however, serve as a sufficient reason to return the hub to Berlin; the crucial decision factor at this point in time was Germany's irreversible trends in industrial development (Redding et al. 2010). Another example would be the decision leading to the construction of New York's Second Avenue

J. Berechman, *The Infrastructure We Ride On*,
https://doi.org/10.1007/978-3-319-74606-7_6

Subway (SAS), which was firmly planted in 1942 after the elevated rail line operating above Second Avenue, on Manhattan's East Side, was demolished. Save for a failed attempt in the 1970s, it took over 70 years before construction actually began.[2] We can therefore conclude that in general, a well-founded idea regarding a project's need, even if raised many years back, can be quite influential many years later, when making the decisions that may lead to its implementation (Rodrik 2014).

The above should not be taken as equating history, as normally understood, with *project history*, especially when considering that implementation takes 20–30 years on average. Within the framework of this book, I regard project history as a distinct path of recordable and documented events linking the project's origins with its culmination.[3] Stated differently, I view a project's history as the longitudinal sequence of events leading from the launching the idea of its *need* to the *choices* made surrounding its construction.[4] As such, this history embraces multiple factors and actors, including institutions, interest groups, engineering issues, urban planning, economic and financial considerations, as well as social movements and cultural changes.

At the risk of overlooking a project's evolution, for purposes of comparison I use the time span between the date the idea for a project was proposed (and documented) and the date when construction began. As the data shown in Fig. 6.1 indicate, that history can be of relatively short duration (e.g., 10 years) but, more often than not, of long duration, meaning more than 50 years, with some projects stretching over 100 years or more.[5]

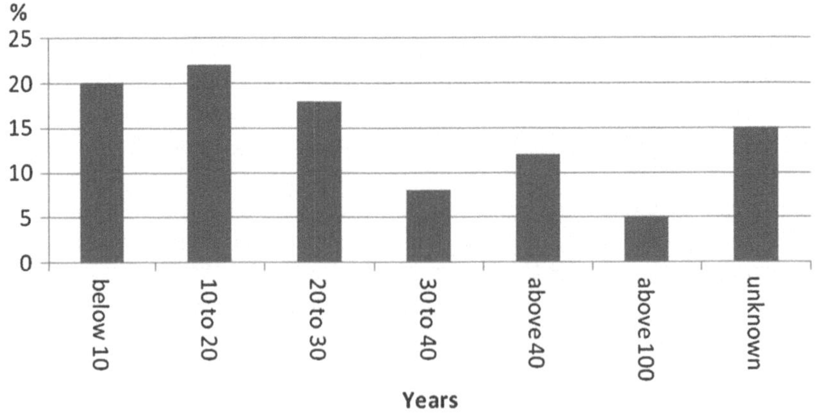

Fig. 6.1 Percent distribution of project histories by years ($N = 60$)

Why is a project's history at all important? Although I do *not* claim that history is *the* decisive factor driving a project's choice, I do argue that history matters in its selection and the surrounding decision-making. History, in this case, is the story told about a project's necessity and the image created to maintain that project as a viable transportation solution in the public's mind, among citizens, professionals and political decision-makers. My main supposition is, therefore, that a project's history has a pronounced effect on the probability that it will be *selected* for construction, but not that it will indeed be implemented. This distinction is crucial from the perspective of theory as well as practice.[6]

We have thus arrived at the point where the main theoretical questions touching on the relationship between a project's history and its choice need to be raised. First, does project choice necessarily follow a distinctive, discernible path? That is, could the same project be selected even if its history had been different?[7] Second, if history is but one determinant, are multiple solutions possible on the way to reaching a decision regarding a project? That is, given the other factors, could the same history have resulted in a different project being selected? If we consider a project's duration as a proxy for its history, will the answer necessarily be *yes*? Third, can changes in fundamental conditions, such as shifting economic conditions, control the project's anticipated path?[8] Evidence suggests that in some cases, pragmatic political factors were the predominant forces diverting a project from its course, duration notwithstanding.[9] Can we therefore conclude that project history plays only a minor role in project choice? Again, the evidence we will present suggests that for the most part, this history does matter. In general, the question of whether project history can be regarded as exogenous to observed patterns of project choice is crucial (Nunn 2007). In what follows, I do treat project history as exogenous to the decision process and use it to explain the project's attributes and associated choices.

Of particular interest is timing of the introduction of new transportation technologies, such as high-speed rail, burrowing techniques or autonomous cars. As a decision variable, technology should be considered as having two segments: its actual introduction and the date of its inclusion in the project. The emergence of a technology is a function of need, relative prices and resource scarcities, but its acceptance is often a function of policy. To illustrate, governments generally prefer rail to bus rapid transit (BRT) even though buses are often as effective as rail but substantially less expensive. Similarly is the case of fossil fuel technology and the transition to clean fuels and electric automobile technologies.

Based on these concepts, this chapter's main objective is to ascertain whether a project's history affects project choice and, if so, how and to what extent. To this end, the chapter presents several conjectures regarding the role of project history in project decision-making. I subsequently report the results of empirical tests of several aspects related to these conjectures while taking advantage of a database of 60 mega-projects. I first examine the impact of a project's history on its likelihood of selection.

6.2 Project History: Impacts

As mentioned previously, a project's history is measured in years from the date of the project's proposal to the year when construction begins. Based on the Nobbe and Berechman (2014) database, described in Chap. 4, Fig. 6.1 shows the distribution of project histories, in years and percentages.

As Fig. 6.1 shows, a project's median history is 20–30 years, with some projects (about 20%) having a history of 40 years or more. But why is this time span important when assessing the proposed impacts of a project's selection?

6.2.1 *Setting the Project's Context and Rationale*

We need first to distinguish between two conceptions of the term *project's idea*. The first is the idea that sparks or drives initial conceptualization of the project. The second is that of the project's rationale. The dismantling of the elevated rail line over New York's Second Avenue gave rise to the idea of constructing the SAS line, whereas its long history of debate sanctioned its status as *the solution* to the area's accessibility. The rationale behind the UK's Channel Tunnel rail link was conceived two centuries ago but it took 35 years from actual project initiation to completion. Here I use the first conception of idea when measuring a project's history and the second when explaining that history's effect on the decision to build.

In general, history serves to prime the public discussion of why a particular project is best for achieving regional economic and transportation goals. Stated differently, a project's history helps congeal the context for promoting the project's idea, ground its rationale and substantiate its overall advantages over potential alternatives. I propose that the longer a project's history is as an idea, the more acceptable it is as the solution to a transportation problem, whether that solution is genuine or not. A good example is the AirTrain to New York's JFK airport. The idea of such a train originated in the 1960s (a history of about 40 years) as a means of connecting the airport to local and regional rail as well as subway systems, thereby improving transit accessibility from lower Manhattan while lessening highway traffic. The project's history served to plant the idea in the minds of the public as well as decision-makers at the same time that it shaped the context for dealing with the question of airport accessibility. Within that context, the AirTrain became *the correct* solution even though other options, such as a new subway line, were viable alternatives.

6.2.2 *Maintaining the Project's Place on the Public Agenda*

The adage "history does not repeat itself" has become so clichéd that we often ignore the fact that people tend to respond to problems in predictable ways. If that tendency is properly manipulated, agencies, planners and politicians can succeed in sustaining the view that their preferred project is the best response to a lingering regional problem. Israel's Ministry of Transportation and the Tel Aviv Municipality had embraced the idea of inter-city light rail with a metro component for close to 50 years before starting to implement the project despite thorny budget constraints. A key element in this story was the authorities' ability to keep the idea of light rail on the public agenda, create community awareness of the proposal and maintain the opinion that this was the *only feasible* project if accessibility to various parts of the metropolitan area, especially Tel Aviv's Central Business District (CBD), was to be improved.

6.2.3 *Prioritization of Competing Investments*

How does a project's history influence prioritization of competing investments? In order to answer this question, I again present two distinctions, that of the project's *objective* and that of its *rationale*. The former responds to the question, "What impacts would a specific project produce?" whereas the latter answers the question, "What is the underlying need for the project?"

To illustrate this distinction in the field of public transit, I return to the case of the SAS. Its original objective was to replace the elevated rail line running along Second Avenue; its rationale was the East Side's perceived poor accessibility to Manhattan's downtown. However, the question of whether that objective of building a new subway provided the correct transportation-economic solution in light of the specific need was never properly addressed. The documentation available indicates that despite the many profound changes in technology, land uses, demography and the region's economy over the years, the project's appropriateness was never questioned. Thus, while the project's objective (build a new subway line) remained essentially unchanged, the underlying rationale (i.e., providing access to the CBD, improving street-level traffic, alleviating crowding on the rest of the subway system, linking other boroughs with Manhattan's CBD, engendering real-estate development, and reducing air pollution) for *this* project certainly did not. Put simply, the SAS's long history was filled with continuous expansion of the list of its alleged benefits, a process meant to justify its huge costs and shape urban transportation policies in its favor. As a result, this particular investment retained its priority when alternative capital investments might have better realized its rationale.

6.2.4 Effect on Potential Opposition

Over the years, a project with a history as long as that of the SAS or Tel Aviv's Light Rail can become a rallying point for public debate, and even the subject of a slogan. Its presence on the public agenda for so long means that its necessity becomes *common knowledge*. Once it achieves this status, the opposition that normally accompanies projects of such magnitude (Chap. 7 discusses the role of opposition per se) may weaken. Under such conditions, the costs of organizing a coalition against the project become prohibitively high.

A conflicting view of the relationship between a project's history and its opposition states that the longer the history, the more likely it is that opposition will be spurred by the changes taking place in the surrounding urban and regional environment, be they new environmental concerns, or external budgetary and fiscal realities. According to this approach, a long history allows more information about the project to become available and consequently encourage people to question its various features and impacts. An example is New York's $2 billion plus Westway project, designed to run along the banks of the Hudson River, which included a limited access highway, a tunnel and a landfill. Despite the many years of planning and the $200 million expended, the project was ultimately voided due to environmentally based public opposition and legal challenges (Buzbee 2014).

To empirically investigate the validity of these two approaches, Nobbe and Berechman (2014) conducted several statistical tests on the relationship between project history and project opposition. The results, discussed in detail in Chap. 7, indicated that political opposition to a project is positively correlated with the length of its history, a finding that contradicts the argument initially stated regarding the positive impact of history on a project's implementation. Similar results were found for financial and other issue-related opposition. We can thus restate this finding as follows: A project's history will be negatively correlated with the absence of opposition, implying that the longer the project history, the less likely that opposition will not arise.

Needless to say, the presence of a statistical correlation between two variables does not amount to either causality or directionality. It is, after all, plausible to claim that contrary to the above, it is political opposition that affects the length of a project's history by delaying the project's approval, often by many years. The latter possibility was indeed supported but by statistically insignificant results.

6.3 History Affects Ambiguity

Perhaps more importantly, history also affects ambiguity in contradictory ways. On the one hand, a project's history can help solidify its rationale and background, thereby reducing ambiguity. On the other, time (meaning the amount of time its details are known) reduces the impetus to update our assessments regarding the project's transportation-economic value with new information. Thus, it enhances ambiguity by blinding decision-makers to the need of incorporating that information to ensure the project's continued relevance. An analysis of the data by Nobbe and Berechman (2014) indicates that when compared with projects having a shorter history, projects with a longer history are less likely to be subjected to either a full or partial Cost-Benefit Analysis (CBA). This observation is quite salient, irrespective of mega-project diversity. It may suggest that decision-makers, when confronting a project with a longer history, find it more expedient to forego a CBA for fear that it might expose the project's currently questionable contributions if they are bent on giving their approval. This tends to occur when the political and economic benefits of not revealing the project's true value exceed the costs of so doing.

The five effects of history so concisely mentioned above should *not* be considered facts or unavoidable outcomes; each dwells in the realm of possibility, as determined by the actors and conditions defining each project's context. In the next section I provide some empirical results from research aimed at assessing just how valid the respective conjectures may be in reality.

6.4 Does Project History Matter?

As stated, I suggest that project's history impacts on the likelihood of a project being selected when it arouses community awareness and positive public attitudes by portraying the project as a solution to a region's needs. In this regard we should consider *project history* as a catch-all term for all the micro-level but also macro-economic factors (e.g., the rate of inflation) that have a bearing on public investments.[10]

Studies on the impact of project history on economic development patterns and decision-making trends have applied various quantitative techniques to ascertain the strength of these effects. In the following chapters, I relate to the three major modeling approaches applied in economic decision-making when determining which infrastructure mega-project will be realized. In doing so I refer to several of the studies previously mentioned although I now stress their methodologies. First, we have the game-theoretic approach that aims at explaining a country's (a region's or continent's) current economic equilibrium by modeling the strategic behavior of key actors. Examples include Nunn's (2007) study of slave traders and colonial rulers in Africa, and Acemoglu and Robinson's (2000) research on democratization in Western societies during the nineteenth century, analyzed in terms of voting rights, taxation and income redistribution (see also Acemoglu et al. 2010). The second approach involves the use of industrial location models to link historical events with current location decisions. One example of such an analysis is that conducted by Redding et al. (2010), who tried to explain the current location of Frankfort's hub airport as a consequence of events relating to Germany's division and then later reunification. The third approach applies statistical regression techniques to panel data for the purpose of estimating the effect of events such as the presence of different types of institutions on current economic parameters, including growth rate (Acemoglu and Johnson 2005; Bogart and Chaudhary 2012).

Keeping in mind the differences between history as such, and project history, the research reported here that belongs to the last approach attempts to establish the possible relationships between a project's history and its outcomes in terms of costs, utilization and decision-making. As explained above, I have employed the time span (the independent variable) between a project's inception as an idea and its selection as a proxy for that project's history. The main advantage of adopting this approach is that it transforms project history into a measurable variable, common to all projects.

Several parametric and non-parametric tests were performed to identify possible relationships between the project's history and its key attributes. These included construction time, total costs, the likelihood that a CBA would be executed, the form of funding and cost overruns. Significant correlation coefficients were found especially between the project's history and cost overruns, as well as the length of that history and the likelihood of the project selection. As to the latter relationship, I found that the longer a project's history, the more probable its selection for implementation.

6.5 Conclusions

Project history can be seen as the convoluted path leading to a particular project becoming a reality. However, due to the great variability in the respective paths, even in the same county, it is impossible to derive verifiable and broadly generalizable conclusions regarding the impact of a project's history on the decision process and final choice. I have therefore used project duration as a proxy for its history. While recognizing that this metric encapsulates a host of divergent issues such as the shifting role of politics and political leadership, technological constraints, and lack of assured funding given rising costs, it remains effective when designing a supportable analysis having generic conclusions.

The key issue nonetheless remains the degree to which a project's history impacts on decision-making. While the data analysis does not provide an unequivocal answer to this question, even when controlling for whether a CBA was performed or not, a positive correlation was indeed found between the length of project history and the likelihood of that project's being selected, the significance of cost overruns, its size and the appearance of opposition.

Notes

1. See for example Nunn (2009); Acemoglu et al. (2005).
2. The call for construction of a subway under Manhattan's Second Avenue originated in a 1919 public transit report prepared for The New York Service Commission. At the time, an elevated rail line operated above Second Avenue from about 60th Street to downtown (City Hall). The report recommended a trunk line under Second Avenue, consisting of six tracks and branching out toward three other boroughs: Bronx, Queens and Brooklyn. The line's construction was initiated in 1929, after the

New York Board of Transportation approved the sum of $98 million for construction of a four-track line from the Harlem River (with a trunk line going north to the Bronx) to 125th Street, and a six-track line from 125th Street to 61st Street (with a link to the 6th Avenue line). From there, a four-track line ran from 61st Street to lower Manhattan (Chambers Street), which continued downtown to Pine Street but with a reduced two-track line. This elevated line was demolished in 1942.

3. It would be reasonable to also examine projects that were only discussed or abandoned at some later stage. Unfortunately, data on such projects is largely unavailable.
4. For a chronological review of the events leading to implementation of the Tappan Zee Bridge project in New York State, a recent example, see Plotch (2015).
5. Besides the Channel Tunnel, Copenhagen's Metro project (Oeresund Link; Øresundsbroen) has a history of 136 years; Greece's Rion Antirion Bridge project can be traced back 100 years.
6. Two categories—*implemented* and *not implemented*—are required if we are to prove this supposition. Yet, as is commonly the case in choice analysis, we cannot observe alternatives cast aside; hence, we are left to deal solely with the set of revealed, or implemented, choices.
7. For example, the light rail project currently (2016) being built in Tel Aviv is based on a 2010 contract signed with the company that won the bid but annulled after the bidder was unable to secure funding. A dedicated agency subsequently took responsibility for the project in the form of a Metropolitan Transit Authority, a step that changed the project's status and key dimensions from a primarily public-private partnership project to an exclusive public sector funded and built project.
8. The literature contains some evidence suggesting that an industry's location is not uniquely determined by fundamentals such as proximity to markets but, rather, shifts in contemporary conditions such as the emergence of new technologies and unforeseen market developments (e.g., see Davis and Weinstein 2002, 2008; Redding et al. 2010).
9. A case in point is the Access to the Region's Core (ARC), a commuter rail project meant to link New Jersey with Manhattan by means of a tunnel constructed beneath the Hudson River. About $600 million was spent on the planning and engineering of the project, which was canceled in October 2010 by New Jersey's Governor for political and taxation reasons.
10. Examples of such variables are a country's growth indicators (e.g., changes in GDP per capita or Gross Output), demographic changes (e.g., urban-suburban shifts) and technological innovations (e.g., modern tunneling and communication techniques).

References

Acemoglu, D., and S. Johnson. 2005. Unbundling Institutions. *Journal of Political Economy* 113 (5): 950–995.

Acemoglu, D., and A. Robinson. 2000. Why Did the West Extend the Franchise? Democracy, Inequality, and Growth in Historical Perspective. *The Quarterly Journal of Economics* 115 (4): 1167–1199.

Acemoglu, D., S. Johnson, and A. Robinson. 2005. The Rise of Europe: Atlantic Trade, Institutional Changes and Economic Growth. *American Economic Review* 95: 546–579.

Acemoglu, D., A. Ozdaglar, and A. Parandeh Gheibib. 2010. Spread of (Mis) information in Social Networks. *Games and Economic Behavior* 70: 194–227.

Bogart, D., and L. Chaudhary. 2012. Regulation, Ownership, and Costs: A Historical Perspective from Indian railways. *American Economic Journal: Economic Policy* 4 (1): 28–57.

Buzbee, W. 2014. *Fighting Westway*. New York: Cornell University Press.

Davis, D., and D. Weinstein. 2002. Bones, Bombs, and Break Points: The Geography of Economic Activity. *American Economic Review* 92: 1269–1289.

———. 2008. A Search for Multiple Equilibria in Urban Industrial Structure. *Journal of Regional Science* 48: 29–65.

Nobbe, P., and J. Berechman. 2014. *A Technical Report*. New York: University Transportation Research Center Region 2, The City College of New York.

Nunn, N. 2007. Historical Legacies: A Model Linking Africa's Past to Its Current Underdevelopment. *Journal of Development Economics* 83 (1): 157–175.

———. 2009. *The Importance of History for Economic Development*. NBER Working Papers, 14899.

Plotch, P. 2015. *Politics Across the Hudson*. New Brunswick, NJ: Rutgers University Press.

Redding S., D. Sturm, and N. Wolf. 2010. History and Industry Location: Evidence from German Airports. http://www.princeton.edu/~reddings/papers/Airports_final_all.pdf.

Rodrik, D. 2014. When Ideas Trump Interests: Preferences, World Views, and Policy Innovations. *Journal of Economic Perspectives* 28 (1): 189–208.

CHAPTER 7

Interest Groups: Advocacy and Opposition

7.1 Introduction

Put most simply, economic changes and policy interventions generate political responses from those who see either threats to their interests or new opportunities to attain benefits (Acemoglu 2010). Because transportation mega-projects belong to that class of projects inciting intense changes, especially at the metropolitan and regional levels, it should not be surprising that they face various forms of opposition coming from multiple sources, ranging from vocal criticism to organized resistance. But mega-projects likewise benefit from vigorous support. In the USA, lobbying for earmarked projects was a common practice at the national (or federal) level until earmarking was prohibited by Congress in 2011.[1] The proliferation of earmarked projects had persuaded advocacy groups to seek additional projects at the price of foregoing the benefits of more worthy projects.[2] In addition, national advocacy organizations (or lobbyists) continue to try to persuade decision-makers by applying sometimes devious tactics but also their professional expertise.[3]

At the local level, expressions of project support, or opposition, range from tacit (dis)approval by citizens to active lobbying and advocacy by business groups, organized labor and dedicated associations (e.g., environmental groups), which obviously include the contractors and consultants who would directly benefit (or suffer) from the project. Such entities commonly referred to as Special Interest Groups (SIGs) employ monetary resources, political pressure as well as moral persuasion to achieve their objectives.[4]

J. Berechman, *The Infrastructure We Ride On*,
https://doi.org/10.1007/978-3-319-74606-7_7

The theoretical underpinnings of just how and why interest groups influence policies have received ample attention, primarily in the political economy literature (e.g., see the insightful book by Grossman and Helpman 2001).[5] Empirical testing and verification of these theories is, however, rather scanty. It is nevertheless clear that an SIG's ability to promote, thwart or stall project decision-making and implementation, regardless of the project's transportation-economic contributions, is a major source of inefficiency as the measures taken require political responses. The need to muster and maintain a supportive coalition covering various jurisdictions, such as municipalities, together with environmental groups and so forth can be costly. Regional and metropolitan rail mega-projects are particularly prone to this interference.[6]

When examining the behavior of SIGs in the context of transportation investments, the most salient questions to be asked are as follows: First, what underlying issues arouse support or opposition? Second, how do SIGs function? And third, what is their impact on actual investment decision-making? This chapter focuses on the last key issue. Before proceeding, it is worth bearing in mind that an SIG's success yields, by and large, benefits limited to the small group of interested parties it represents. In contrast, the costs of those successes are distributed over much larger populations, especially taxpayers. This explains why an SIG's involvement in political and economic processes is so problematic.

When explaining how SIGs subvert equilibrium policies (i.e., policies that balance a project's costs and benefits for investors and users), the political economy literature makes one of two assumptions: that the underlying issues are well defined and agreed upon so that all SIG members can identify with them; or that SIG members are able to reconcile or resolve their own internal disagreements in order to rally around common ideas and beliefs. However, reconciliation of a group's internal conflicts often requires extensive financial and/or motivational costs, that is, the costs associated with bringing diverse motivations in line behind one SIG as opposed to coping with a consortium of SIGs representing multiple motivations. In effect, to understand the behavior of even one, let alone a coalition of SIGs, we must take into account the role of leadership in surmounting internal conflicts and unifying contending actors around a common goal.[7] This role is not less important than representation and advocacy. How the leadership does so, and at what costs, is normally excluded from theoretical (including game-theoretic) models even though leadership may be crucial for effectively influencing a project's future.[8]

Given the scope of this book, we only touch upon these issues in this chapter. As in other chapters, the empirical analysis and evidence is based primarily on the 60 mega-project database discussed in Chap. 4 (Appendix).

At the project's promotion stage, the major disagreements arising usually circle around core policy issues such as mode (rail vs. highway).[9] At the project's decision-making stage, however, conflicts often verge toward values such as equity or neighborhood cohesion. In either case, the very basic conflicts are hardly ever about technical issues or data; most often, they are over the project's political objectives.[10]

Lastly, it might be argued that the kind and strength of the impacts that SIGs have on mega-projects' decision-making is case-based because they vary considerably by project, depending on local conditions, politics and the population's socio-economic composition. Nonetheless, similar to what was stated about other effects discussed in this book, we contend that the collection of data on a large number of mega-projects can help us extract valuable generic empirical insights into the degree to which SIGs affect projects' decision-making. This is what we do here.

7.2 SIGs: Advocates and Opponents

As we have intimated, one factor that consistently influences the choices made by public decision-makers is who exerts the most effective economic and political power; stated differently, which group has the greatest impact on mega-project decision-making? We distinguish between two main groups: project advocates and project opponents. Both share three common factors. The first is their goal: to persuade decision-makers to act in their favor, which they do by applying various tactics, including lobbying, information dissemination, campaign contributions, political endorsement or opposition, and legal means.[11] The second factor involves attempts to bring specialized information on the subject to the attention of decision-makers as a means of validating their position. Examples of such information are estimates of the health impacts and escalated congestion rates arising from the greater traffic to be observed should a proposed new highway be built. The third common factor is the cost of SIG activities, which includes data collection outlays, the costs of public relations campaigns and legal fees.

An important comment to be made here is that the amount of effort and funds an SIG expends can serve as a signal indicating the credibility of its claims. This observation tends to carry greater weight if an SIG's aims conflict or compete with those of other SIGs. We should never forget that in cases of competition over public projects and agendas, credibility is a crucial resource. Any gaps in credibility between two SIGs over the true value of a project's impacts can definitely affect the organizations' bargaining power and influence.

I nevertheless do not want to convey the impression that an SIG's efforts to persuade decision-makers have only two possible outcomes, namely, project selection and construction, or obstruction of its implementation. In reality, numerous outcomes are possible. One major and more-common outcome is modification, that is, project may be scaled down or up, or may acquire a different form (e.g., an above-ground rather than an underground rail line), or altered in terms of location or capacity. However, we should recall that our subject here is not the particular form of a project's outcomes following an SIG's intervention; what interests us is how and to what degree SIGs affect decision-making in the transportation sector. We begin our analysis by identifying SIGs belonging to the two types we have mentioned, with a focus on the USA.

7.2.1 *Project Advocacy SIGs*

On the national level we find several SIGs whose main objective is influencing the allocation of federal funding. One of these is the ASCE, which represents infrastructure designers and builders, including transportation infrastructure. To achieve their objective they provide expert testimony during Congressional hearings and conduct research that highlights transportation issues. ASCE activities are also aimed at promoting infrastructure's public profile by issuing reports, a major one being the bi-annual *Report Card for America's Infrastructure*, which assigns a letter grade to the state of the country's infrastructure by location and type. Another such SIG is the American Public Transportation Association (APTA), which advocates development of public transport. It engages in policy research, directs lobbying, as well as public awareness campaigns. The APTA also helps coordinate local transportation initiatives by providing data and consultation. Other SIGs involved in similar activities are the Alliance of Automobile Manufacturers, the various airline alliances, the Association of American Railroads, Smart Growth America, and the Coalition for Clean Air, to name just a few.

At the project level, SIGs serve their members from outside administrative agencies and local governments. Flyvbjerg and Van Wee (2008) claim that the main supporters of mega-project development are the firms that profit from the huge amount of money and prestige involved in mega-project planning, technical design and construction. Consulting firms and contractors who negotiate the contracts are obvious winners. To illustrate this trend, we need only mention that the proposed JFK Access to Lower Manhattan shuttle[12] was promoted by powerful real-estate and financial interests that billed the project as crucial for New York City's ability to compete globally.[13]

Another, more elaborate layer of supportive interest groups is comprised of sometimes tacit coalitions of politicians, local authorities, developers, land owners, labor unions and consultants, who all stand to gain from a project.[14] Non-pecuniary rewards are of prime importance especially to the politicians who manage to push through projects meant to serve as monuments to their public service legacy.[15] In a similar manner, the engineers and architects assigned to plan the highest bridge or longest rail tunnel by means of advanced technologies are also enthusiastic project supporters, irrespective of a project's true social welfare contribution (Frick 2008).[16] In addition, institutions that may benefit from expensive projects, thanks to the subsequent expansion of their authority, financial power and, most importantly, assurance of their organizational survival, will likewise tend to support the relevant projects. Finally, we should note that for a variety of reasons, not all SIG project support is visible, meaning that their activities remain behind the scenes. This lack of transparency is quite rampant and often practiced even by those politicians and local authorities who publicly advocate a project's acceptance.

7.2.2 Project Opposition SIGs

By and large, SIGs opposing a project tend to be quite visible, consequent to the observable media, political and judicial measures they use to exert pressure on decision-makers. The transportation industry, by its very nature, displays a network-like structure. Whereas the negative aspects of mega-projects, primarily environmental nuisances, may remain local, the positive aspects, such as agglomeration and accessibility spillovers, are likely to be distributed throughout the larger network. Seaports and airports are extreme examples of this phenomenon in that the congestion caused by traffic to and from the port affects mainly the adjacent communities whereas the distribution of passengers and freight is regional or national.[17] Moreover, when a significant portion of funding comes from federal coffers, there is a built-in incentive for local groups to demand all sorts of externality-mitigating measures (e.g., tunneling or underground construction to lessen noise), their costs notwithstanding. The possibility of federal funding thus feeds into the ferocious local opposition that mega-projects commonly face. To illustrate this effect, consider the cost of the Boston Central Artery project (known locally as the Big Dig), which ballooned from $2.6 billion in 1987 to $15.8 billion 16 years later, in great part due to local demands for noise reduction.

In general, however, whereas opposition-oriented SIGs tend to relate to a range of issues, advocacy-oriented SIGs tend to focus on funding, the pivotal factor determining project selection (see Chap. 8). But can we be more specific when discussing the impacts of SIGs on project attributes and decision-making? An empirical response demands data, which are easier to find regarding project opposition than promotion.[18] For this reason, I next examine data only on opposition to mega-projects.

7.3 Empirical Findings

Here I make use of the database first presented in Chap. 4, Appendix. For each project, the database contains information on four opposition categories:

1. Political opposition
2. Funding opposition
3. Issue-oriented opposition (e.g., environmentalists)
4. No opposition

7.3.1 The Distribution of Opposition by Type

Obviously, opposition to a project can center on more than one issue. This becomes more evident from Table 7.1, which indicates the distribution of opposition by type. Because opposition can fall into more than one category, neither the number of cases, nor the percentages, adds up to 60 or 100, respectively.

As the above table indicates, issue-oriented opposition, which relates mainly to environmental nuisances, was found for over 50% of the projects in the database. Demands for funding a competing project comes next (about 33% of all cases), followed by political opposition (about 27%). About 28% (17 cases) of the 60 projects experienced opposition of more than one type. Finally, in about 24% of all the cases, no noticeable opposition was either observed or reported. We can therefore conclude that over 75% of all mega-projects in the database faced opposition of at least one type.[19] Given this sizeable proportion, it is reasonable to expect that opposition has some bearing on the choice of projects and their attributes.

We can now ask whether the type of project affects the pervasiveness of opposition. By dividing the data according to highway, rail, tunnel and other projects, it quickly becomes clear that each type of project is associated with different kinds and levels of opposition, as shown in Chart 7.1, below.

Table 7.1 Distribution of 60 mega-projects by opposition category

Opposition category	*Number of cases*	*Frequency (%)*
Political	16	26.6
Funding	20	33.3
Issue-oriented	31	51.6
No opposition	14	23.3
No information	1	1.6

Source: Nobbe and Berechman (2013)

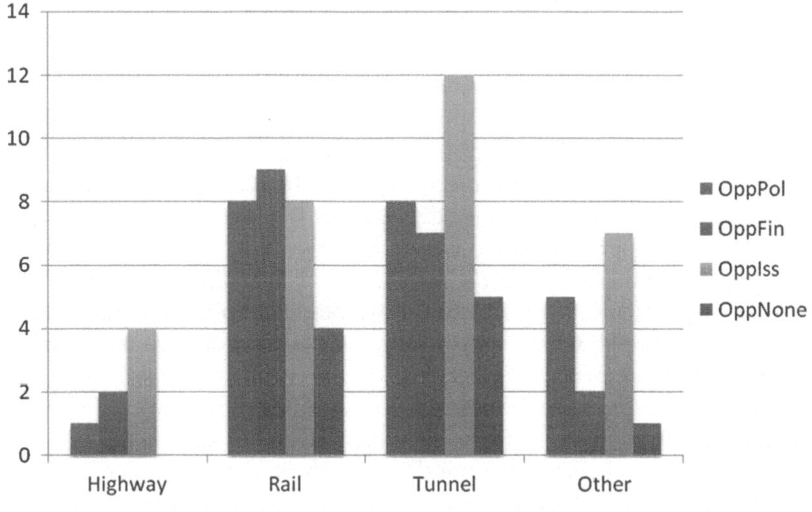

Chart 7.1 Distribution of opposition category by project type. *OppPol* Political opposition, *OppFin* Financial/funding opposition, *OppIss* Issue-oriented opposition, *OppNone* No opposition. Source: Nobbe and Berechman (2014)

Chart 7.1 confirms the conclusions reached from Table 7.1: A majority of mega-projects do face some type of opposition. The most common category of opposition is issue-oriented, although rail projects tend to more frequently face funding-oriented opposition. Furthermore, all project types face considerable political opposition.

But what happens when we examine countries other than the USA, given their different political and institutional environments? With respect to Europe, Asia, South America, Australia and North America, the data in our database reveal some variation in type of opposition. Although issue-oriented opposition tends to predominate in these countries as well, funding is the dominant source of opposition in Asia.

Lastly, we investigated the distribution of opposition by location, that is, inner city versus surrounding areas, with the latter referring to the metropolitan, regional, national and international level. Our underlying premise was that inner cities, due to the density of activity, will demonstrate relatively more opposition than might other locations. The data indeed confirmed this premise, with issue-oriented opposition being twice as frequent for inner-city projects, than for projects to be executed in other locations (we return to this point below).

7.3.2 *The Effect of History*

The project decision-making paradigm shown in Fig. 4.1, Chap. 4, assumes that a project's history is related to its opposition. To test this idea, I hypothesized that *history*—measured in years—affects the likelihood that a project will face opposition of some type. Stated differently, I proposed that the longer a project's history, the higher the likelihood of opposition to it emerging. Once defined this way, we can argue that causality can also operate in the opposite direction, namely, the presence of opposition lengthens a project's history. The results of testing such reverse causality were found, a bit surprisingly, to be statistically insignificant.[20]

As already noted, with respect to the database, history was measured as the number of years elapsing between inception of the project's idea and commencement of its construction. Opposition was measured as a binary variable: present (1) or not (0). This enabled us to test for the possible effect of project history on opposition. We therefore used a Logit model to test for this probability by project type.[21] The results showed that history does indeed have a positive and significant (at 0.01 level) effect on opposition.[22] For instance, if a project's history increases by one year, the probability of political opposition emerging increases by 0.25%.

Although delays can be caused by any number of factors (e.g., conflicts among agencies, unsecured funding, an antagonistic administration[23]), the analysis confirmed that the longer a project's history, the more likely that opposition of some kind will arise. This indicates that contrary to our conclusion, stated in Chap. 6, that political opposition does not explain a project's history on a statistically significant level, we cannot rule out this effect from a conceptual point of view. As a project's history becomes more protracted, the likelihood grows that local, state and federal governments as well as administration officials will change their minds, and with that the willingness to express opposition. Similarly, the longer the history, the more probable that the underlying local and regional conditions, which initially rationalized the project, will change and thus stimulate opposition to the project in its original form.

7.3.3 *Other Attributes of Project Opposition*

Altshuler and Luberoff (2003) have argued that inner-city projects draw, on average, more opposition than do regional or national projects. Our empirical analysis confirmed this claim. The main explanations for this outcome are, first, that inner-city projects directly affect a large number of residents; given population density, projects are more complex and thus costlier to execute, whether above or below ground.[24] In addition, dense infrastructure tends to be already in place, which means either moving or demolishing existing infrastructure prior to its replacement. Most importantly, these projects provide an opportunity for local decision-makers to increase their visibility at the regional and state level by either voicing opposition or support to parts or the entire project. As a corollary to this situation, we found that in European countries as well, projects proposed or financed by the national government faced weaker opposition than did local projects.[25] Finally, we also considered the possibility that some opposition, while overtly championing environmental issues, are really about locational (Not in my Back Yard (NIMBY)) issues. Given the lack of publicly available data, we can only speculate about the frequency of these instances.

Related to a transportation mega-project's potential impacts and the time it takes for an agency or political leaders to promote that project (for a case study, see Plotch 2015) is opposition to the project's cost. We did find that history is statistically correlated with a project's cost per mile (or km), primarily with respect to highway projects; we also found that history affected opposition per se. While the causal relationships expressed by these statistical associations have yet to be unequivocally established, it stands to reason that any delay in a project's implementation will most probably result in escalated costs. Some of the examples sprinkled throughout this and previous chapters demonstrate the validity of this expectation irrespective of any statistical analysis conducted.

7.4 Conclusions

Opposition to and support for major transportation infrastructure projects are manifested by the formation of SIGs, associations representing vested interests. This chapter examined the nature of SIGs and their impacts, positive and negative, on project realization. In theory, SIGs can influence a project's future in three principle ways: they can completely forestall it, delay its implementation or facilitate its execution. Based on our database, it appears that advocacy-oriented SIGs are more likely to work behind the scenes either tacitly or at low levels, mainly to conceal the interests at stake. In contrast, opposition-oriented SIGs tend to be much more vocal and visible. The findings from our study show that most opposition centers on issues such as environmental nuisances, followed by funding.

Finally, a project's opposition appears to be affected by its history, measured in years. Notwithstanding a project's complexity and unexpected events, the statistical results regarding the association of opposition and time are significant, though the direction of causality remains uncertain. For all project types, project history is positively associated with opposition. At this point, we can only suggest that a longer history presents more opportunities for opposition-oriented SIGs to become organized and operational.

Needless to say, organized opposition and support affect decision-making. The issues motivating the formation of SIGs, their organized quality, the strength of the interests they represent and the resources they can amass all play a role in the process. I return to this issue in Chap. 11.

Notes

1. US federal legislation, "Safe, Accountable, Flexible, Efficient Transportation Equity Act: a Legacy for Users", (Public Law 109-59; SAFETEA-LU), passed in 2005, appropriated $244 billion over five years. It contained an unprecedented number of earmarks: 6373 separate projects amounting to nearly 10% of the total bill (Giuliano 2007).

2. Once earmarks were eliminated, lobbyists had to devise new strategies. One critical result is the political gridlock, as legislators no longer have a way to pay for the crucial votes, accompanied by jobs and construction contracts.
3. The American Association of State Highway and Transportation Officials (AASHTO) and the American Society of Civil Engineers (ASCE) are two such organizations. They are engaged in setting standards in addition to publishing the building specifications and guidelines used in highway design and construction throughout the USA. They represent air, rail, water and public transportation as well.
4. Here I use the acronym *SIGs* to identify any organization engaged in economic and political activities with the aim of obtaining benefits for its members by influencing decisions favoring their interests. In our case, their success is measured in the form of mega-project revision, implementation or obstruction. For other definitions and the assumptions underlying their operation, see Knight (2004) and Grossman and Helpman (2001).
5. For the role of opposition and advocacy groups in transportation policy-making, see Dunn (1998).
6. An example is the Copenhagen Metro, a 22 km rapid transit system that faced ideology-based funding issues. It took 15 years to complete the project, with cost overruns of over 200%.
7. In Chap. 6, I discussed the role of project history in establishing and sustaining the *project's idea*, which serves as a rally point for support.
8. Olson (1971) regards leadership or *political entrepreneurs* as a key determinant in solving collective action problems. Acemoglu and Jackson (2011) suggest a game-theoretic approach to modeling leadership. In their model, leaders are regarded as prominent agents, whose actions are more clearly observed by more agents.
9. For example, the cross-Israel highway project (Highway 6) was originally considered in terms of highway versus rail options. Similar arguments were made before construction of the Canada Line, an above- and under-ground rail line in Vancouver, BC. For a more general discussion, see Dunn (1998).
10. Leading textbooks in policy analysis focus mainly on technical issues rather than on political structure and players (e.g., see Weimer and Vining 2005).

    More recent policy studies have underscored the importance of understanding the political contexts of decision-making (e.g., Weible 2006). More recently, Rodrik (2014) has emphasized the importance of ideas and the need for their systematic inclusion within a political-economic analysis. The interaction between ideas and institutions, with the latter often using the former to enhance their power, has still not received proper attention in the germane literature.

11. See Grossman and Helpman (1994) for a model depicting how an SIG's political contributions can influence trade policy.
12. A commuter super-shuttle service linking Lower Manhattan and downtown Brooklyn to Long Island and the JFK AirTrain at an estimated cost of $2.4 Billion (2004 prices).
13. A good example of a political champion of such interests is Manhattan borough President George McAneny who, in 1911, became the acknowledged main supporter of the New York City subway expansion scheme. According to public accounts, his leadership was indispensable in overcoming major development and construction interests, who had previously dithered in deciding how they would proceed (Derrick 2001).
14. New York's Second Avenue Subway, already mentioned here, is a classic case in point. ARC project, which will bring the Long Island Railroad to Grand Central Station in Manhattan, is another.
15. Extension of Manhattan's Number 7 subway line (a one-mile one-station project running from 42nd Street to 34th Street along 11th Avenue at a cost of $2.4 billion) was executed mainly due to the decisive advocacy of New York's previous mayor, Michael Bloomberg.
16. See Plotch (2015) on the Tappan Zee Bridge in upstate New York.
17. See Berechman (2009) for the negative impacts of port expansion projects.
18. One possible source of information on proponents' activities is the documentation used for environmental impact analyses (Environmental Impact Statement—EIS), which by law must be published. Unfortunately, an EIS is often carried out years before a comprehensive CBA is completed, which itself can predate decision-making by several years.
19. Given the limitations of the database (see Appendix, Chap. 4), we do not know how many mega-projects that faced opposition were ultimately not selected for implementation. However, we can safely conclude that 75% is a lower bound for the occurrence of some kind of opposition.
20. To that end we used a statistical test known as the Granger causality test, which in our case means testing the hypothesis that opposition prolongs history as measured in years.
21. In its binary form, the Logit model is expressed by the function $P_1 = \frac{1}{1+e^{-(\beta \cdot v_1)}}$, where P_1 is the probability of the occurrence of the phenomenon studied (i.e., opposition) and v_1 represents its explanatory variable (project history in this case). The null hypothesis, that history has no effect on opposition (the coefficient $\beta = 0$), states the alternative ($\beta \neq 0$).
22. The constant for this model is −1.263, at a significance level of 0.01%.

23. See the 2013 case where New Jersey's governor terminated the Cross Hudson Tunnel, known as "ARC", a $9.8 billion project in the works for nearly 20 years.
24. New York's Second Avenue Subway, an inner city project, cost about $2.2 billion per km.
25. This finding may not be applicable in the USA as a top-down project is more likely to run into local opposition than one locally initiated.

References

Acemoglu, D. 2010. Theory, General Equilibrium, and Political Economy in Development Economics. *Journal of Economic Perspectives* 24 (3): 17–32.

Acemoglu, D., and M. Jackson. 2011. *History, Expectations, and Leadership in the Evolution of Social Norms*. Working Paper No. 17066. Washington, DC: National Bureau of Economic Research. http://www.nber.org/papers/w17066.

Altshuler, A., and D. Luberoff. 2003. *Mega-Projects*. Washington, DC: Brookings Institution Press.

Berechman, J. 2009. Estimation of the Full Marginal Costs of Port Related Truck Traffic. *Journal of Evaluation and Program Planning* 32 (4): 390–396.

Derrick, P. 2001. *Tunneling to the Future: The Story of the Great Subway Expansion That Saved New York*. New York: New York University Press.

Dunn, J., Jr. 1998. *Driving Forces: The Automobile, Its Enemies, and the Politics of Mobility*. Washington, DC: Brookings Institution Press.

Flyvbjerg, B., and B. Van Wee, eds. 2008. *Decision-Making on Mega-Projects: Cost-Benefit Analysis, Planning, and Innovation*. Cheltenham and Northampton, MA: Edward Elgar.

Frick, Karen Trapenberg. 2008. The Cost of the Technological Sublime: Daring Ingenuity and the New San Francisco-Oakland Bay Bridge. In *Decision-Making on Mega-Projects: Cost-Benefit Analysis, Planning, and Innovation*, ed. Hugo Priemus, H. Bent Priemus, B. Flyvbjerg, and B. Van Wee. Cheltenham and Northampton, MA: Edward Elgar.

Giuliano, G. 2007. The Changing Landscape of Transportation Decision Making. *Transportation Research Record* 2036: 5–12.

Grossman, G., and E. Helpman. 1994. Protection for Sale. *American Economic Review* 84 (4): 833–850.

———. 2001. *Special Interest Politics*. Cambridge and London: MIT Press.

Knight, B. 2004. Parochial Interests and the Centralized Provision of Local Public Goods: Evidence from Congressional Voting on Transportation Projects. *Journal of Public Economics* 88: 845–866.

Nobbe, P., and J. Berechman. 2013. *The Politics of Large Infrastructure Investment Decision-Making: The Case of the Second Avenue Subway Case Study*. New York: University Transportation Research Center, City College of New York.

———. 2014. *The Politics of Infrastructure Investment Decision-Making: Report of the Statistical Analysis of Selected Hypotheses.* University Transportation Research Center Region 2, CCNY, CUNY, Final Report.

Olson, M. 1971. *The Logic of Collective Action: Public Goods and the Theory of Groups.* Cambridge, MA: Harvard University Press.

Plotch, P. 2015. *Politics Across the Hudson: The Tappan Zee Megaproject.* New Brunswick, NJ: Rutgers University Press.

Rodrik, D. 2014. When Ideas Trump Interests: Preferences, World Views, and Policy Innovations. *The Journal of Economic Perspectives* 28 (1): 189–208.

Weible, C. 2006. An Advocacy Coalition Framework Approach to Stakeholder Analysis: Understanding the Political Context of California Marine Protected Areas. *Journal of Public Administration Research and Theory* 17: 95–117.

Weimer, D., and A. Vining. 2005. *Policy Analysis: Concepts and Practice.* 4th ed. Upper Saddle River, NJ: Prentice Hall.

CHAPTER 8

The Decisive Role of Project Funding

8.1 Introduction

A voluminous literature has been written on the topic of transportation funding. This literature has dealt mainly with the rapidly growing discrepancy between infrastructure investment, maintenance and operation needs on the one hand, and funding on the other. It dwells on the underlying causes of the gap created by the scarcity of funds as well as the gap's grave effects on system performance but also on various potential sources of funding while arguing their relative merits and shortcomings. The inability to secure a steady source of adequate funding has undoubtedly furthered the deterioration of existing facilities as well as made long-term planning and system development an increasingly frustrating undertaking.

Why funding transportation is so complicated an endeavor? Why cannot transportation systems be self-sustaining, meaning free of the constant need for external subsidies?[1] The answer lies, in part, in the nature of transportation infrastructure as a public good, a feature that precludes self-financing through optimal pricing. That is, when operating under less than full capacity, as is the case during off-peak hours, the cost to the system of serving an additional unit of output (e.g., a trip) is close to zero. Under such conditions, the introduction of an efficient pricing scheme, where marginal cost equals demand, would generate losses for operating the system at the respective hours, ultimately making it impossible to cover capital costs.[2] A second, frequently mentioned explanation for the lack of

J. Berechman, *The Infrastructure We Ride On*,
https://doi.org/10.1007/978-3-319-74606-7_8

self-sustaining funding is the impact on equity of low transit fares, which purportedly helps meet the accessibility needs of low-income users. A third and final explanation is embedded in the political nature of transit system decision-making, which favors low fares and externally subsidized systems, an arrangement perceived as increasing the leadership's political leverage.

Transportation infrastructure investments are also unique in some other key ways, which complicate capital funding issue. First of all, investments are largely irreversible, thus implying significant sunk costs. Transportation infrastructure facilities are also indivisible, meaning that capacity can be added only in fixed units, whether as carriages or miles of track, thus making optimal financing rules hard to set. Moreover, transportation investments tend to generate network and spillover externalities over many jurisdictions, large populations, numerous activities and diverse land uses. The main economic implication of these externalities is that the assessment of an optimal investment's benefits and costs requires a global, systemic view rather than a facility-based approach. As to policy, the network-like impacts of such investments are that they affect scores of stakeholders, especially the local governments that tend to exert political pressure to gain local benefits irrespective of the project's broader economic or transportation viability.

Given this portrayal of public transport investment and pricing, together with the gap between funding needs and availability, we should not wonder why securing funding is a matter of utmost importance. For our purposes, however, the main question asked in this chapter can be phrased as, how does capital funding affect decision-making with respect to a project's value and investment choices? Does funding availability supersede all other investment criteria, including the project's net transportation-economic contribution? And given the sources of funding, how do these affect key attributes such as capital and operating costs, equity effects and operating attributes?

In my book *The Evaluation of Transportation Investment Projects* (Berechman 2009), I distinguish between the notions *source of funding* and *form* or *method of financing*. The source of funding points to the level of government, the agency or the private source, contributing the money. Sources thus range over federal, state or local governments, transportation agency self-financing formats, and Public Private Partnership (PPP) project consortia. The method of financing, in contrast, indicates the specific type or form of financial support, be it grants, bonds or equity. Funding often flows from more than one source, concluding in a mix of financing forms. For example, the funding of the Alameda Corridor, a 32 km below-grade rail and road passageway in Southern California (to which we return later), came from three sources: federal, local and institutional (the port of Los Angeles); it was financed with bonds and grants. Based on this distinction, we can ask the following question: How do actual funding practices, given their sources and methods, affect project choice? For instance, if the largest share of the money needed to build a new subway line is in the form of a federal or state grant, will this affect the local decision-makers' predisposition to build the project even if, from a transportation-economics viewpoint, it is a boondoggle?

Underlying these questions is a fundamental issue, namely, the correct sequence of funding decision-making. That is, as I argue below, it is necessary to know the relationship between the source of funding and the method of financing with reference to key variables (e.g., cost of capital, annual cash flow and financial risk) before we can correctly evaluate a project's transportation-economic value. Hence, the source of funding and its method should be determined by the time the project is appraised. Yet, if funding has been made certain prior to the project's comprehensive evaluation, will that knowledge be the deciding factor in the project's choice, regardless of its value (as is often the case)? Alternatively, if these factors are known only subsequent to the evaluation, can the project be properly assessed? Given this predicament, the core issues that we face after having secured funding are as follows: To what degree does funding availability become a necessary *and* a sufficient condition for a project's selection, irrespective of its value? Second, from a normative standpoint, should the funding-evaluation process be sequential, with assessment before funding, or funding before assessment, or simultaneous but reiterative? If the latter, how should the process best be designed and executed?

8.2 Funding Alternatives

Transportation projects rest on a range of funding options: general taxation (grants), dedicated taxation (e.g., gasoline tax and sales tax), farebox revenues, cross-subsidies (e.g., charges levied on car users and sometimes on non-travel-related commodities)[3] and debt (bond issues). Additional sources range from taxes on travel inputs and outputs (e.g., tires and miles traveled), to value-capture revenue mechanisms (e.g., transit-stimulated development).[4] In selected types of PPP projects, capital is provided by the private sector, which implies specific types of financial risk.

From an economic perspective, a tax or a charge, of any kind, produces three main types of outcomes: welfare, equity and anticipated revenues. To assess the probability of achieving these outcomes, which indicates the project's efficiency, economic theory applies Pareto Optimum conditions as criteria. The studies conducted in this vein have shown that taxes tend to distort the meeting of these objectives, thus producing inefficiency and welfare losses, caused by the discrepancy that taxes introduce between the effective prices that consumers and providers face and described by the tax-induced deadweight loss.[5] When considering alternative taxes to fund transportation, the question of which tax has the least distortionary effect on welfare is therefore highly consequential.

Taxes also engender income distribution effects as the population that actually bears the tax burden may not benefit from it. In Chap. 10, I deal with equity issues. Here it will suffice to point out that the distribution of the tax burden, otherwise known as the tax incidence, may vary relative to multiple variables such as project location, transportation mode and users' socio-economic status, each of which affects the overall equity effect resulting from that tax. The final core funding issue to be mentioned here is how much revenue will actually be collected. Computation of this amount calls for the use of an equilibrium model approach aimed at estimating travel demand, by a mode, subsequent to the tax's introduction.

Turning to policy, a crucial element of any tax proposal is the probability that it will be passed given public sentiments and other political realities. Often, proposals to raise transit-supporting revenues by imposing car-user charges end up on the legislature's floor. A case in point is the proposal made by the former mayor of New York to levy a charge (the so-called congestion charge) on vehicles entering a cordoned midtown area. The proposal fell through when state legislators rejected it.[6]

Another policy consideration concerns the tax collection mechanism. Quite often, this issue presents an arduous hurdle to implementation of a proposed tax. For example, a distance-based tax, currently being proposed in the USA as a substitute for the gasoline tax, requires the use of a tracking technology to collect the necessary data. However, use of such technology raises difficult privacy issues, which has provoked motorists' opposition.

Lastly, there is the question of what to do with the tax's proceeds and who makes that decision. It often happens that the authority receiving the tax revenues from, let us say, a public transit property, is not the one that decides its rates or incidence, decisions that are frequently made elsewhere, such as the highway toll authority (see Chap. 9 for a discussion on the role of institutions in mega-project decision-making). This split often points to the political rivalry waged by institutions over money issues, a situation that affects the actual amount of revenue reaching the agency needing that revenue.

The key lesson to be learned from this short discussion is that the factors mentioned must be addressed when judging the pros and cons of any tax proposal. Consider the US experience. Thanks to a string of legislative acts called *earmarked legislation* (informally referred to as *pork barrel legislation*), the federal government has come to support the stipulated large-scale transportation investments in the form of dedicated grants taken from general coffers. This type of legislation is generally initiated by legislators wishing to direct money, in the form of a project, to benefit their home district or state. While earmarks tend to eliminate the free-rider problem of public goods, their inefficiency and equity income distribution impacts are quite significant as they serve designated populations but not necessarily the needy populations (e.g., Mwangi et al. 1990). With regard to project choice and selection, the main drawback of earmarked funding is that it effectively renders irrelevant comprehensive appraisal of the project. As a result, earmarked funding does not guarantee that the best project is selected. Just think of the significant number of unworthy projects that have already been funded (see Chaps. 2 and 3).

At the other end of the funding spectrum are dedicated taxes, such as the US motor fuel tax, levied at a fixed rate per unit of gasoline. This tax, which has been used as the main source of funding for constructing and maintaining the highway network, is exhibiting rapidly decreasing effectiveness primarily due to the continuous technological improvement in vehicle fuels.[7] This reality, which has been compounded by the rising needs and costs of highway construction, is the main reason driving the myriad proposals aimed at its replacement with other dedicated taxes and user charges, such as the previously mentioned distance-traveled tax. Although such dedicated taxes are often regarded as mechanisms to discourage highway travel and thus reduce negative externalities like air pollution, the desired results are contingent on the presence of a viable public transit system with sufficient capacity to handle the shifted demand. In the absence of such a system, low-income groups suffer disproportionally from such a tax.

Highway, bridge and tunnel tolls have also been a main source of funding for transit. But like the distance-traveled tax, tolls suffer from a range of efficiency, distributional and technological shortcomings. For example, tolls not based on time of day, as they should be, introduce welfare inefficiencies because off-peak and peak-hour users will pay the same charge even though the latter generate more-significant congestion externalities. Additionally, since local and inner-city roads are typically not tolled, motorists residing far from center city employment locations will pay relatively much more than people who reside closer to these locations.

Many other proposals to raise revenues for transit have been suggested, ranging from indexation of tax rates (e.g., gasoline) to taxing of crude oil. But even non-tax proposals, such as asset sales, land leasing and land swaps, although popular among some transit properties, carry efficiency effects because transit authorities enjoy monopoly status in some markets (particularly land); their actions thus tend to distort prices and threaten competition with private sector enterprises. In general, prior to their introduction, a tax's relative merits with respect to the above issues, mainly efficiency, equity and estimated total revenues, must be demonstrated. The remainder of the chapter deals with the two key questions raised at the outset: How do the source and method of financing affect a project's true costs, and how does guaranteed funding affect project choice and decision-making?

8.3 Project Fund by Source and Method

To properly analyze the impact of funding on project costs and decision-making, we need to first differentiate between the *source of funding* and the *method of financing*. Table 8.1 summarizes these notions.

In Table 8.1, the *Source of funding* column distinguishes between the various governmental levels that participate in project funding: national, local, state or provincial, transportation agency, international,[8] and private sector. In Vancouver, for example, funding for the Canada Line rail project (total cost: $Can 1889 billion in 2003 prices) came from the federal government (Transport Canada, 22%), the Province of British Columbia (12%), the Greater Vancouver Transportation Authority (a conglomerate of local governments, 16%), the Vancouver Airport (12%), the City of Vancouver (1.4%) and the private sector (34%[9]), with the balance coming from multiple other sources.

In some cases, funding comes from one main source. For instance, private sources fully funded Australia's CityLink, a 22 km road project in Melbourne. In contrast, national sources funded Italy's Frejus Road Tunnel in its entirety. But these are exceptions. Figure 8.1 summarizes the data on funding sources from our mentioned database of 60 mega-projects (Nobbe and Berechman 2014).

Table 8.1 Sources of transportation project funding and methods of financing

Source of funding	*Taxation*	*Bond and debt*	*Equity*
Local (city)	Property, impact (value captured), tolls, asset sales and various fees	Municipal bonds	
State or Province	Income, payroll, other taxes (e.g., fuel), tolls and fees	State bonds	
Federal or Central government	Direct and indirect taxes (general tax revenue); grants	Treasury bonds	
Public agency		Agency bonds	Investment income
Private sector		Corporate bonds, loans	Private funds
International	Grants, loans		

Source: Based on Berechman (2009)

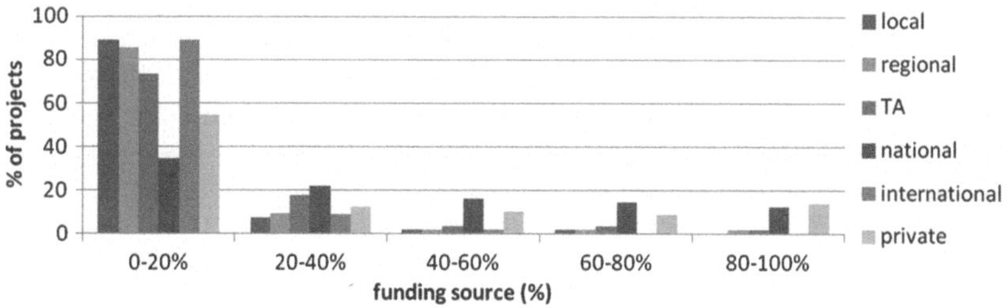

Fig. 8.1 Average project funding by source (in %). *TA* Transit Authority. Source: Nobbe and Berechman (2014)

It is obvious from these data that in only a few projects (0%–20%) does the majority of funding come from local sources. In general, national (federal) funding dominates all but this first cluster. That is, national-level agencies provide most of the investment capital for projects in the 20%–40% and 60%–80% ranges and just about equal international funding in the 80%–100% cluster (mostly European projects with cross-national impacts).

At this point it is pertinent to ask what rationale underlies the allocation of federal grants to transportation, a significant proportion of which are dedicated grants that benefit local populations. One answer is that for various reasons, lower-level governments are financially unable to fund capital-intensive projects, especially if they are mega-projects. A second answer is the internalization of positive externalities in the form of positive transportation spillovers to adjacent metropolitan areas or even to neighboring states (De Borger and Proost 2012). Yet, how valid are these arguments? In reality, not very. The inability of local governments to pay for the capital costs of infrastructure projects can be resolved by non-dedicated grants or tax revenue-sharing. Furthermore, dedicated grants distort resource allocation and, as I elaborate below, are closely associated with unworthy projects. With regard to the spillover argument, it is doubtful if many projects, even large ones, indeed engender sufficiently extensive externalities to warrant federal funding.[10]

In justifying these arguments, we should explore just how efficient this federal mechanism truly is. In the USA, federal matching grants for megaprojects as provided by the Federal Highway Trust Fund (FHTF) can reach 80% of total project cost. This level of funding is based on technical criteria not necessarily akin to the project's welfare contribution. While legislators generally do not directly decide on a project, congressmen from the target districts can insist on execution of the so-called preliminary *demonstration projects*, financed from other federal sources, which serve as a condition for approval of the respective funding package. This system strongly encourages regional representatives and local politicians to compete for higher shares of total funding allocations, behavior highly likely to produce gross inefficiencies (Besley and Coate 2003).

8.3.1 Methods of Finance

In the USA, for example, the major financing method used by local and state authorities is debt accumulation in the form of bond issues. Federal and state grants represent another significant channel in many countries. Yet, in the majority of cases, financing is obtained by a mix of means and sources. One succinct example is California's Alameda Corridor project, mentioned above. As shown in Fig. 8.2, about half of the funds for this project came from revenue bonds while the other half came from grants contributed by the federal government, a transit agency and others sources.

In another instance, the $4.75 billion capital costs of New York's Second Avenue Subway (SAS) was financed as follows: $1.3 billion in the form of a federal grant (the New Starts program), $3 billion in grants from state and local sources, and $450 million by means of the 2005 State Transportation Bond Act.[11]

In PPP projects, the funding methods commonly used are bonds, bank debt and equity. Australia's CityLink project, a PPP undertaking, was financed with 61% bank debt (including 2% subordinate debt), 23% equity

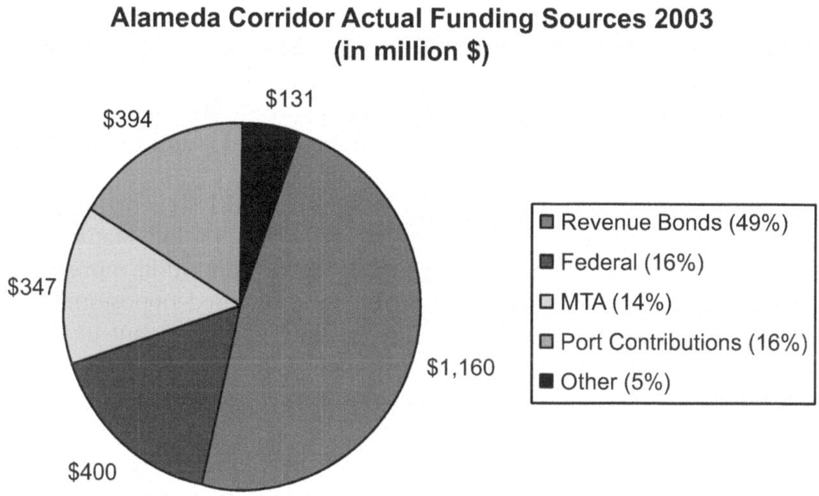

Fig. 8.2 Funding the Alameda Corridor. Source: Nobbe and Berechman (2014)

and 16% bonds. The project's source of direct income was toll charges, collected electronically. New York State's Tappan Zee Bridge is currently being built with private investment and a loan from the federal government, which is expected to leverage more private dollars.

Data culled from the Nobbe and Berechman (2014) database indicate that a mix of bonds, loans and grants (from general revenues) represent the key methods chosen to finance mega-projects. Only a small number of projects use grants and bonds exclusively. The importance of identifying the financing package lies in the fact that no two projects are financed by the same mix. But because that mix affects the project's cost of capital and annual debt service costs, it impacts on the computation of its worthiness.

8.4 Effects of Funding on Decision-Making

We made use of our database to statistically test several hypotheses regarding the relationship between a project's funding, properties and choice.[12] Some of the results are discussed next.

A noticeable result of the analysis is that funding methods differ across project types. That is, compared with highway projects, rail tends to be financed less by bonds and grants than by loans and dedicated revenues and, to a lesser extent, by equity. A key reason for this trend is that in many developed countries, railway firms own or control the rolling stock and services as well as the infrastructure; they therefore use financing methods akin to those common in the private sector. As to the highway sector, we find the separation of infrastructure ownership and vehicle service provision, which explains the greater reliance on bonds and grants as the major financing methods.

Another phenomenon revealed by the statistical analysis is that opposition to a project is indirectly related to the method of funding. Statistically, private funding was found to be associated with opposition more than were other forms of funding. Moreover, issue-oriented opposition was strongly correlated with bond-backed projects whereas grant-financed projects were comparatively opposition-free.[13] How can these results be explained? My response is that grants are normally provided by a government entity, whether local, state or federal, a source that conveys the image of being socially more responsible and attuned to the citizens' *true* needs. Since grants are provided from public coffers, their use to finance a project also carries the clout of formal fiscal responsibility and transparency. Yet, most federal highway, transit and safety funds are distributed through formulas that only indirectly relate to needs and may have no connection to performance. Furthermore, local authorities, as recipients of federal and state money, tend to regard such *external funding* as costless; they tend to consider grants as political benefits, not costs. In any case, the public deems private funding, the bulk of which is delivered by means of equity and private loans, as serving narrow interests, meant to generate profits for private firms through real-estate development, for example. This may explain the greater opposition to private financing than to public grants.[14]

Another finding, as noted above, is the effect of the specific financial package used on the project's true cost of capital and, it follows, the discount rate of its future streams of costs and benefits, as well as the size of the annual debt service payments. In reality, this is not the case for multiple reasons, including political expediency. Most countries use a uniform, mandatory discount rate, known as the Social Discount Rate (SDR), for all transportation infrastructure projects, regardless of type and financing method. The discounting of benefits and costs at an incorrect rate is liable to produce erroneous estimates of an investment's economic value and, in consequence, the choice of unwarranted projects.[15]

At the country level, an interesting result from the statistical analysis is that equity funding is negatively associated with a country's wealth.

That is, wealthier countries tend to fund public infrastructure projects through grants significantly more than do poor countries. The latter need to find external sources of funding, mainly from institutions like the World Bank or the private sector. It is not surprising, therefore, that equity funding of infrastructure plays a less-substantial role in European than in Asian or Latin American countries.

We now come to the key question of the relationship between the source of funding and project choice. That is, does the source of funding, especially if it lies outside the project's administrative boundaries, determine its selection? And if so, by how much? I investigated this issue as follows. First, using the Nobbe–Berechman database, I identified those project attributes related to its funding source. These include risk level, years to completion and the likelihood of not subjecting the project to a Cost-Benefit Analysis (CBA).

The statistical analysis revealed a strong positive association between federal or national-level funding and a project's risk level. That is, national funding is associated with riskier projects than are local or agency sources. It therefore appears that national governments are more willing to support riskier projects. This may be due primarily to their ability to internalize risk, to withstand financial insolvency and, perhaps, to view needs on the national level. The negative side of this correlation is that these same projects are also associated with longer construction periods and larger cost overruns. After controlling for a project's risk level, I obtained a related result: national governments tend to take on disproportionately cost-inefficient projects.[16]

This also implies, as might be imagined, that funding source is also associated with the number of years required for a project's completion. Thus, when private (mostly PPP) sources are involved, completion times go down, probably due to strong cost minimization and efficiency-enhancing efforts. We may therefore tentatively conclude that national sources are associated with longer completion times because cost savings and efficiency may not be clear, high-priority objectives.[17]

Surprisingly, the analysis also showed that compared with projects funded at the sub-national levels, the number of cost-benefit studies done when national funding is involved was the same. We would also expect, a priori, that national governments follow guidelines more stringently with respect to CBAs. Yet, as the data disclosed, national government involvement in a project does not automatically imply that its choice will be based on a bona fide CBA. For example, Proost et al. (2010) found that more than half of the projects on the Trans European Transport Investment priority list did not pass the cost-benefit test.

Switching to the effect of funding source on local decision-making, our analysis showed that when the major share of funding comes from federal or national sources, the propensity of local decision-makers to select larger projects escalates as compared to the projects selected when the main share of funding comes from local sources. That is, we found that local projects (urban and metropolitan) funded mainly from federal sources are much greater in scope than those projects whose major share of funding comes from non-federal sources (e.g., bonds, loans and cross-subsidies). Regional and national projects are much less prone to this effect. This finding should nonetheless be considered in light of the association of national funding with higher levels of project risk. The importance of these results cannot be overstated.

Given the negative impact of rising taxation and debt payments on local decision-makers' willingness to undertake capital investments, this result is not surprising. When the bulk of funding for a local transportation project must be raised locally, decision-makers therefore tend to favor smaller and less-risky projects than when most of the funding comes from national coffers. Since the ability to raise local funds is limited economically, statutorily and politically, transportation projects necessarily compete among themselves and with non-transportation investments. These factors explain, at least in part, the behavior of local decision-makers.

I now return to the observation that funding for transportation infrastructure, including new facilities and the upgrading of existing ones, is dwindling as traditional sources, such as the FHTF, are rapidly experiencing depletion of their resources.[18] A bi-product of this reality is the creation of new mechanisms meant to raise revenues, each of which has potentially distortionary effects on resource allocation. A key example is cross-subsidization, which occurs when highway toll revenues or tax revenues from other services (e.g., telecommunications) are used to subsidize transit operations and capital investments, or to back up the sale of bonds for the same purpose (Hirschman et al. 1995).[19] When coupled with distortionary pricing schemes,[20] these other markets (e.g., highway travel or telecommunications) become grossly inefficient. While it can be argued that the degree to which the increased use of public transit reduces auto-related externalities such as air pollution, such subsidies are warranted even though direct taxation of these externalities would be an economically superior step. Even so, the distortionary effects of transit subsidies on other sectors should be weighed before adopting these mechanisms.

An additional factor affecting project choice is rent-seeking,[21] mainly through lobbying for government contracts. For instance, once funding has been secured, special interest groups such as consulting and construction firms initiate frantic lobbying activities with the aim of acquiring monopolistic advantages related to the project's implementation (e.g., appointment as the project's chief engineering firm). Some of these efforts may in fact commence even earlier, just as the process of securing funding takes its first steps. Lobbying to persuade local officials to secure funding at the national level is very common. The manipulation of transportation agencies to obtain lucrative contracts once funding has been obtained (if not before) is another example. In general, as the intricacy of project funding escalates, the economic and political struggles intensify, together with the potential veto points, which tend to emerge over sources and the contributions of the respective stakeholders (Giuliano 2007).

In sum, once a project's financial package has been finalized, history teaches us that funding availability becomes a necessary but *also* a sufficient reason for its implementation. A case in point is New York's SAS. A partial CBA was conducted as part of the project's environmental impact statement many years before work began. An informal CBA done in 2003/2004 indicated the project's marginal transportation-economic value (Berechman and Paaswell 2005). Yet, the ability of key stakeholders to finalize a financial package in 2005 was sufficient for construction to commence in 2007.

8.5 Grants and Risk in PPP Projects

As I pointed out above, grant availability tends to encourage acceptance of riskier projects, with relatively fewer CBA studies performed to ascertain their value. This means that a thorough risk analysis, formally required by all CBA procedures, is usually not carried out. And so, with the number and size of grants dwindling, other funding recipes, mainly PPP, are becoming more prominent. But what about the risks involved with projects funded partly by government grants and partly by private equity?

The response to this question directly relates to the type of PPP selected. Generally speaking, a choice is made between the two main types of PPP: in the first, a contractor is chosen for a turnkey project; in the second, an actual risk partner is involved. Under the first, the private party receives a guaranteed income for his work and assumes only the project's cost-related risks. A prudent contractor therefore incorporates a risk premium into his bid, which reflects his anticipated level of cost volatility and risk aversion. Under the second, the private partner assumes some of the project's risks, those mainly related to cost, demand and revenues, regulation and financing. The question of how to allocate risks between the public and private partners is thus the central issue determining the specific PPP arrangements (Ke et al. 2010). This is particularly the case when the government's objective is to minimize project costs given the desired level of output, whereas the private entity's aim is to reduce its related risks (e.g., by inflating the costs agreed upon in the contract). Contract renegotiation, that is, when a bidder subsequent to winning the contract tries to renegotiate its terms, is a common tactic used by private partners to achieve this objective.

The result is a sub-optimal level of investment which entails the main drawback of PPP funding, whereas its advantages are expanded budgets, shorter construction times and more-efficient project management. In an environment of declining public funding for transportation projects, especially mega-projects, it is not surprising that decision-makers are predisposed to this method. The data verily show that the total value of PPP contracts is on the rise (Kappeler and Nemoz 2010).

8.6 The Sequence of Funding and Investment Decisions

It would not be trivial to state that the sequence in which decisions are made often determines their outcomes. This is especially true in the public sector. We therefore find that the best net welfare-improving transportation projects all too often remain on paper. This reality reflects why decision-makers agree that funding is the decisive factor in the mega-project choice process (see Chap. 4, Fig. 4.1). Funding thus dominates all other considerations when it comes to project choice. It also explains the frantic attempts by project proponents to secure funding even before, or regardless of, the evaluation of its transportation-economic value.

A classic sequence initiated to pay for mega-projects, what has come to be known as the notorious Robert Moses approach to funding (Caro 1975), entails acquisition of funding sufficient to begin planning, designing and even some construction; at that point, the project initiator uses the sunk cost argument to acquire the rest. But why is this sequence reprehensible? From a policy perspective, funding should be secured for a project only after its transportation-economic value has been clearly demonstrated. However, in order to conduct a CBA we need to know the method of project financing for the reasons discussed previously. This rationale raises a clearly fundamental question concerning the sequence of funding-evaluation-choice, where funding refers to both source and method. Should the correct sequence be (a) secure funding then conduct a CBA; or (b) perform a CBA and then secure funding; or (c) iteratively identify funding sources, perform a CBA, and then secure funding conditional on the CBA's results?

In order to conduct a genuine CBA, we require information about key financial factors such as annual expenditures and cost of capital, the assessment of which can be calculated only if we know the funding source and method. Yet, as argued, such a requirement may inadvertently predetermine a project's selection. Given the three optional approaches indicated, it appears that the most appropriate way to eschew such a predicament is to adopt the third option, an iterative process in which funding is secured if and only if a CBA has confirmed the project's net welfare contribution. Once funding is secured, a new CBA can be conducted to establish that the financial package negotiated does not negatively influence the project's assessed value. Crucially, given the lengthy time often elapsing between the CBA and actual implementation, such an iterative process would ascertain whether the project is still viable at any point in time.

But is such a process achievable in practice? The answer is, probably not. First, iterative procedures are time-consuming and rather cumbersome. Second, political decision-makers tend to regard secured funding as a political gain and thus closed to review. Third, under current political and planning realities, where a significant number of mega-projects do not undergo any or only a partial CBA, the suggested sequence appears improbable. Observed practice is therefore likely to prevail, with secured funding often serving as a necessary and sufficient condition for project choice.

8.7 Conclusions

There is little doubt that in most Western countries, current funding of transportation projects is too ad hoc and falls short of urgent investment and maintenance needs. As a result, transportation agencies fiercely vie for whatever funds are available. Once obtained, even in part, that funding supersedes any other project selection criteria. This effect is so strong that about half of the funded and/or implemented projects in our database were not required to undergo any CBA to validate their transportation-economic net value.

Following a brief review of funding alternatives, this chapter therefore focused on the role of funding, by source and method of financing, in project selection. Based on the statistical analysis, we can derive the following conclusions.

Federal or national government grants constitute a significant portion of mega-projects' total funding. Yet, in many European and North American countries, the share of federal grants in total project funding has eroded over time while that of state and local governments, transportation agencies and the private sector has increased. Bonds, government loans and grants from dedicated revenues have become the main financing instruments. Other methods include revenues from user charges, diverse sources (mainly, cross-subsidization) and private equity. Funding responsibility is being increasingly delegated to lower levels of government that, in light of the small number of financial instruments available to them, seek more and more private funding in the form of PPP projects. Patterns do vary, however, by transportation sectors.

A key finding of our analysis is that the source of funding has an effect on the degree of opposition to a project. That is, projects funded by public grants statistically generate much less opposition than do projects funded by private money (PPP). The explanation offered is that the public views the former source of funding as serving its true needs whereas the latter is viewed as serving narrow, mainly private interests. The analysis further reveals a strong positive association between national-level funding and selected project attributes. These include the tendency to undertake projects that are riskier, require longer construction periods and exhibit larger cost overruns, in short, disproportionately cost-inefficient projects.

Another core conclusion is that the share of federal money out of the project's total budget positively affects the propensity of local decision-makers to select larger projects. That is, when funded mainly by federal sources, urban and metropolitan projects tend to be much larger than those funded mainly from non-federal sources.

The dwindling of traditional sources of transportation project funding has compelled state and local decision-makers to develop various alternative mechanisms, aimed at raising revenues. Many of these have significant distortionary effects on the local economy.

Lastly, this chapter has drawn attention to the fact that in order to avoid the conclusive impact of secured funding on project selection, an iterative process of funding followed by a CBA should be adopted. However, given current political and bureaucratic realities, marred by investment decisions too often driven by politics, institutional rivalry, rent-seeking and administrative inefficiency, we can only conclude that the existing pattern of funding will prevail as a project's *raison d'être*.

Notes

1. In 2012, total state and local tax revenues in the State of New York allocated to subsidizing New York City transit came to $7.7 billion, not counting the subsidy to commuter rail. The bulk of this money, over $4.5 billion, was used to maintain low transit fares by covering the system's maintenance and operating costs, leaving only $3.2 billion for capital investments (Aggarwala 2014). See Nash and Matthews (2013) for a survey of efficient pricing and subsidy regimes in transportation sectors.
2. We should not neglect the free-rider effect that, for public goods, implies the built-in tendency of individuals not to reveal their true preferences, thereby avoiding payment of the real price of supplying the good.
3. For example, to fund the Tappan Zee Bridge replacement—a $5 billion investment in upstate New York—it was proposed that the State's Environmental Facilities Corporation's Clean Water Fund loan money to the project. This money is typically used for sewage improvements and clean water projects, not transportation.
4. For reviews of the subject, see Cervero et al. (2004), Goldman and Wachs (2003) and Litman (2013).
5. It is often claimed that taxing cars to cross-subsidize transit also benefits car users, for example, by lowering congestion. Notwithstanding the degree to which this claim holds true, taxes affect efficiency as they alter the relative prices of mode use, thereby producing a deadweight loss.
6. In contrast, the London congestion scheme, introduced in 2003, is still in place. It levies a charge on most motor vehicles operating within the Congestion Charge Zone in Central London. The charge's aims are to reduce high traffic flow in the central area and raise funds for London's public transport system. At the time of writing, it is considered a *success* in terms of these two criteria.
7. In the USA, the federal tax per gallon has been 18.4 cents for gasoline and 24.4 cents for diesel fuel since 1993. The Congressional Budget Office has since estimated a decline of 21% in total revenues by 2040, when new federal fuel economy standards will be fully phased in.
8. For some national or cross-national projects, funding can come from international sources such as The World Bank, the Inter-America Development Bank, or the European Bank for Reconstruction and Development.

9. To finance Transit BC L.P., a limited partnership was formed mainly by SNC-Lavalin Inc., the British Columbia Investment Management Corporation (bcIMC) and the Caisse de dépôt et placement du Québec.
10. For a discussion of these issues in the context of the EU, see de Rus and Socorro (2010).
11. A support coalition, comprised of several regional special interest groups that included labor unions, business associations and consulting firms, actively lobbied for the Act, which became a key factor in completing the project's financing package and its consequent implementation.
12. The results were obtained using correlation, regression and Logit models (see Nobbe and Berechman 2014). The reader should keep in mind the distinction between correlation analysis, where two effects are statistically correlated, and causality analysis, where statistical measures test the degree to which one variable (e.g., source of funding) affects another (e.g., size of a project). Results from statistical tests notwithstanding, causality arguments must be supported by a theoretical line of reasoning.
13. Using a Logit model, the results show that the probability of opposition to a project declines with the relative size of the grants in the total funding package. This effect is stronger for projects that are add-ons to existing networks than to entirely new enterprises.
14. In the USA, some states impose tolls while others rely more heavily on fuel and other taxes. Levinson (2001) explains this observation on the basis of a state's share of non-resident workers, the policies of neighboring states, historical factors and population makeup.
15. For example, since 2007, Canada's obligatory SDR is 8%. Based on a consumption rate of interest and a growth model for projects of 50 years or less, assuming no crowding out of private investments, the rate should have been 3.5% (Boardman et al. 2010). The effect of using a higher discount rate is to discourage projects that could have been judged as worthy would a lower discount rate be used.
16. It should be noted, however, that in recent years and across several countries, national-level funding is diminishing relative to other sources. As a result, the complexity of funding arrangements has increased. This trend is particularly strong in non-European countries, where projects are funded through a mix of financial instruments.
17. This result was obtained from a Logit model analysis, where the probability of longer completion period was estimated relative to the source of funding.
18. This fund is financed mainly by dedicated taxes on gasoline, collected by a federal agency. A recent report by the American Society of Civil Engineers estimated that by 2020, $3.6 trillion will be needed for nationwide infrastructure renewal, of which transportation costs are a major component

(ASCE 2013). On July 31, 2014, the US Congress approved a measure transferring $10.8 billion into the FHTF; the measure was later reauthorized and extended through May 2015.

19. A 1980 Metropolitan Transportation Authority (MTA) study found that $14.4 billion was needed for its long-term plan to bring its systems to a state of good repair. To obtain these funds, the MTA proposed selling bonds backed by tolls on bridges and tunnels and by a range of future operating revenues. The New York State government, on its part, offered to commit $80 million annually to support the sale of $800 million of *service contract* bonds to cover 1982–1986 capital costs. The proceeds from the sales of these bonds were added to the traditional funding provided by the federal government (about one-third of the total package) and the City of New York (Derrick et al. 2012).
20. These include fare level irrespective of distance travelled and time of day, non-tolled congested roads and bridges, and price discounts to specific groups of users (see Aggarwala 2014).
21. The term describes the behavior of economic entities (e.g., firms), that seek to increase their share of existing wealth (such as government funding of a project) through activities that do not create new wealth (e.g., lobbying and political pressure).

References

Aggarwala, R. 2014. Why High Fares Would Be Good for Public Transit. *Atlantic CityLab.* http://www.citylab.com/commute/2014/07/why-higher-fares-would-be-good-for-public-transit/374314/.

American Society of Civil Engineers (ASCE). 2013. *Report Card for America's Infrastructure.* http://www.infrastructurereportcard.org/a/#p/home.

Berechman, J. 2009. *The Evaluation of Transportation Investment Projects.* New York: Routledge.

Berechman, J., and R. Paaswell. 2005. Evaluation, Prioritization and Selection of Transportation Investment Projects in New York City. *Transportation* 32 (3): 223–249.

Besley, T., and S. Coate. 2003. Centralized Versus Decentralized Provision of Local Public Goods: A Political Economy Approach. *Journal of Public Economics* 87: 2611–2637.

Boardman, A., M.A. Moore, and A.R. Vining. 2010. The Social Discount Rate for Canada Based on Future Growth in Consumption. *Canadian Public Policy* xxxvi (3): 323–341.

Caro, R. 1975. *The Power Broker, Robert Moses and the Fall of New York.* New York: Vintage.

Cervero, R., F. Dunphy, M.M. Dock, D. Porter, and C. Swenson. 2004. *Developing Around Transit: Strategies and Solutions That Work*. Washington, DC: Urban Land Institute.

De Borger, B., and S. Proost. 2012. Transport Policy Competition Between Governments: A Selective Survey of the Literature. *Economics of Transportation* 1: 35–48.

de Rus, G., and M. Socorro. 2010. Infrastructure Investment and Incentives with Supranational Funding. *Transition Studies Review* 17 (3): 551–567.

Derrick, P., R. Paaswell, and D. Petretta. 2012. Transportation Policy and Politics in New York State. In *Oxford Handbook of New York State Government and Politics*, ed. G. Benjamin. New York: Oxford University Press.

Giuliano, G. 2007. The Changing Landscape of Transportation Decision Making. *Transportation Research Record* 2036: 5–12.

Goldman, T., and M. Wachs. 2003. A Quiet Revolution in Transportation Finance: The Rise of Local Option of Transportation Taxes. *Transportation Quarterly* 57 (1): 19–32.

Hirschman, I., J. Berechman, C. McKnight, J. Pucher, and R. Paaswell. 1995. Bridge and Tunnel Toll Elasticities in New York: Some Recent Evidence. *Transportation* 22 (22): 97–113.

Kappeler, A., and M. Nemoz. 2010. Public-Private Partnerships in Europe, Before and During the Recent Financial Crisis. *Economic and Financial Report*. http://www.eib.org/epec/resources/efr_epec_ppp_report1.pdf.

Ke, Y., S.Q. Wang, and A.P.C. Chan. 2010. Risk Allocation in Public-Private Partnership Infrastructure Projects: A Comparative Study. *Journal of Infrastructure Systems* 16: 343–351.

Levinson, D. 2001. Why States Toll – An Empirical Model of Finance Choice. *Journal of Transport Economics and Policy* 35 (2): 223–238.

Litman, T. 2013. *Local Funding Options for Public Transit*. Paper 13-3125, Transportation Research Board Annual Meeting, Washington, DC.

Mwangi, K., D. Lee, and R. Tollison. 1990. Efficient Lobbying and Earmarked Taxes. *Public Finance Review* 18 (1): 104–113.

Nash, C., and B. Matthews. 2013. Transport Pricing and Subsidy. In *Handbook of Transport Studies*, ed. Jean-Paul Rodrigue, Theo Notteboom, and Jon Shaw. Thousand Oaks, CA: Sage.

Nobbe, P., and J. Berechman. 2014. *The Politics of Infrastructure Investment Decision-Making: Report of the Statistical Analysis of Selected Hypotheses*. University Transportation Research Center Region 2, CCNY, CUNY, Final Report.

Proost, S., F. Dunkerley, S. Van der Loo, N. Adler, J. Bröcker, and A. Korzhenevyc. 2010. *Do the Selected Trans European Transport Investments Pass the Cost Benefit Test?* Discussion Paper 10.02, Leuven, Belgium, KULeuven, Center for Economic Studies.

CHAPTER 9

Overseeing Institutions

9.1 Introduction

Transportation agencies can be viewed as specialized institutions whose mission is to supply transportation facilities and services within defined geographic regions. How well do they accomplish their mission, especially with respect to the choice of worthy transportation projects?

The economic literature defines institutions as a set of formal and/or informal rules and norms that people abide by and that govern the type and distribution of their incentives and opportunities.[1] Here we deal with the organizations that embody those rules and norms, particularly the public agencies or authorities set up to decide upon and administer the numerous aspects of rail, road and sometimes air and marine transportation. Many additional institutions become involved at the point of actual selection and implementation of a specific project.[2] The entire structure therefore consists of non-transportation agencies such as housing authorities, the legal system, urban planning agencies, operational subsidiaries (e.g., bus and commuter rail companies), and state, regional and local governments to which we should add, depending on the project, branches of the central (national or federal) government. Here we focus primarily on the local economic institutions that plan, execute and oversee transportation policy and investments.

The goal of this chapter is to examine mega-project decision-making in a multi-layered political world. I will respond to three main questions: First, how do agency characteristics, including their organizational structure

J. Berechman, *The Infrastructure We Ride On*,
https://doi.org/10.1007/978-3-319-74606-7_9

and sources of funding, affect capital investment decision-making? Second, does the multiplicity of organizations, which raises issues of inter-agency competition, have a bearing on the choice of mega-projects? Third, can the relationships between the political system and transportation agencies explain infrastructure decisions?

9.2 Transportation Agencies: Their Roles and Functions

Transportation agencies are publicly established organizations through which transportation policies are enacted and capital investments planned and implemented. Their pivotal place in the overall system justifies consideration of their nature. Like other public bureaucracies, transportation agencies fill many roles, serve many interests and have diverse institutional dimensions.[3] Given our focus here on the selection of transportation mega-projects, one way to view these agencies is as a three-layered body. The top layer consists of the overseeing elected politicians, such as transportation ministers, which we label here as the *officials*. Under the officials are the agency's head and governing board, known as *directors*.

Beneath this layer are the bureaucrats (administrators) or the technical *professionals*. Formally, the role of officials is to set overall agency scope and strategy, obtain the necessary resources, and take policy complementarities and equity issues into account. Officials appoint the directors, whose key role is to define and manage realization of the policies that reflect the officials' transportation goals. The main task of the professionals is to quantify, identify and design the specific transportation system in detail.

A related approach to the study of transportation agencies is to consider them as bureaucracies that strive to solve an optimization problem, given an objective function. According to this model, agency directors, working with the framework of the overall goals delineated by officials, set specific objectives while professionals determine the transportation-economic value of each project option. Put differently, given the objectives defined by the agency's heads, and given the various physical, financial and planning constraints, the organization's main role is to find a feasible solution (i.e., a project) that will comply with needs in light of the constraints. By and large, these projects represent second- or third-best solutions that raise the least resistance.[4]

While useful as a theoretical framework for thinking about the structure and function of public institutions such as transportation agencies, these models are quite difficult to empirically validate for several reasons. To begin with, the above approaches assume that elected officials are motivated by the desire to advance their public standing, implying their chances for re-election, whereas directors and professionals are motivated by professional career objectives. They further posit *ex-ante* motivations, roles and objectives for each layer. The corroboration of these assumptions is difficult because in reality, these objectives and roles may be blurred or mixed as directors often worry about their public reputation while tenured professionals often regard intra-agency politics as more valuable than professional performance in furthering their careers.[5] Moreover, the time horizons of elected officials normally are shorter than those of appointed directors and much shorter than those of tenured professionals. Elected officials may thus have little interest in long-term investments, a position that may conflict with the objectives of professionals interested in long-term job security.

For the sake of the current discussion, I therefore focus directly on the specific tasks that metropolitan transportation agencies perform in order to fulfill their mandates:

1. Reduce congestion and improve accessibility through capacity expansion and pricing
2. Reach and maintain existing facilities in a state of good repair
3. Improve mobility options for different socio-economic and demographic groups
4. Improve system reliability and efficiency
5. Reduce disruptive impacts, mainly negative environmental externalities
6. Increase traffic safety
7. Improve quality of life
8. Further urban and regional economic development and competiveness
9. Achieve adequate and sustainable funding

I further group these functions into five categories: policy design, regulation, funding, project implementation and project leadership.

9.2.1 *Policy Design and Information Gathering*

Goal setting, strategic planning, as well as generation of alternatives and their evaluation are fundamental policy-oriented activities assigned to transportation agencies at all levels of government but especially the municipal level, which tends to be most directly involved in serving the project's diverse users. In Chap. 2, I summarized the formal procedures in place that agencies should follow when executing these roles. Assuming that these procedures are followed, a key concern becomes the availability of the necessary information: demographic trends, land uses, current and future demand, trip patterns and mode choice, reliable cost estimates, present and future network structure, but also a host of macro (e.g., income distribution) and micro (e.g., demand and cost elasticities) data. Irrespective of their necessity, data collection and manipulation are very costly undertakings, requiring much time and highly skilled labor. As a result, agencies often attempt to minimize these costs by reducing the scope of data collection and maintenance, by excluding important information during project evaluation and, most importantly, by making unfounded assumptions regarding key parameters and trends (e.g., demand estimates and mode choice elasticities) to support predetermined results and thereby avoid the gathering of potentially problematic information. Deliberate data omission and manipulation have also been mentioned as an explanation for this practice (see, Flyvbjerg 2005, 2006). To illustrate this point, consider the $1.4 billion Evergreen Line in Vancouver, BC (Canada). In a report prepared by Vancouver's Auditor General (Evergreen Line 2013), it was claimed that when forecasting ridership, the overseeing agency (TransLink) had applied unwarranted, speculative assumptions regarding future investment in other parts of the transit system and increases in the cost of using cars after 2021, which together suggested that the cost of car driving would jump 70% between 2021 and 2031. The Auditor General concluded that the demand estimates used for the project's evaluation were groundless and probably biased. Poor data collection and analysis were also reflected in the failure to conduct risk assessments for the entire transit system, which had serious implications for appraising the project's true value. In general, the main result of these types of failures is the increased possibility of under-performing projects being selected.

9.2.2 Regulation

Public transportation agencies, including metropolitan authorities, exercise substantial monopolistic power within their domains. As such, they function as regulators of all public (and often private) transportation activities in their respective jurisdictions. Metropolitan transportation agencies are typically assigned several regulatory functions. They control the use of key inputs such as capital and labor, bus fleet size, train cars and routes, number of drivers, acquisition of electric versus fuel-powered vehicles and so forth. They also regulate output prices such as fare levels and parking fees. They further control who, and under what conditions, can provide public transport services, meaning private providers or public subsidiaries.

Three salient aspects of regulatory agencies warrant noting due to the sometimes contradictory expectations regarding the outcomes of their actions. First, people often do not want relief from regulation but, rather, the protection that regulation can provide. Some of these protections are implicit while others are explicit. Labor, local business and real-estate interests, for example, all want protection from competition. Transportation agencies, in their regulatory capacity, tend to provide such protection in the form of preferential projects and regulations meant to appease interest groups and politicians.[6]

From these examples, we might conclude that transportation agencies, in complying with their regulatory role, do not necessarily try to minimize societal costs, as theory would suggest; instead, they try to minimize their own (agency) costs, which include the costs of mistakes and enforcement. They also try to avoid the political costs of misreading what politicians, interest groups and legislators want (Yandle 1983).

A third salient aspect of regulatory power is its effect on project choice. First, by regulating the technology in use, an agency can inhibit introduction of less-costly technologies. For example, given the existing demand and network structure, a region's Bus Rapid Transit (BRT) often provides adequate service (sometimes only in a particular corridor), thereby preventing adoption of a much more expensive yet technologically more sophisticated rail system. Should an underground rail technology have powerful supporters, they may try to exert pressure on the agency to install or maintain their preferred system. A case in point is the Tel Aviv Light Rail (about $5 billion project, currently under construction), which the regulatory agency claims will provide service superior to the operating BRT system per dollar investment, even though this contention has never been corroborated by a systematic study. The reason why may be found in the coalition of local and national politicians who, supported by the agency's vested interest in managing large-scale projects, promoted the metro alternative over the years.

As noted above, agencies, in their regulatory capacity, often protect inputs by stipulating the use of unionized labor or domestically produced raw materials (e.g., steel). In so doing, they award the providers of these factors monopolistic rents because lower-priced substitutes (e.g., non-unionized labor or imported steel) are prohibited. Project costs consequently escalate. When this occurs in periods of severe budgetary constraints, some projects, including potentially profitable ones, can become unfeasible.

9.2.3 *Funding*

A necessary and at times even sufficient condition facilitating the execution of an infrastructure project, especially a transportation mega-project, is the acquisition of funds at adequate and sustainable levels. While different countries have different sources of funding for such projects (see Chap. 8), stakeholders typically characterize funding methods and resources as inadequate and too unpredictable. Given this reality, it is no wonder that political and administrative actors direct major efforts at obtaining and securing adequate funds.

As explained in Chap. 8, funding for metropolitan and regional transportation projects comes from a variety of sources, with the main contributors being central (federal) governments. Local governments and agencies provide the balance, comprised of a mix of taxes, debt issues and, to a lesser extent, farebox revenues. However, in reality, funding is generally subject to acute uncertainties regarding availability at an assured level in the short as well as long run. One key result of this situation is that rather than starting with the fundamental question of what project, or combination of projects, is good for the region, an agency's point of departure is, all too often, captured in the question, "what projects are immediately eligible for funding" (Paaswell and Berechman 2006). Needless to say, given such insecure environments, the chances of selecting the *best project* in terms of its social welfare contribution are rather slight.

Finally, as also discussed in Chap. 8, the assurance of federal funding of local capital projects, irrespective of their transportation-economic efficiency, provides a massive incentive to select capital-intensive projects. When responding to this incentive, local agencies tend to view these funds as cost-free and politically beneficial.

9.2.4 *Implementation*

One somewhat neglected area of study of transportation agency performance, perhaps to avoid embarrassing inquiries, pertains to the quality of capital project implementation. The choice of worthy, transportation-economic, capital-improving projects is one thing; their efficient implementation is altogether another. One key indicator of effective implementation is the length of a project's planning and construction time. Ample evidence has shown that a major cause of project cost overruns are construction schedule delays (Berechman and Chen 2011; Flyvbjerg et al. 2004). Among the explanations so far submitted are extended bidding and contracting, legal hurdles such as lawsuits that drag out land acquisition or introduce unexpected environmental concerns, and bureaucratic inefficiencies. The question is, however, are these the only reasons? We can only conclude here that the gap between the plan and its execution requires study.

9.2.5 *Project Promotion and Leadership*

Transportation agencies, like the majority of official entities, come to play dual roles as a result of their mandate's character: They promote new capital investment projects but also, as part of those projects' approval processes, find themselves acting as the projects' champions, a position that forces them to engage in lobbying activities.[7] That is, agencies soon act as special interest groups (see Chap. 7) working to advance their own interests, which include expanding their mandate and influence over the sector they control.

In their roles as advocates, agencies attempt to sway politicians and general public opinion in favor of their projects' implementation. Because public funds are scarce and competition over investment choice is often fierce, the agency's leadership often becomes a crucial player when determining a project's fate.[8] It is therefore not surprising that agencies vigorously generate and disseminate favorable information about a project's expected transportation-economic benefits, its impact on regional wellbeing and, mostly importantly, justifications for why the particular agency is the best vehicle for the respective project's implementation.

9.3 Organizational Efficiency

How does a transportation agency's organizational structure and efficiency level affect project decision-making? This section deals with these issues.

From my perspective, organizational structure pertains to the agency's scope of governance (i.e., its mandate) and the way its head and top managers are appointed. For example, Greater Toronto's Metrolinx, the transportation oversight agency, has a board of directors appointed by the provincial government that is accountable to Ontario's Minister of Transport. In Greater London (UK), the city's mayor appoints the board of trustees of London's principle transportation agency (TFL). In Stockholm, the same power to appoint top management lies in the hands of the Stockholm County Council, which governs the metropolitan transportation agency (SL).

A crucial and related governance issue pertains to how key investment decisions are actually made. That is, in complex bureaucracies such as transportation agencies, which specific department or administrative level is responsible for making these decisions? One way to examine this issue involves using the paradigm set out earlier, where the organization's director(s) sets its objective(s) and lower administrative levels strive to find solutions that can overcome constraints. Another useful approach involves thinking in terms of the *principal-agent* problem. That is, how can *the principal*—the governing body (e.g., the minister or the province)—motivate and ensure that *the agent*—the bureaucracy—will, in fact, act in what the principal defines as its best interests? To illustrate this approach I turn to the case of TransLink, the main transportation agency of Vancouver, Canada. It has been reported that Metropolitan Vancouver's mayors (the principal) want their interests to be taken into account by TransLink (the agent), implying the effective replacement of the multibillion-dollar transit organization's current board of directors (*The Vancouver Sun* 2013; see also Lim 2013). Such a conflict between principals and agents is not exceptional. The literature cites numerous instances where agencies have followed their own agenda, taking steps that secure self-preservation and expansion but that, in so doing, often abandon accountability to the principal as well as to their clients, the public (Altshuler and Luberoff 2003; Doig 2001, 2012). While it seems plausible to assert that the specific organization's structure (and its institutional culture) does affect its investment policy and decision-making, it is difficult to empirically establish a clear causal direction or pattern. I return to this issue in Sect. 9.5.

We should not, however, forget that in order to execute their policies, governments need administrative agencies. Due to their mission and management of implementation mechanisms, administrative institutions possess the capacity to constrain executive power and thereby manipulate investment decisions (Greif 2008). For example, transportation authorities, by effective use of the technical and administrative means at their disposal, can suppress the power of federal or state governments to levy airport taxes, a step that prevents government from extracting monopolistic rents from airport users.

But the opposite can also be true: By means of their technical knowhow and ability to impede implementation in practice, institutions can raise travel costs beyond those inferred by government policies. This possibility is not far-fetched because government endeavors to change or replace incumbent administrators are often very costly. The higher these costs, the more difficult it is for political policy-makers to execute their first-best policies without acquiring the respective agency's consent and cooperation.

The above portrayal of a transportation agency's institutional power raises the important question regarding the status of those agencies' unused capacity or *X-inefficiency*,[9] relative to their current operations and maintenance activities but also relative to investments in new infrastructure. Chapter 5 dealt with cost estimates, which are often based on extrapolation of existing figures. What is not clear, however, is whether current costs reflect the level of administrative efficiency despite the theories striving to minimize costs as indicators of institutional competence. I am unaware of any recent studies that systematically examine this question.[10] Yet, sporadic reports do reveal that in many cases, inputs, particularly labor, are inefficiently utilized even after adjusting to public sector input prices (e.g., wages) and work rules.[11] These inefficiencies are not confined to routine operational and maintenance activities; new agency-approved construction appears to suffer from the same malaise.

9.4 Institutional Multiplicity, Competition and Rivalry

A useful way to think of mega-project decision-making is to consider the process as governed by vertical and horizontal administrative layers. In general, if more than one public transportation agency operates in the same metropolitan area or region, they frequently find themselves competing over revenues and spheres of control. Agencies consequently attempt to impose tax (tolls), set prices (transit fares or parking fees) and decide on capacity investments for facilities that serve users from other jurisdictions. Considered vertically in terms of administrative level, project funding, taxation, regulation and implementation often result from interactions between federal, state and city governments within the framework of a country's specific political organization. Horizontally, a project's promotion, evaluation, selection as well as output prices are often decided during interactions between local agencies.[12] The key problem created by inter-agency competition is inefficiency, whether it results in the loss of consumer welfare, deadweight losses and under- or over-supply of infrastructure.[13] That is, planning can become confounded by competing proposals and multiple non-fungible sources of funding.

To illustrate the magnitude of the problem, consider the bureaucratic landscape of New York City's transportation's sector. Eight federal, state and local agencies directly contend with the city's transportation planning and investment programs.[14] Also involved are several subsidiaries, transport authorities and companies controlled by the city's main transportation oversight agency (the MTA).[15] A similar picture emerges in many other metropolitan areas.[16] Each agency has a mission, with projects required to meet specific organizational as well as regional goals. Each also has differential access to the capital expended to implement its projects.

While each metropolitan area is unique in terms of size, population makeup and underlying political and legal systems, the presence of several transportation agencies gives birth to similar kinds of problems. First is the multiplicity of agencies operating in one jurisdiction, a structure that complicates project selection. In their study of New York region's transportation investments, Berechman and Paaswell (2005) found that the large number of participating agencies was accompanied by an equally large number of planning objectives and ideologies. For instance, "some were proposed to solve transportation problems, while others are meant to mainly boost real-estate development and economic growth in specific locations." These authors concluded that the involvement of such a quantity of actors interferes with rational project selection: "[T]he raison d'être of these projects did not emerge from a comprehensive analysis of regional needs; rather, they have been posed by various stakeholders putting forth agency-sponsored projects, some of which are over a decade old" (ibid. p. 225).

In another study, the same authors highlighted the political rivalry often characterizing inter-agency relationships in the course of their competition over resources and influence within the same geographical sphere (Paaswell and Berechman 2006). Since each agency pursues its own preferred project, the end result is that the chosen projects may not be optimal from a regional perspective and are often inferior according to transportation-economic criteria or in comparison with alternative projects. This means that if one agency expands highway capacity, it might negate efforts by another agency to promote public transit use within the same metropolitan area. Because the transportation industry is structured and operates as a network, marked by high connectivity, when an agency expands transit capacity in one part of the system for the purpose of reducing congestion elsewhere in the region, its actions may force another agency to follow suit (i.e., invest in a similar project for the same purposes) even though this may not be the most efficient type of project.[17]

A recent report on the structure and operation of the Port Authority of New York and New Jersey (PANYNJ) highlighted the key issues affecting this agency's functioning (Moss and O'Neill 2014). Of particular importance was the finding that, in addition to the previously noted malaise of mismanagement and rivalry, the agency's departure from its core business model undermined efficiency. This deviation emerges when an agency seeks to expand its sphere of activities into areas remote from its core transportation functions. Once introduced, these digressions may make it impossible for the agency to recover capital, maintenance and operating costs, and for a variety of reasons. But why should this entry into foreign fields occur in the first place? One reason is that the business model that worked for the agency in the past, especially when it was newly established, may no longer be appropriate. In other cases, an agency may find it politically expedient to engage in activities diverging from its original mission, such as urban planning or overseeing other transit systems. Economic models become unsustainable especially when political interests interfere in the agency's operations.[18] In the 60 mega-projects included in the

Nobbe and Berechman international database (see Chap. 4), a large proportion (55%) of projects were the products of political meddling.

The issue of politics leads us to another important question: Do transportation agencies and stakeholders evaluate and select projects differently according to organizational type, and, if so, why? Theoretically, we can submit an agreed-upon set of criteria for evaluating projects so that, in principle, one should observe consistent project-selection behavior on any given level of government. When the criteria conflict across levels, does the level that contributes the most money dominate or is it the level most affected by the project? I am unaware of any study that methodically answers these questions, but it seems that at the federal level, project evaluation criteria as well as evaluation procedures differ from those applied at the local level (Berechman 2009, Chap. 2).

With respect to funding, data on those same 60 mega-projects indicate that in over 70% of the cases, the national/federal government was involved in the project's capital funding, followed by private funding (58%), transportation agency funding (45%) and state/provincial government (30%). When it came to decision-making, the national/federal government was involved in 70% of all cases, followed by state/provincial government (40%), transportation agency/authority (23%) and local government (21%). This leads us to conclude that the proportion of funding does not unequivocally ensure parallel control over project decisions.

What follows from this reality is that decisions concerning transportation mega-projects are subject to negotiation and approval by many institutional stakeholders. It further follows that the competition among these stakeholders, and thus their impact on project advocacy, directly reflects the likelihood of obtaining significant federal and state funds. Situations of this sort lead, in turn, to the promotion of the least-controversial but not necessarily the best project in terms of its transportation-economic contribution.

Lastly, the existence of a relatively large number of agencies within the same region raises the likelihood of resource wastefulness for three main reasons: (a) competition for the same funds, which commonly come from the same sources; (b) friction between agencies due to unclear administrative boundaries and control;[19] (c) loss of the economies of scale that result from the subordination of common activities under the same organizational roof. However, given the political reality, the establishment of multiple agencies is unavoidable because of the power and means of control it provides legislators and politicians.

9.5 Summary: Institutions, Politics and Investment Decisions

As already depicted in Chap. 4 (Fig. 4.1), transportation agencies and authorities closely interact with political institutions at all levels of government, and for highly practical reasons when considering the agency's perspective. As we have found, government's organizational complexity promotes these interactions. Political institutions generally appoint an agency's board of directors and top management. National and local legislators often approve the operational and capital budgets of those same agencies. In addition, agency policies regarding pricing (e.g., transit fare), taxation (e.g., road tolls) and investments are subject to political endorsement.

In light of these facts, how do these intertwined institutional-political relationships affect the choice of project capital investments? Who, in fact, controls transportation investment policies? When speaking of control, we are referring to the range of managerial, financial and decision-making factors encapsulated in that term. In Western countries, the political system generally consists of federal legislators and ministries (e.g., transportation, treasury, environment, etc.), state or provincial legislators, governors, city councils and mayors. The veto power possessed by these entities enables them to neutralize or hinder the policy as well as the practical decisions made on other political levels.[20] The resulting competition, which is acted out with the help of political machinery, deflects transportation agency goals to external benefits such as political influence or job creation. The end result is the selection of projects that are politically feasible but do not necessarily contribute most to the public's welfare. A corollary of this observation is that in order to achieve acceptable amounts of funding, the political machinery on its various levels must consent to common standards and goals since, otherwise, operational and investment quandaries will arise and endure.[21]

At present, only a scant number of empirical analyses have been conducted on the consequences of these intricate relationships for the investment decisions made by transportation agencies. As could be expected, the main instruments by which the political machinery affects project decision-making are the size and allocation of budgets. I examined the overall question of transportation finance and its impact on mega-projects in Chap. 6. Here I summarize the three main conclusions reached on the basis of empirical evidence from the European Union (EU) and the

USA. First, the conjecture that government's supply of a public good, such as transportation, is uniform over regions should be disputed (Knight 2004). Rather, national (federal) or state (provincial) political agents often favor some regions over others. Second, the allocation of funds is highly inefficient and generates much waste (Besley and Coate 2003; Proost et al. 2010). Inferior and unworthy projects are conspicuous manifestations of this outcome. Third and following from the above discussion, the type of government in place does matter with respect to which evaluation criteria will prevail. Coate and Knight (2009), for example, found that projected spending on projects is lower under mayor-council than under council-manager types of municipal government because the latter requires council support exclusively. The same argument also applies to the revenue side. In New York State, for example, republican administrations typically favor funding public transportation through farebox revenues rather than subsidies financed by direct or indirect taxes (Derrick et al. 2012).

Finally, analysis of the 60 mega-project database has produced some germane results regarding the political system's role in project decision-making. First, whenever the proportion of national funding out of total project funding increases, the likelihood of cost overruns also increases. Second, project funding methods in centralized economies differ from those in countries enjoying federal structures. Countries having federal governments are required to develop funding packages that are simultaneously agreeable to state and local governments as well as the implementing institutions. Such a need may not arise in countries with centralized economies. These results also point to the possibility of introducing a decision-making process that dispenses with transportation-economic efficiency considerations. A salient example is China's High Speed Rail (HSR), a huge mega-project covering a network of 13,000 km long, constructed over a short period of time without any cost-benefit analysis or transportation-economic rationale (Fu and Nie 2011). Hence, when deciding on a project, the formal requirement that a project undergoes *and* passes a transportation-economic feasibility test a priori is neither a necessary nor sufficient condition. Other considerations, mainly funding and political acceptability, are revealed as the key criteria. In consequence, the process unavoidably fosters the implementation of inferior projects, including economically unworthy ones.

Notes

1. For studies on the origin and evolution of national institutions, see Helpman (2008) and Acemoglu and Robinson (2013). See also Acemoglu and Johnson (2005) on property rights as institutions.
2. One can distinguish between political institutions, which allocate and control political power and thus the distribution of resources, and economic institutions, which determine how markets function, including their economic outcomes. On the roles of these two types of institutions in determining differences in economic growth between countries, see Acemoglu et al. (2004).
3. The vast organizational literature can be roughly divided into several strands. Some early authors like Smith (1776), Durkheim (1893) and Taylor (1911) modeled institutions as rational decision-makers striving to achieve production efficiency. Others, recognizing their structural complexity, viewed organizations as rational agents whose goals do not necessarily correspond (Buchanan and Tullock 1962; Niskanen 1971). Still others (e.g., March and Simon 1958) emphasized bounded rationality as characterizing organizational decision-making. For more recent and extensive studies, see Williamson (1995) and Hatch and Cunliffe (2006).
4. For a formal analysis of these paradigms, see Alesina and Tabellini (2004) and Cres et al. (2012).
5. A pertinent example is the case of upstate New York's Tappan Zee Bridge, a $5 billion project where inter-agency politics played a major role in prolonging its planning and implementation for many years (Plotch 2015).
6. An example is the proposed JFK Access to Lower Manhattan—a super shuttle service linking Lower Manhattan and downtown Brooklyn to Long Island commuters and the JFK AirTrain, at a cost of an estimated $2.4 billion (2004 prices). The project was advocated by powerful real-estate and financial bodies and billed by politicians as crucial to New York City's ability to compete globally.
7. An example would be the New York Metropolitan Transportation Authority (MTA) and its role in the promotion of the Second Avenue Subway (SAS) (Smith 2012).
8. Jones and Olken (2005) demonstrate that leadership matters at the state level; see Bertrand and Schoar (2003) for a discussion at the firm level.
9. Economic theory suggests that an agency's (or a firm's) management endeavors to minimize costs by efficiently employing inputs required to produce a given level of output. However, when faced with no market competition (e.g., a monopoly), or when agents do not act to maximize the utility of the principals, slack occurs. This happens when agencies employ more resources (e.g., labor) than are actually needed to produce a given level of output. Unused capacity results in X-inefficiency.

10. On the efficiency of regulators as opposed to administrative agencies, see Coelli (2003).
11. See, for example, a report by the MTA's Inspector General on gross inefficiency in managing labor at the Long Island Railroad (Kluger 2012). For an econometric analysis of the operational efficiency of Israel's regulated bus transit sector, see Appelbaum and Berechman (1991).
12. The Metropolitan Transportation Authority (MTA) and the Port Authority of New York and New Jersey (PANYNJ) are examples. For a review of these dynamics, see De Borger and Proost (2012).
13. Notice that horizontal competition is often carried out over the same network, road or rail. See de Palma and Lindsey (2000), De Borger et al. (2005). Levinson (2001) has discovered rivalry between neighboring US states. If a state uses highway tolls to raise revenues, an adjacent state is likely to counter by imposing its own tolls. Rork (2009) found a similar phenomenon: states compete with those states from which they receive and/or send many commuters by using toll-tax exporting behavior.
14. These agencies include the MTA, the PANYNJ, the Port Authority Trans Hudson (PATH), the New York State Department of Transportation (NYSDOT), the New Jersey Department of Transportation (NJDOT), the Federal Department of Transportation (DOT), New Jersey Transit (NJT), and the New York Metropolitan Transportation Commission (NYMTC), which is a Metropolitan Planning Organization (MPO).
15. These subsidiaries include the Triborough Bridge and Tunnel Authority, the New York City Transit Authority, the Manhattan and Bronx Surface Transit Operating Authority, the Long Island Railroad Company, the Metro-North Commuter Rail Company, the Staten Island Rapid Transit Operating Authority, the Metropolitan Suburban Bus Authority, the MTA Bus Company, the MTA Capital Construction Company and the First Mutual Transportation Assurance Company.
16. In Vancouver, Canada, in addition to the main oversight agency, TransLink, the other agencies and institutions include Canada's federal government (Transport Canada; Brown et al. 2005); the British Columbia Ministry of Transportation; local municipalities; the Port of Vancouver; boards of trade; and the Vancouver Foundation in addition to other NGOs and stakeholders that contribute to the discussion. A number of TransLink subsidiaries, such as the Coast Mountain Bus Company, are also present.
17. For analysis of these and similar cases, see De Borger et al. (2007).
18. A case in point is the New York Port Authority's acquisition of a money-losing public transit system. A leading senator from NY State (Charles Schumer) was reported to have said, "The Port Authority has come to be seen as the proverbial honey pot, a cookie jar, a rainy day fund—whatever metaphor you prefer—for state projects outside the Port's core mission"

(WNYC News, Andrea Bernstein, May 6, 2014, http://www.wnyc.org/story/incredible-sinking-port-authority/?utm_source=Newsletter%3A+WNYC+Daily+Newsletter&utm_campaign=df8e456897-Daily_Brief_Jan_27_20141_26_2014&utm_medium=email&utm_term=0_edd6b58c0d-df8e456897-68854853).

19. During the construction of a new transportation facility, a question often arises with respect to who is responsible, administratively and financially, for the relocation of a non-transportation facility, such as an existing water system. Should the transportation agency pay for and manage the project, or should this be the responsibility of the pertinent local government?
20. Consider the 2007 congestion pricing scheme proposed by Michael Blumberg, the mayor of NY, which was effectively blocked by the NY State Assembly. For a review of transportation-oriented political issues in New York, see Derrick et al. (2012).
21. An example is the resignation, in 2009, of the MTA's chief executive officer due to the inability of NY State and NY City governments to come to terms on the MTA's financial predicament, caused by the 2007–2009 US economic crisis that severely affected New York State's finances.

References

Acemoglu, D., and S. Johnson. 2005. Unbundling Institutions. *Journal of Political Economy* 113 (5): 949–995.

Acemoglu, D., S. Johnson, and J. Robinson. 2004. *Institutions as the Fundamental Cause of Long-Run Growth*. NBER Working Paper No. 10481. Washington, DC: NBER.

Acemoglu, D., and J. Robinson. 2013. Cows, Capitalism and Social Embeddedness. *Why Nations Fail*, Blog, October. http://whynationsfail.com/blog/2013/10/23/cows-capitalism-and-social-embeddedness.html?utm_source=feedburner&utm_medium=email&utm_campaign=Feed%3A+whynationsfail+%28Why+Nations+Fail%29.

Alesina, A., and G. Tabellini. 2004. *Bureaucrats or Politicians?* National Bureau of Economic Research, Working Paper 10241, Cambridge, Massachusetts.

Altshuler, A., and D. Luberoff. 2003. *Megaprojects: The Changing Politics of Urban Public Investment*. Washington, DC: Brookings Institution Press.

Appelbaum, E., and J. Berechman. 1991. Demand Conditions, Regulation, and the Measurement of Productivity. *Journal of Econometrics* 47: 379–400.

Berechman, J. 2009. *The Evaluation of Transportation Investment Projects*. New York: Routledge.

Berechman, J., and L. Chen. 2011. Incorporating Risk of Cost Overruns into Transportation Capital Projects Decision-Making. *Journal of Transport Economics and Policy* 45 (1): 83–104.

Berechman, J., and R. Paaswell. 2005. Evaluation, Prioritization and Selection of Transportation Investment Projects in New York City. *Transportation* 32: 223–249.

Bertrand, M., and A. Schoar. 2003. Managing with Style: The Effect of Managers on Firm Policies. *Quarterly Journal of Economics* 118 (4): 1169–1208.

Besley, T., and S. Coate. 2003. Centralized Versus Decentralized Provision of Local Public Goods: A Political Economy Approach. *Journal of Public Economics* 87: 2611–2637.

Brown, D., G. Hoover, A. Howaston, and J. Schulman. 2005. *Canada's Transportation Infrastructure Challenge: Strengthening the Foundations.* Ottawa: The Conference Board of Canada. http://books.google.ca/books/about/Canada_s_Transportation_Infrastructure_C.html?id=MQTTZwEACAAJ&redir_esc=y.

Buchanan, J., and G. Tullock. 1962. *The Calculus of Consent: Logical Foundations of Constitutional Democracy.* Ann Arbor: University of Michigan Press.

Coate, S., and B. Knight. 2009. *Government Form and Public Spending: Theory and Evidence from U.S. Municipalities.* NBER Working Paper No. 14857, Cambridge, Massachusetts.

Coelli, T. 2003. *A Primer on Efficiency Measurement for Utilities and Transport Regulators.* Washington, DC: World Bank Publications.

Cres, H., I. Gilboa, and N. Vieille. 2012. *Bureaucracy in Quest for Feasibility.* A Seminar Paper. www.fas.nus.edu.sg/ecs/events/seminar/seminar-papers/10Sep13.pdf.

De Borger, B., F. Dunkerley, and S. Proost. 2007. Strategic Investment and Pricing Decisions in a Congested Transport Corridor. *Journal of Urban Economics* 62 (2): 294–316.

De Borger, B., and S. Proost. 2012. Transport Policy Competition Between Governments: A Selective Survey of the Literature. *Economics of Transportation* 1: 35–48.

De Borger, B., S. Proost, and K. Van Dender. 2005. Congestion and Tax Competition on in a Parallel Network. *European Economic Review* 49: 2013–2040.

de Palma, A., and R. Lindsey. 2000. Private Toll Roads: A Dynamic Equilibrium Analysis. *Annals of Regional Science* 34 (1): 13–35.

Derrick, P., R. Paaswell, and D. Petretta. 2012. Transportation Policy and Politics in New York State. In *The Oxford Handbook of New York State Government and Politics.* New York and London: Oxford University Press.

Doig, J. 2001. *Empire on the Hudson: Entrepreneurial Vision and Political Power at the Port of New York.* New York: Columbia University Press.

Doig, W. 2012. Should It Take Decades to Build a Subway? *Salon*, February 4, 2012. http://www.salon.com/2012/02/04/should_it_take_decades_to_build_a_subway/.

Durkheim, E. 1949 [1893]. *The Division of Labor in Society.* Glencoe, IL: The Free Press.

Evergreen Line. 2013. *Decisions on Scope of Evergreen Line Not Fully Informed – Auditor General.* (Kelly Sinoski, Vancouver Sun 03.28.2013), The Vancouver Sun, Vancouver, Canada. http://www.vancouversun.com/news/decisions+scope+evergreen+line+fully+informed+auditor+general/8165417/story.html.

Flyvbjerg, B. 2005. Measuring Inaccuracy in Travel Demand Forecasting: Methodological Considerations Regarding Ramp Up and Sampling. *Transportation Research A* 39 (6): 522–530.

———. 2006. Design by Deception: The Politics of Megaproject Approval. In *Urban Planning Today*, ed. William S. Saunders, 131–148. Minneapolis and London: University of Minnesota Press.

Flyvbjerg, B., M.K. Holm, and S.L. Buhl. 2004. What Causes Cost Overruns in Transport Infrastructure Projects. *Transport Reviews* 24 (1): 3–18.

Fu, H., and L. Nie. 2011. Economy and Efficiency Oriented Passenger Flow Organization: Train Stop Scheduling for High-Speed Railways. *Journal of Beijing Institute of Technology* 20: 79–83.

Greif, A. 2008. The Impact of Administrative Power on Political and Economic Developments. In *Institutions and Economic Performance*, ed. E. Helpman. Cambridge, MA: Harvard University Press.

Hatch, M., and A. Cunliffe. 2006. *Organization Theory.* 2nd ed. New York and London: Oxford University Press.

Jones, B., and B. Olken. 2005. Do Leaders Matter? National Leadership and Growth Since World War II. *The Quarterly Journal of Economics* 120 (3): 835–864.

Kluger, B. 2012. Improving the Management of Crews in the MTA Long Island Rail Road's Structural Maintenance Division. http://mtaig.state.ny.us/assets/pdf/12-05.pdf.

Knight, B. 2004. Parochial Interests and the Centralized Provision of Local Public Goods: Evidence from Congressional Voting on Transportation Projects. *Journal of Public Economics* 88: 845–866.

Levinson, D. 2001. Why States Toll – An Empirical Model of Finance Choice. *Journal of Transport Economics and Policy* 35 (2): 223–238.

Lim, C. 2013. *TransLink Governance Review, A Report.* Acuere Consulting Inc. http://www.scribd.com/doc/131890569/TransLink-Governance-Review.

March, J., and H. Simon. 1958. *Organizations.* New York: John Wiley and Sons.

Moss, M., and H. O'Neill. 2014. *A Port Authority That Works.* New York: Rudin Center for Transportation, The Wagner School, New York University.

Niskanen, W. 1971. *Bureaucracy and Representative Government.* New Brunswick, NJ: Aldine Transaction.

Paaswell, R., and J. Berechman. 2006. Models and Realities: Choosing Transit Projects for New York City (Chap. 5). In *Policy Analysis of Transportation*

Networks, ed. Marina van Geenhuizen, Aura Reggiani, and Piet Rietveld. Farnham: Ashgate.
Plotch, P. 2015. *Politics Across the Hudson: The Tappan Zee Megaproject*. New Brunswick, NJ: Rutgers University Press.
Proost, S., F. Dunkerley, S. Van der Loo, N. Adler, J. Brocker, and A. Korzhenevyc. 2010. *Do the Selected Trans European Transport Investments Pass the Cost Benefit Test?*" Center for Economic Studies (CES), Catholic University of Leuven, Belgium, Discussion Paper 10.02.
Rork, J. 2009. Yardstick Competition in Toll Revenues: Evidence from US States. *Journal of Transport Economics and Policy* 43 (1): 123–139.
Smith, A. 1957 [1776]. *The Wealth of Nations*. New York: Appleton Century Crofts.
Smith, S. 2012. New York's MTA Doesn't Need Any More Money. *Bloomberg*, October 10, 2012. http://mobile.bloomberg.com/news/2012-10-10/new-york-s-mta-doesn-t-need-any-more-money.html.
Taylor, F. 1911. *The Principles of Scientific Management*. New York: Harper.
Vancouver Sun. 2013. Metro Mayors Want the Keys to TransLink. March 22. http://www.canada.com/vancouversun/news/westcoastnews/story.html?id=59fada0a-e927-44a8-bfb3-61e9150f96de.
Williamson, O. 1995. *Organization Theory: From Chester Barnard to the Present and Beyond*. New York and London: Oxford University Press.
Yandle, B. 1983. Bootleggers and Baptists: The Education of a Regulatory Economist. *Regulation* 7 (3): 12–17.

CHAPTER 10

Alternative Decision Criteria: Equity, Economic Development and Environmental Externalities

10.1 Introduction

Economic welfare theory suggests that decision-makers, when selecting an infrastructure investment, should strive to maximize net welfare, measured mainly as the change in consumer surplus subsequent to the investment. In terms of transportation investment analysis, such a criterion is measured in terms of the value of reduced travel times and costs, improved accessibility to locations, spatial coverage, improved safety, favorable modal shares, and improved system capacity and connectivity.

Transportation investments nevertheless generate myriad other effects that can also be applied as criteria in project selection. These can be categorized into distributional and externality effects, with the latter further divided into economic development and environmental impacts. Distributional effects encompass two different concepts: *benefits*, which accrue to disadvantaged individuals and socio-economic groups, and *local benefits*, which accrue to the residents of a particular locale. After observing real-world cases, we can conclude that mega-project investment policies are more often than not rationalized in terms of locale-related distributional effects as well as economic development.

From a normative, social perspective, we cannot dismiss such an approach. That is, even an economically beneficial project, if shown to adversely affect equity for some disadvantaged groups, probably should not be executed. But the opposite can also be argued: If a project carries positive equity affects but engenders insignificant net transportation-economic

J. Berechman, *The Infrastructure We Ride On*,
https://doi.org/10.1007/978-3-319-74606-7_10

benefits, it should not be implemented. Unfortunately, such reasoning is not always applied; a considerable number of projects were and still are implemented on the basis of assumed equity and anticipated economic development impacts, irrespective of the project's actual transportation-economic contribution. Moreover, these distributional and economic development effects tend to be inferred or assumed, not actually measured or compared with factors such as improved income distribution, job creation, real-estate development or environmental enhancement. Put simply, when selecting a project, these criteria are too often used as substitutes for, rather than complements to, the project's transportation-economic value.

In consideration of these observations, this chapter's main aim is to examine the significance of equity and economic growth criteria in project choice. That is, we explore the extent to which transportation infrastructure indeed generates distributional and economic externality effects, how they are measured, and how they enter the decision process. Environmental externalities, which are often among the prerequisites for funding provision, are also discussed.

To be sure, this chapter does not examine the theoretical or even detailed economic dimensions of equity and externalities in relation to transportation investment. These subjects are adequately explored in the literature; see, for example, my books on transportation investment and economic development (Banister and Berechman 2000) and on project evaluation (Berechman 2009, Chaps. 11, 12, and 13). Instead, I prefer to focus here on equity, economic development and environmental externalities in their roles as project choice criteria.

10.2 Distributive Impact Considerations

The equity effects of transportation investments have long been a source of conflict and power struggles.[1] Broadly speaking, these effects can be interpreted as an investment's impact on the distribution of benefits and costs across different groups, differentiated by social identity, ethnicity, income, location, physical wellbeing and access to transportation networks.[2] While each definition implies unique methods of measurement and assessment, they all convey the concepts of fairness, equality and justice, terms used interchangeably in the literature.[3] In our analysis, we distinguish between state- or regional-level equity and local- or project-level equity. For example, in a federal system such as that operating in the USA, where grants from the federal government extensively fund highway projects, equity is often taken to mean the share of grants a state receives relative to its contribution to the Federal Highway Trust Fund (FHTF) (Altshuler 2013).

10.2.1 Defining Equity in Transportation Investment

Before delving into the necessary questions, we should recall the following. The use of any form of tax, progressive (e.g., income tax) or regressive (e.g., sales tax), to finance public expenditures, including those aimed at transportation, produces two main effects: economic inefficiency and income redistribution. The former is expressed by tax-related burdens, measured as deadweight losses, which are manifested by reduced disposable income and thus diminished sales. The redistribution effect is expressed by changes in the post-tax income level of a given income group, relative to its pre-tax position. If the tax revenues are earmarked to finance a transportation investment, for example, the tax's net effect must be considered in terms of the welfare losses *and* gains of the respective socioeconomic groups subsequent to project completion.[4]

The literature on equity and justice in transportation has long argued that income distribution alone, however measured, cannot capture the gamut of equity effects. For instance, income per se does not indicate the degree of access to specific modes of travel by elderly or mobility-impaired populations. So, how should measures of transportation-related equity be derived? The answer depends on which philosophical grounds are employed.

In the 1950s, when Cost-Benefit Analysis (CBA) became prevalent in transportation project analysis, *libertarianism*, a philosophical school, reigned in the discussion over equity, its main tenet being that individual liberty is and should be a society's primary political value. Accordingly, the free market was defined as a system ensuring the right of individuals not to be coerced and to be free from government interference (Arthur and Shaw 1991). Thus, under libertarianism, unimpeded accessibility to destinations is the primary transportation justice criterion (Van Wee and Geurs 2011).

Following the appearance of his seminal book *The Theory of Justice* (Rawls 1971) on the philosophy of distributive justice, John Rawls' theory found its way into the economic and, subsequently, the transportation literature. Rawls construed justice as fairness, which could be achieved under what he termed the *veil of ignorance*, implying that members of society should make choices under conditions of freedom from group identity (e.g., ethnicity, religion or gender) and without any knowledge about their relative status in society. Once under the veil of ignorance, people will choose a ***minimax*** strategy, namely, the distribution of maximum benefits to whomever is born with a minimum of tangible, or intangible, assets. Distributive justice is thus the principle that provides maximum benefits to those with minimal natural assets, and rejects every allocation of benefits that does not improve the situation of the least-advantaged.[5] In transportation terms, the travel times and costs of reaching desired destinations, work- and non-work-related, primarily for disadvantaged groups, represent such equity criteria.

Still another philosophical approach to equity and justice is the *capabilities approach* first articulated by Sen (1992) and later refined by Nussbaum (2006). These two philosophers based their arguments on the principle of individual capability, meaning what individuals are able to achieve given their skills and socio-economic wellbeing, implying that the range of opportunities placed before individuals should be the core criterion for assessing equity. It follows that denying sufficient access to transportation curtails a person's capacity to realize his or her full potential. Under this approach, the maximum distance, by mode, which can be reached within a determined time frame or the maximum price of transportation for residents of an area, by income, serve as transportation equity criteria (Hananel and Berechman 2016).

In the field of economics, it is common to distinguish between vertical and horizontal equity. The former considers equity as the fair or equivalent treatment of people belonging to *different* socio-economic groups (e.g., income strata). In contrast, the latter is defined as the fair or equivalent treatment of people belonging to the *same* socio-economic group or level. Vertical inequality can be observed when different people belonging to different socio-economic groups, and living in same city, pay same road tolls (e.g., see the study by Peters and Gordon (2008), described below).

The literature also offers the concept *environmental justice* when referring, even if implicitly, to the distribution of a project's environmental impacts with respect to diverse groups (Hartgen 2013). Typically, assessments of environmental justice are made by first indicating where disadvantaged populations live, say, along a proposed highway project, in light of the fact that they may bear the brunt of its environmental costs in terms of fumes, noise and other forms of pollution. The question thus becomes, how are such equity effects measured in practice?

10.2.2 Measuring Equity in Transportation

As currently practiced, we can distinguish between equity analyses conducted at the national or state level and the same analysis conducted on the regional or local level. As an instance of the first in the European Union context, researchers have used *social cohesion* to assess equity effects from infrastructure investments while defining social cohesion as the share of benefits received by poor regions in Europe relative to the share received by rich ones (Bröcker et al. 2010). This is a Rawlsian-type measure, which was embedded within a general equilibrium model for the purpose of discovering the regional cohesion effects of Trans-European Networks (TEN-T) rail investments.[6] Results from their statistical analysis revealed that out of the 22 projects considered, only seven had conferred a high share of benefits to low-income European regions.

In contrast with this continent-level approach, a more commonly used measure of equity is the relative distribution of benefits and costs among the socio-economic groups residing within the impacted area. Common metrics applied include access and mobility, measured by travel times and costs, between the Origin-Destination (O-D) locations comprising the network (Levinson 2002).

Equity concerns differ, sometimes quite strikingly, when examined within the framework of modal investment policies, primarily highway versus mass transit. Highway investments, which affect mainly car and truck users, tend to focus on network capacity constraints and traffic management policies, such as High Occupancy Vehicle (HOV) lanes and congestion charges. Vehicles' travel times and costs, by location, are thus the main equity considerations in these cases. In contrast, public transit projects that, among other objectives, aim at improving the mobility and accessibility of low-income groups, have been and still call for heavy subsidies by governments. Hence, equity in these cases has become defined in terms of geographical incidence, ease of access to the transit system, price of use (fares) and level of service (e.g., train or bus headways) as they accrue to diverse socio-economic groups.

In a study of the equity implications of road tolls in New Jersey, Peters and Gordon (2008) used income-related metrics of equity. These included per capita toll collection in a region, percent of income spent on tolls, and per capita toll burden by location. The authors' key result was that the burden of road tolls in New Jersey fall disproportionally on lower-income groups. These results accord with those obtained in other studies that showed low-income and travel-constrained populations to be disproportionally burdened by transportation investments and policies.[7]

According to Thomopoulos et al. (2009) as well as Manaugh et al. (2015), the equity measures typically used in transportation are as follows:

1. accessibility to work and non-work destinations by socio-economic group
2. relative travel times and costs to destinations by mode
3. relative mobility costs by income group
4. share of household expenditures on transportation
5. spatial coverage of mass transit by population type

To these we might add a quasi-equity measure, namely, the degree to which benefits from a project accrue to residents of a given area irrespective of their socio-economic status. This criterion may be more properly considered a *political-equity* measure because, as argued below, it falls within the sphere of interests guiding decision-makers who represent a designated locale and who are therefore concerned almost exclusively with the welfare of their constituents. Table 10.1 summarizes the equity measures just discussed.

As Table 10.1 clearly shows, measures of equity in fact pertain to different effects and use different metrics, variables affecting the type and comparability of the benchmarks influencing policy judgments.

Table 10.1 Measures of equity

	Horizontal equity	*Vertical equity*
Macro level	Distribution of benefits and costs across regions	Costs of travel by socio-economic group
Micro level	Share of household expenditures on transport	Accessibility to destinations by socio-economic group
Modal	Availability of car and public transit in a region	Travel times and costs by mode
Socio-economic group	Carless, elderly, disadvantaged, mobility-impaired	Accessibility to destinations by socio-economic group
Political equity	Distribution of benefits and costs across locales	Accessibility to destinations by residents of a given locale

10.2.3 Equity and Decision-Making

If equity and its measurement is so crucial to transportation decision-making, the question requiring an answer is just how much do equity considerations enter project decision-making? Responses should rest, first and foremost, on the distinction between what policy-makers say when trying to rationalize their investment decisions and the degree to which equity concerns actually play a role in any specific decision. Consider the following statement made by Christina Romer, past Chairwomen of President Obama's Council of Economic Advisers, which is typical of how policy-makers refer to equity in relation to transportation investments: "If increasing income equality is the goal, it might be wiser to put money into infrastructure than to subsidize manufacturing. Construction also pays good wages but with lower educational requirements. And America's infrastructures are enormous" (*New York Times*, February 5, 2012).

And yet, in practice, redistribution rarely constitutes an explicit policy goal; these effects are, by and large, inconsequential even in public transit investments (Altshuler 2013). In an empirical, socio-economic study of transit use, Pucher and Renne (2003) report that in the USA, low-income transit users depend mainly on buses for their daily commutes whereas the bulk of transit subsidies are allocated to rail projects, which is used much less often by low-income commuters.[8] As Winston and Maheshri (2007) found, rail investments in the USA have actually reduced welfare and, for reasons of high costs and often low benefits, are unlikely to become socially desirable. It is therefore unlikely that rail investments can increase equity.

If we broaden the notion of equity to encompass the political benefits accruing to constituents residing in a given area, the question of whether or not and to what degree a given project actually benefits residents can play an important role in decision-makers' attitudes toward the project. To illustrate this point I return to the Second Avenue Subway (SAS), constructed in Manhattan's East Side. A key figure influencing the project's choice was the representative of Manhattan's Lower East Side (later the Speaker of the New York State Assembly), who refused approval of any proposed budget if it excluded the SAS. Support for the region's transportation plan was thus made contingent on securing a project that conferred benefits to residents of a particular area irrespective of their socio-economic profile but apparently in recognition of their political clout.

In sum, equity criteria, while championed by proponents of infrastructure projects and often mentioned in CBA documents, are unlikely to enter the actual decision process, not the least because of the difficulty of endorsing an agreed-upon definition of equity, especially as a benchmark for fairness. As Altshuler and Luberoff (2003) point out, policy-makers will, at best, reject an investment that would clearly harm a disadvantaged group (they label this as *the do no harm* approach). Alternatively, a key factor often determining support for a project is the declared bestowal of benefits to residents of a circumscribed area.

10.3 Economic Development

"I'm not going to lie to you," he says. "[The Gateway Program] is about the economy, it's about the movement of goods, it's about securing the economic future of our children and grandchildren. But the side beneficiary [sic] of all of that is that it will be a great benefit to commuters. There's no doubt about it."[9]

These and similar assertions are often used to justify implementation of transportation projects.[10] Yet, we still need to ask whether such claims are credible and actually used to prioritize project alternatives, to select the *best one*. What are these development impacts and how are they measured?

10.3.1 Economic Development Effects

As demonstrated above, the argument that the benefits engendered by a transportation investment will include the so-called, external, secondary or wider benefits is commonly used by decision-makers, including economists. Theoretically, however, the actual materialization of these external benefits rests on the assumption that in some markets, prices do not correctly reflect the marginal costs of the resources used, and that the improved accessibility promised can ameliorate these conditions, thereby generating economic benefits.[11] Many markets are imperfect to some extent as prices deviate from marginal costs. Hence, what matters is the potential of improved accessibility to effectively trigger market changes and, in turn, economic development.[12] For example, suppose that due to entry barriers, labor prices (workers' wages) in some markets diverge from their respective marginal costs to employers (actually, wage rate divided by the marginal product of labor). Improved accessibility to these markets, if they lessen these barriers, could improve labor productivity, thus bringing down marginal costs, thereby encouraging employment. Other markets, such as freight logistics, real estate and agglomeration of urban commercial activities, may experience similar effects. Notice that these external effects can be either positive (e.g., economic growth) or negative (e.g., environmental degradation, accidents). Here we are concerned with the former.

The above conceptual and analytical issues raise concerns regarding the misuse of hypothetical external benefits to justify project selection. As the previous quotations attest, policy-makers commonly cite alleged project benefits without considering, for whatever reason, just how valid or credible they may be.

Growth-related positive externalities have often been cited in the literature on transportation infrastructure investment (Banister and Berechman 2000; Lakshmanan and Chatterjee 2005). The list covers outcomes ranging from greater competition (which may weaken local monopolies), expansion of labor markets, improved productivity, increased tax revenues from heightened economic activity, land development, intensified scale and agglomeration economies, activity clustering and regional specialization (which raise productivity), new production chains and improved logistics. The very listing of these effects notwithstanding, the critical question is how to identify and measure them *ex ante*. Moreover, many of these effects are, in essence, consequences of the capitalization of the project's primary benefits—travel time and cost savings; hence, even if correctly measured, their inclusion as part of the project's overall benefits amounts to double counting. That is, increased accessibility may be counted once as a primary benefit and then as an enhanced activity (e.g., rise in real-estate prices), which actually reflects the capitalized accessibility benefit in the relevant market (real estate), and not an additional benefit caused by a positive externality. Below I demonstrate these issues by focusing on the two main effects—that project proponents most often claim when championing their position.[13]

10.3.2 Job Creation

Job creation has remained the most prominent argument touted to justify an infrastructure project.[14] As already mentioned, politicians, stakeholders and other decision-makers, when voicing their support for a project, freely allude to the number of jobs expected to be created in the course of its execution.[15] From a project analysis perspective, the key problem is how to actually measure and validate that number. The problem becomes even more acute when the expected jobs need to be categorized by type for long-term economic reasons, such as tax revenues and regional growth. After all, not every job is equivalent in this respect.

Analytically, specification of the functional relationships between a transportation investment and employment rests on two conditions: First, that the direction of causality is in the desired direction, that is, the investment generates jobs rather than the opposite, meaning that the increased employment raises the demand for travel and, in consequence, further transportation investments. Second, the actual presence of positive externalities in labor markets is waiting to be ignited by the improved accessibility and its translation into additional jobs.

Assuming these two conditions hold, how are we to measure job growth forecasts? One fundamental condition is that we differentiate between short-term and long-term employment. The former covers workers employed in the construction of the project, meaning that their employment lasts only until the project's completion. An outgrowth of short-term employment is associated with the so-called investment multiplier effect, implying that the funds invested engender further spending by their recipients. That spending generates additional economic activity (e.g., retail sales) and thus more jobs. However, it should not be forgotten that the bulk of this employment is sustained primarily during the project's construction due to the investment-related spending.

If the investment is financed wholly or partly by taxation, some of the related multiplier effects acquire the form of pure transfers from taxpayers to local residents. Additional economic gains are enjoyed by local businesses as increased purchases by residents in the project's vicinity shift their spending from other areas. However, if demand for local goods increases as a result of the investment funds infused, prices may go up, with the increases in producer surplus partially offset by a decline in consumer surplus (Berechman 2009, Chap. 13).

Long-term employment results, in contrast, from the reduction in market entry barriers, such as prohibitive travel costs. That is, employees who respond to the decline in travel times and costs find it economically advantageous to participate in labor markets that were previously regarded as inaccessible. This increased employment is considered long-term as the investment's primary benefits from accessibility last for many years.

The magnitude of short-term employment can be estimated in terms of the dollar amount of the investment and its economic multiplier. The same cannot be said of long-term employment. Assuming proper causality (transportation improvements encourage employment) and the existence of positive externalities in travel and labor markets, the estimation of long-term employment is quite intricate. It calls for specification of an econometric model that accounts for changes in accessibility engendered by the investment, and the consequent change in employment, by type, consequent to the changes in accessibility, all the while controlling for a range of socio-economic variables (Berechman and Paaswell 2001).[16]

Studies on the effect of transportation investments on economic development—mainly jobs and regional output—have produced a myriad of numerical results whose values depend on the region or country studied, the type of database and econometric model used, and the type of transportation infrastructure (rail, highway, etc.).[17] On the basis of these results, several general conclusions can be stated. First, long-term employment does not grow monotonically with the size of the investment. Depending on the transportation network in place and the region's stage of development at the time of the investment, employment tends to increase initially and then to taper off even if accessibility levels increase further (Banister and Berechman 2000; Berechman 2009, Chap. 13; Berechman et al. 2006). Second, other variables, mainly wage rates, level of education and type of household (e.g., single parent, two breadwinners), do a better job of explaining changes in labor market participation rates than does accessibility. Third, the empirical results reveal that some jobs are more responsive to changes in travel costs than are others. Retail jobs, for instance, are much more sensitive to these changes than are construction and transportation jobs.

Decision-makers should bear in mind that proponents of a project, when touting its anticipated employment benefits, often lump short- and long-term employment together. The figures they quote frequently represent short-term job growth because estimating long-term employment is either too intricate a task or, perhaps, may lead to contrary results. Decision-makers should therefore be aware that the figures presented may be misleading and not base their judgments primarily on such data.

Research has also indicated that substantial time lags separate implementation of an investment from its economic benefits. These often emerge three to five years subsequent to the investment's completion although changes in real-estate values especially (expressed in rising prices) may be observed prior to the investment's implementation in anticipation of future events.

Benefits can also spill over. Given the size and nature of the investment as well as the structure of the regional transportation network, development effects can be detected in areas far from the investment's site, meaning that different numerical results are obtained according to whether the analysis is conducted at regional or state scales versus county or municipal scales. Most importantly, local conditions—especially transportation level, regional income and employment—influence the nature and extent of the respective development benefits (Berechman et al. 2006).

10.3.3 Real-Estate Development

Like job creation, real-estate development is frequently used to rationalize an investment. The fact that transportation investments positively affect real-estate values and new construction has been substantiated by numerous studies,[18] with the rationale behind this phenomenon well-understood. The basic argument runs like this: reduced travel times improve relative accessibility to disparate locations, thus enhancing the consumer surplus to be gained. Improved accessibility is likewise capitalized in producer surpluses for residential and commercial real estate, which are further reflected in land and building values (Anas 1995). The subsequent rise in tax revenues is, of course, considered another, highly attractive benefit.

However, we should recall that assessments of changes in property values are performed *ex ante*, before any decision to invest is made. This raises several analytical and methodological questions regarding the use of changes in property values to assess a project's contribution to economic development. Hence, the choice of method used to estimate these values has become a crucial element in investment decision-making. The availability of methods for estimating future changes in property values must therefore be carefully considered. How can we account for the decline in values? And how can we avoid double counting the respective benefits?

The *hedonic price regression model* has become the main approach used throughout the industry to assess a transportation investment's effect on property values. The model requires regressing property values against their proximity, in km, to the planned facility, given property characteristics and type, location and neighborhood amenities.[19] The parameter estimates obtained provide indications of how the respective markets value accessibility, for example. A common result obtained with this model indicates that the values of properties located in areas having commuter rail tend to be about 10% higher than those of properties located in areas lacking this mode of rail stations (Armstrong and Rodrigues 2006).

Empirical studies have also shown that changes in property values are distributed in an uneven pattern across space. That is, the values of properties located very close to transportation facilities (e.g., transit terminals or railway stations) are typically quite lower than those of properties located at some distance away, mainly due to noise and traffic. While peaking at short distances, property values tend to diminish with distance, reflecting the increasing costs of access, demanding the use of other transport modes, such as automobiles, to reach the main transportation facility. When compared with their pre-project values, more-distant properties may verily experience a loss in value, an outcome of this intra-regional redistribution of demand for real estate. In contrast, the research results show that the values of commercial properties tend to peak near the transportation facility, although they, also, taper off with distance.[20]

These patterns raise difficulties in using changes in property values as an indicator of development benefits. To begin with, after modeling the values of properties in the relevant region, how can we balance the increase in value for some properties with the decline in value of others? Moreover, real-estate supply (e.g., the number of building permits) tends to grow in anticipation of increases in value. The net effect of this relationship is likely to be a rather small aggregate change in property values. Most studies nevertheless consider only those real-estate markets that are located near a new project, resulting in the over-estimation of the net capitalized value of the improved accessibility. Adding to these distortions are market imperfections, such as zoning regulations, which often prohibit high-density construction near transportation facilities.

Lastly, but most importantly, unless improved accessibility can be explicitly shown to overcome existing barriers to real-estate development, the use of improved property values per se amounts to the double-counting benefits occurring when travel time and cost savings accruing from the investment are capitalized in the form of higher property values, which are then treated as additional benefits and included in total investment calculations.

In daily reality, investment analysts rarely perform a meticulous *ex-ante* analysis for the purpose of more accurately estimating the future aggregate value of real estate. Similar to the observation made with respect to new employment figures, proponents of a project frequently float unsubstantiated real-estate values to reinforce their position. In the case of the

ARC project (footnote 14), advocates claimed that the increase in rail capacity would raise the value of homes within the train stations' vicinity by a total of $18 billion. And yet no one has ever demonstrated the credibility of this figure.

10.3.4 Economic Development and Decision-Making

If we accept the scenario of promoters using economic development to rationalize acceptance of their project, how frequent is this phenomenon and what is its actual impact on project decision-making? Figure 10.1, below, shows the findings of a review, conducted by Berechman and Paaswell (2005), of proposed transportation infrastructure investments in New York. This table indicates the prevalence of this practice by showing the Present Value (PV) of direct transportation benefits and of their development benefits both as percentages of the PV of each project's capital costs.

It immediately becomes evident that the PV of the economic development benefits from these projects, mainly jobs, real-estate expansion and tax revenues, by far exceed the primary transportation benefits that engendered

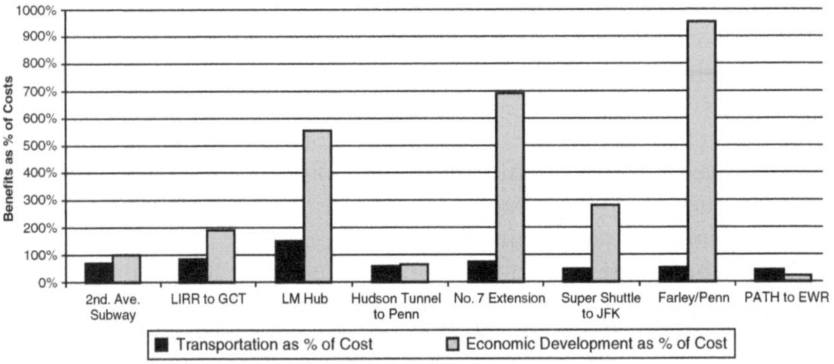

Fig. 10.1 Transportation and economic development benefits as percent of capital costs, by project (2002–2004). Present Values of benefits and costs. 2nd Ave. (Second Avenue Subway); LIRR to GCT (LIRR connection to Grand Central Station, East Side Access); LM Hub (Fulton Transit Center and Permanent PATH Station); Hudson Tunnel to Penn (Access to the Region's Core: NJ Hudson Tunnel); No. 7 Subway line extension; Super Shuttle to JFK (LIRR and/or JFK Access to Lower Manhattan); Farley/Penn (Penn Station and Farley Post Office); PATH to EWR (PATH Extension to Newark Airport). Source: Berechman and Paaswell (2005)

development in the first place. If the projects cited had been selected according to the aggregate size of their expected benefits, the economic rather than the transportation effects would have been considered the dominant choice criterion. However, would we want our choice of projects to be dictated by often only alleged development benefits rather than by the project's primary transportation benefits, those that motivated the project in the first place? In my view, the answer would be affirmative *no*.

10.4 Environmental Externalities

Many countries require an explicit analysis of anticipated environmental externalities when considering a transportation project. Such a study, known as an Environmental Impact Statement (EIS), implies that only projects meeting a mandated set of environmental criteria will be considered for implementation. In many places, preparation of the EIS thus frequently precedes preparation of the CBA, often by several years. Many consequently treat the EIS as a *pre-feasibility study*.

In response to current public opinion, government sensitivity to environmental effects and their heavy social costs has escalated, an attitude explaining why so many governments regard a positive EIS as a mandatory condition for project approval. Key categories of environmental externality costs include air pollution, noise, climate change, as well as effects on water, soil and human health. Infrastructure wear and tear, congestion and accidents costs may also be included. In the area of transportation, decision-makers should nevertheless consider a positive EIS as a necessary but not a sufficient condition for undertaking a project: An EIS-approved project may still produce insignificant transportation benefits.

The literature on the calculation of environmental costs is veritably voluminous (e.g., see Berechman 2009, Chap. 12; European Commission 2014; VTPI 2013). Its main objective is to estimate the magnitude of these costs by mode, location and trip type. Depending on data sources, year and method of analysis, the results may vary widely although they persistently amount to a significant percentage of a country's GDP. Quinet (1997), for example, using European data, reports that noise costs range from 0.02% to 2% of GDP. A 2000 European Union study estimated the external costs of transport to be about 8% of GDP in 1995 (INFRAS/IWW 2000). Delucchi (1998, 2000), using US data for the years 1990–1991, reports total external costs ranging from 1.9% to 13.9% of GDP.

Table 10.2 Full marginal costs, by category, for a trip distance of 9–15 miles (in $US)

Private (internalized) costs			*Infrastructure costs*	*Non-internalized externality costs*			
Operating	*Congestion*	*Accidents*	*Maintenance*	*Congestion*	*Accidents*	*Air pollution*	*Noise*
1.389	3.786	0.664	0.062	0.635	0.345	0.114	0.158

Source: Ozbay et al. (2001)

Another indication of a project's economic efficiency is captured by the marginal costs of an additional trip. Consider the results obtained by Ozbay et al. (2001, 2007) with respect to these costs for a peak-hour trip of 9–15 miles, which is average highway trip length in Northern New Jersey (see Table 10.2).

What these figures show is that private costs, the direct expenditures (e.g., fuel, toll) borne by auto users, in addition to the value of time spent in congested traffic, constitute the bulk of peak-time car trip costs. Among these, unpaid costs—namely environmental and accident externalities—amount to a significant proportion of total auto travel costs. These costs represent social costs, borne by society and normally not paid-for by users.

In light of the data provided above, and given the focus of this book, the subject of environmental externalities raises three key questions. First, since an EIS is, by and large, carried out long before a project is implemented, sometimes even years before, are the estimated externality effects still applicable to the project's final engineering design and travel properties? The answer is probably *no*. And yet, currently project analysis protocols do not stipulate the execution of an EIS proximate to the computation of its comprehensive CBA. Second, the environmental costs of a project are generally not internalized, with users paying neither directly nor indirectly for the external costs they produce. For example, motorists commonly do not pay for the pollution and noise caused by the additional fumes and noise cars emit in the wake of higher traffic volumes once road capacity has been expanded. When the project selection process does not account for these costs, suboptimal projects are likely to be implemented.

Lastly, how should environmental effects enter the decision-making process? Should they enter the calculation of a project's value and in what form? From a theoretical perspective, environmental impacts, like CBA results, should be part of the social welfare function that the project is assumed to optimize.[21] Yet, given the tangled project decision-making process, it remains unclear whether this is done. At present, EIS findings, if acceptable, serve mainly as a precondition for project funding rather than for project choice.

10.5 Conclusions

Like any other public service, the provision of transportation services through infrastructure investment is accompanied by efficiency, equity and externality effects. While the definition and measurement of a project's contribution to efficiency is relatively straightforwardly, that is not the case for equity. Equity estimation is far more complex, mainly due to the problem of arriving at an agreed-upon benchmark for fairness and, it follows, the equitable versus inequitable distribution of benefits and costs. Considering the intricacies of defining and measuring equity, it is no wonder that the analysis of equity is confined to delineation of the area over which project-induced changes in accessibility can be measured.

Equity and economic development, while prominent in the pronouncements of politicians and project proponents, are rarely properly analyzed, or measured, a failure preventing their use as criteria in project selection. Beyond the conceptual and technical issues, the main obstacle preventing their application is the difficulty of achieving a consensus among stakeholders on the level at which these effects become important. Complicating this feat is the fact that stakeholders often support, or oppose, a project based on what they view to be the potential influence of equity, economic and environmental results on their constituents. From a project's choice perspective, ascertaining its transportation-economic contribution should be a prerequisite when measuring a project's economic development externalities. But, as pointed out in Chap. 2, a significant number of standing mega-projects did not undergo such a comprehensive CBA.

Finally, due to the time lapse between analysis of a project's environmental effects and its final approval, travel and economic conditions may change. We must therefore conclude that at best, an EIS should be stipulated mainly as a precondition for a project's inclusion among the potential investment set but never as a substitute for a bona fide CBA. Unfortunately, international evidence demonstrates the contrary.

Notes

1. A dramatic manifestation of this struggle is found in Caro's (1974) seminal book on the massive transportation investments masterminded and championed by Robert Moses in mid-twentieth century New York.
2. But notice the difference between equity and income inequality. The former relates to the distribution of benefits from a project at a given location. The latter refers to the share of income, by income group, of total state income, resulting from a range of socio-economic, educational, monetary and fiscal factors.
3. On the theory of justice and equity, see Young (1994) and Sen (2010).
4. The field of public finance deals extensively with this issue. See for example (Gruber 2011, Chaps. 18 and 19).
5. Rawls' theory and inferences have been criticized extensively. Campbell and Marshall (2006), for example, question the tenet that free and equal citizens would choose the *original position* of equality behind the veil of ignorance. They added that even if this choice was made, could we assume that liberty would be prioritized or that a low-risk rather than a utilitarian option would be chosen?
6. More specifically, they correlated the relative welfare benefits from a project, measured as a percentage of regional GDP, with the region's GDP per capita.
7. For impacts on the carless, see Berechman and Paaswell (1975); for those on the elderly, see Wachs (1979).
8. They also report that in 2001, 75% of US low-income households (annual income under $20,000) used automobiles for their daily trips in comparison to the 4.6% who used transit. These figures are national averages. We should note that in metropolitan areas, the use of transit by low-income groups is significantly higher.
9. Transportation Minister Kevin Falcon, referring to a project planned for the Province of British Columbia, Canada (*The Vancouver Courier*, February 17, 2006).
10. The following quote is an interesting reminder that not everyone agrees to or accepts the economic development argument. Franklin Roosevelt (US President, 1933–1945) once said, "Refrain from claiming that public works create indirect jobs as a result of spending by construction workers" because he did not want to create the impression that the government could create prosperity by spending large amounts of borrowed money (William 2014).
11. We must also assume that the enhanced accessibility did not result from technological improvements because the external effects could not be attributed to the project per se but to the new technology. Installment of

Internet connections on existing transit modes can prompt economic development effects even without any accessibility improvements, such as travel time savings.

12. For most enterprises, transportation costs constitute only a small fraction of their total costs so that transportation infrastructure improvements will have only a small effect on their manufacturing or commercial performance. This necessitates accurate assessment of the impact of improved accessibility on market structure and behavior.
13. Travel safety, including a reduced rate of traffic accidents, is usually listed among a transportation project's primary benefits.
14. Consider the now-canceled Access to the Region's Core (ARC) project, a $9.8 billion commuter rail investment meant to connect New Jersey and Manhattan, which would have included a new tunnel under the Hudson River. Claims had been made that the ARC would generate 44,000 permanent jobs and 5700 construction jobs. Despite the strong support for the project, it was terminated by New Jersey's governor on political grounds.
15. The representative of Manhattan's East Side district claimed that the first phase of SAS, a $4.35 billion project, will create 16,000 jobs and generate $842 million in wages. The credibility of these figures remains unclear.
16. Another method is called the input-output model. It is based on accounting tables that establish links between economic sectors, using fixed coefficients to indicate the unit input contribution of one sector to the output of another sector (Batty 1976).
17. For such results, see Berechman (2009, Table 13.1).
18. For a survey of these studies, see Cervero and Duncan (2002), Hess and Almeida (2007) and Huang (1995).
19. A second modeling approach often used involves assessing the amount of new residential and commercial floor space that would be added in response to the investment. This method uses fixed coefficients to convert floor space into employment and income figures. Because the magnitudes of these coefficients are crucial, they are generally based on the observed floor space and employment densities found near other transportation facilities. However, unlike the hedonic model, this approach provides no credible way for statistically ascertaining the validity of its results.
20. For a review of the empirical residential and commercial literature, see Vessali (1996). For a case study of the effect of light rail transit on commercial properties, see Weinberger (2001).
21. This observation also holds for public private partnership projects when it is unclear as to who is responsible for the proprietary rights over emissions (Rouhani and Niemeier 2014).

References

Altshuler, A. 2013. Equity as a Factor in Surface Transportation Politics. *Access* 42: 2–9.

Altshuler, A., and D. Luberoff. 2003. *Megaprojects: The Changing Politics of Urban Public Investments*. Washington, DC: The Brooking Institute Press.

Anas, A. 1995. Capitalization of Urban Travel Improvements into Residential and Commercial Real Estate: Simulations with a Unified Model of Housing, Travel Mode and Shopping Choices. *Journal of Regional Science* 35: 351–375.

Armstrong, R., and D. Rodrigues. 2006. An Evaluation of the Accessibility Benefits of Commuter Rail in Eastern Massachusetts Using Spatial Price Function. *Transportation* 33 (1): 21–43.

Arthur, J., and W.H. Shaw. 1991. *Justice and Economic Distribution*. 2nd ed. Englewood Cliffs, NJ: Prentice-Hall.

Banister, D., and J. Berechman. 2000. *Transportation Investment and Economic Development*. London: University College London Press.

Batty, M. 1976. *Urban Modeling*. Cambridge: Cambridge University Press.

Berechman, J. 2009. *The Evaluation of Transportation Investment Projects*. New York: Routledge.

Berechman, L., D. Ozmen-Eretkin, and K. Ozbay. 2006. Empirical Analysis of Transportation Investment and Economic Development at State, County and Municipal Levels. *Transportation* 33 (6): 537–551.

Berechman, J., and R. Paaswell. 1975. The Urban Disadvantaged and the Search for Locational Opportunity. *Traffic Quarterly* 30 (1): 85–100.

———. 2001. Accessibility Improvements and Local Employment: An Empirical Analysis. *Journal of Transportation and Statistics* 4 (2/3): 49–66.

———. 2005. Evaluation, Prioritization and Selection of Transportation Investment Projects in New York City. *Transportation* 32 (3): 223–249.

Bröcker, J., A. Korzhenevych, and C. Schürman. 2010. Assessing Spatial Equity and Efficiency Impacts of Transport Infrastructure Projects. *Transportation Research B* 44: 795–811.

Campbell, H., and R. Marshall. 2006. Towards Justice in Planning: A Reappraisal. *European Planning Studies* 14 (2): 239–252.

Caro, R. 1974. *The Power Broker: Robert Moses and the Fall of New York*. New York: Random House.

Cervero, R., and M. Duncan. 2002. Benefits of Proximity to Rail on Housing Markets: Experience in Santa Clara County. *Journal of Public Transportation* 5 (1): 1–18.

Delucchi, M. 1998. *The Annualized Social Cost of Motor Vehicle Use in the United States, Based on 1990–1991 Data, UCD-ITS-RR-96-3*. Davis, CA: University of California, Institute of Transportation Studies.

———. 2000. Environmental Externalities of Motor-Vehicle Use in the U.S. *Journal of Transport Economics and Policy* 34: 135–168.

European Commission. 2014. *DG MOVE, 2014, Update of the Handbook on External Costs of Transport, Ricardo-AEA/R/ED57769* 1, 8 January.

Gruber, J. 2011. *Public Finance and Public Policy*. 3rd ed. New York: Wirth.

Hananel, R., and J. Berechman. 2016. Justice Theories and Transportation Project's Decision Criteria. *Transportation Policy* 49: 78–85.

Hartgen, D. 2013. Hubris or Humility? Accuracy Issues for the Next 50 Years of Travel Demand Modeling. *Transportation* 40 (6): 1133–1157.

Hess, D., and T. Almeida. 2007. Impact of Proximity to Light Rail Rapid Transit on Station-Area Property Values in Buffalo, New York. *Urban Studies* 5/6: 1041–1068.

Huang, W. 1995. *The Effects of Transportation Infrastructure on Nearby Property Values: A Review of the Literature*. Berkeley, CA: University of California, Institute of Urban and Regional Development.

INFRAS/IWW. 2000. *External Costs of Transport: Accident, Environmental and Congestion Costs in Western Europe*. Zürich/Karlsruhe, March. http://ecocalc-test.ecotransit.org/CE_Delft_4215_External_Costs_of_Transport_in_Europe_def.pdf.

Lakshmanan, T.R., and A.R. Chatterjee. 2005. Economic Consequences of Transport Improvements. *Access* 26: 28–33.

Levinson, D. 2002. Identifying Winners and Losers in Transportation. *Transportation Research Record* 1558: 24–24.

Manaugh, K., M. Badami, and A. El-Geneidy. 2015. Integrating Social Equity into Urban Transportation Planning: A Critical Evaluation of Equity Objectives and Measures in Transportation Plans in North America. *Transport Policy* 37: 267–276.

New York Times. 2012. Romer Christina, Do Manufacturers Need Special Treatment? February 4.

Nussbaum, Martha. 2006. *Frontiers of Justice*. Cambridge, MA: Harvard University Press.

Ozbay, K., B. Bartin, and J. Berechman. 2001. Estimation and Evaluation of Full Marginal Costs of Highway Transportation in New Jersey. *Journal of Transportation and Statistics* 4 (1): 81–104.

———. 2007. Alternative Methods for Estimation Full Marginal Costs of Highway Transportation. *Transportation Research A* 41 (8): 768–786.

Peters, L., and C. Gordon. 2008. Measuring the Equity Burden in Public Service Provision: The Case of New Jersey Toll Roads. *Economic Papers* 27 (4): 381–392.

Pucher, J., and J. Renne. 2003. Socioeconomics of Urban Travel: Evidence from the 2001 NHTS. *Transportation Quarterly* 57 (3): 49–77.

Quinet, E. 1997. Full Social Cost of Transportation in Europe. In *The Full Costs and Benefits of Transportation Contributions to Theory, Method and Measurement*, ed. D. Greene, D. Jones, and M. Delucchi, 69–111. Berlin: Springer.

Rawls, J. 1971. *A Theory of Justice*. Cambridge, MA: Harvard University Press.

Rouhani, O., and D. Niemeier. 2014. Resolving the Property Right of Transportation Emissions Through Public-Private Partnership. *Transportation Research D* 31: 48–60.

Sen, A. 1992. *Inequality Reexamined.* Oxford: Oxford University Press.

———. 2010. *The Idea of Justice.* London: Penguin.

Thomopoulos, N., S. Grant-Muller, and M. Tight. 2009. Incorporating Equity Considerations in Transport Infrastructure Evaluation: Current Practice and a Proposed Methodology. *Evaluation and Program Planning* 32: 351–359.

Van Wee, B., and K. Geurs. 2011. Discussing Equity and Social Exclusion in Accessibility Evaluations. *European Journal Transportation Infrastructure Research* 11 (4): 350–367.

The Vancouver Courier. 2006. Kevin Falcon comments on the Gateway Program (BC Highways). February 17.

Vessali, K. 1996. Land Use Impacts of Rapid Transit. *Berkeley Planning Journal* 11: 71–105.

Victoria Transport Policy Institute (VTPI). 2013. *Transport Costs Literature Review.* http://www.vtpi.org/tca/tca02.pdf.

Wachs, M. 1979. *Transportation for the Elderly: Changing Lifestyles-Changing Needs.* Berkeley, CA: University of California Press.

Weinberger, R. 2001. Light Rail Proximity Benefit or Detriment in the Case of Santa Clara County California. *Transportation Research Record* 1747: 104–113.

William, B. 2014. *American's Fiscal Constitution, Its Triumph and Collapse*, 539. New York: Public Affairs.

Winston, C., and V. Maheshri. 2007. On the Social Desirability of Urban Rail Transit Systems. *Journal of Urban Economics* 62: 362–382.

Young, H.P. 1994. *Equity: In Theory and Practice.* Princeton, NJ: Princeton University Press.

CHAPTER 11

Why Unworthy Mega-Projects?

11.1 Introduction

In Chap. 2, I presented estimates of the enormous resources that developed countries require to maintain, upgrade and expand their in-place transportation infrastructure systems. The data also showed that over time, only one-third to one-half of these needed resources are actually invested. Against this dismal picture one would expect that only the best welfare-contributing infrastructure projects would be selected for implementation. Yet, as demonstrated throughout this book, this is not the case. A significant number of the implemented transportation projects, especially mega-projects, display unacceptable *ex-ante* or *ex-post* transportation-economic properties: inferior economic performance, grossly missed schedules, way-off budgets and non-delivery of promised benefits. Furthermore, the formal requirement to conduct a Cost-Benefit Analysis (CBA) or one of its variants notwithstanding, the data show that few projects in developed countries have actually undergone a comprehensive CBA prior to their selection. This phenomenon is especially disturbing because it implies that, at least in these countries, a significant proportion of the scarce resources allocated to transportation infrastructure improvement are being misused or wasted.

Why is this occurring? Why do so many transportation infrastructure projects turn out to be unworthy or inferior relative to other investment alternatives, implying that they should have not been chosen in the first place? This is the dilemma confronted by this book. Its guiding question is,

J. Berechman, *The Infrastructure We Ride On*,
https://doi.org/10.1007/978-3-319-74606-7_11

therefore as follows: What is the underlying process that leads to the selection of inferior or unworthy transportation infrastructure investment projects?

The answer advanced in this book is that this reality represents the outcome of several factors, as detailed in previous chapters. We have thus reached the point where I can summarize key findings related to these factors and their impacts on project choice. Prior to doing so, however, I need to point out that among practitioners—especially engineers, planners and managers—the prevailing belief is that cost overruns, demand shortfalls and implementation delays are unavoidable. Without accepting them as inherent to project complexity, nothing much will ever be built.[1] To my mind, this way of thinking is seriously flawed: In addition to being misleading and thus dishonest, it ignores the immense opportunity costs associated with wasted resources. These costs come in the form of society's deprivation of needed goods and services, including effective transportation projects.

My key argument here is that the factors explored in this book, whether separately or in conjunction, adequately explain why inferior and unworthy projects are implemented. And yet, other explanations might also be valid. These range from the behavior of key decision-makers in an uncertain world, to deliberate manipulation for the sake of political gains, to project choice as the result of interactions between a group of stakeholders (as modeled by group choice theory).[2] I succinctly examine some of these arguments below, mainly in the form of the research questions engendered by these approaches. Before closing this chapter, I dwell on the question of what can be done to remedy this reality where unworthy and inferior mega-projects are executed.

11.2 Lessons Learned

Is there an observable choice pattern characterizing all transportation infrastructure investments? It might be argued that each project is idiosyncratic relative to spatial and network characteristics, engineering requirements and socio-economic attributes, which imply a choice process unique to each project, even if executed in the same country. However, the sketchy but verifiable information available on actual decision-making, worldwide, makes such an investigation highly improbable at this point. Yet, in terms of evaluation requirements and transportation-economic effects, all mega-projects, worthy or not, display similar attributes, particularly in the travel impacts they produce, such as accessibility and modal-use change, massive investment cost, changes in urban structure, environmental externalities and equity effects requiring public approval. These observations provided the rationale for the construction and empirical analysis of our mega-project dataset.

What, then, can we add to our understanding of the main factors influencing project choice and explaining the choice of unworthy investments? My answer, as elaborated in this book, was based on the critical assumption that fundamentally similar key elements, together with their interplay, enter into all transportation project decision-making but with varying degrees of impact, by case. These are depicted in the decision-making framework presented in Chap. 4 (Fig. 4.1). As this figure shows, all the enumerated factors operate within a political environment where political concerns (e.g., public opinion, political control and consensus-building) play a major role.

Chapter 5 analyzed the underlying causes that can bias the estimates of a project's costs and demand (e.g., future traffic). A particularly interesting finding is that the distributions of those estimates are not random. If cost and demand estimates were subject to random error, one would expect their normal (bell-shaped) distribution, where the likelihood of over- and under-estimated costs and demand were about equal. Yet, data on transportation mega-project cost and demand estimates show skewed distributions. Costs systematically tend to be under-estimated whereas demand tends to be over-estimated. Such results can imply deliberate manipulation by project proponents (see below) but, as the analysis in Chap. 5 demonstrates, flaws in the models and methods used by transportation analysts to derive these estimates may also explain such distortions. Partial or outdated data further contribute to these results.

To the extent that cost and demand estimates are used at all in project decision-making,[3] other factors were also revealed as influencing the choice of unworthy projects. A project's history, which for purposes of statistical analysis was defined as the time elapsed between a project's conception and its actual implementation, is such a factor (Chap. 6). On average, transportation mega-projects are conceived 20 years prior to their implementation, although longer periods, even 100 years or more, were recorded in a significant number of cases. While project history per se is not considered a decision factor, a long history facilitates public acceptance of the project by keeping it on the public agenda and transforming it into a *well-known must*. Hence, even if the problem that initially rationalized the project has long faded away due to transformations in land uses and developments in other transportation modes, a long history helps keep the project afloat. It can even prevent the performance of a comprehensive evaluation to ascertain the project's worthiness because its *need* is eventually perceived as a self-evident, *proven* truth.

Chapter 7 dealt with the issues surrounding the competition between transportation investments, especially mega-projects, for public funds and other resources as well as the multiple travel and non-travel effects they engender. This structure tends to prompt support or opposition to the project's effects by Special Interest Groups (SIGs). What, however, is the weight of SIGs among project choice factors? The conclusion reached in Chap. 7 is that opposition to projects centers on specific, often local, issues such as environmental nuisances, inequality effects and community cohesion. Funding, by mode (rail or highway) is found only second place when it comes to prompting opposition, especially when competing projects are involved, a situation often too complex to allow informed decision-making among average citizens. In all cases, opposition tends to prolong implementation, thereby raising project costs and construction time. However, unlike generalized community opposition, which tends to be vocal and quite visible, SIGs tend to operate behind the scenes, mustering political influence to advance their cause, be it pro or con, regarding a project.

The cliché stating that even the best project remains just an idea if funding is not secured is nevertheless limited in its application. What should interest us happens in the opposite situation, when securing funding becomes a necessary and sufficient condition for project implementation? In Chap. 8 I demonstrated that the impact of funding on project choice is often so consequential that a great deal of political capital is spent in its pursuit, irrespective of the project's actual transportation-economic value. Against a background of political commitments and legislative processes, funding, once obtained, renders a project *implementable*, regardless of its true contribution to public transportation needs. Confirmation of this process is found in our database of implemented, that is, funded projects. In other words, funding was acquired by all despite the fact that over half of these projects were never subjected to any CBA and about one-third of the remainder underwent only a partial CBA.

Turning to structural issues, the active participation of a large number of institutions in transportation planning and investment decisions has become a key feature of how major metropolises in developed countries make policy and implement infrastructure projects. This institutional network includes transportation agencies, operators, land-use planning organizations and neighboring local municipalities, each having its specific interests and agenda. They all vie for funding that commonly comes from same coffers while fervently protecting their own organizational interests, especially control over their spheres of influence. As argued in Chap. 9, for mega-projects extending over large areas and several jurisdictions, this reality intensifies the necessity for compromise. As a result, the projects selected tend to reflect the often fragile balance of interests and resources, implying that these projects are seldom the best or even worthy from a transportation-economic perspective.

In their attempts to promote a particular mega-project, politicians and transportation agency executives tend to emphasize its positive external benefits, with job creation, economic development and regional competitiveness in particular used to rationalize their choice. Research in various countries (see Chap. 10) has shown that such claims are, by and large, unsubstantiated, with the figures cited especially by politicians grossly inflated. Rarely is any distinction made between short- and long-run employment; double counting of benefits (e.g., improved accessibility and real-estate values) is also rather prevalent. Alleged equity in service provision is also frequently touted but here, again, there is little evidence that such considerations carry much weight in actual decision-making. To the degree that spatial and socio-economic distribution of benefits enters the choice equation at all, they appear in the form of benefits to the constituents living within the jurisdictions of the key politicians involved making choices.

Environmental effects nevertheless represent a different class of choice considerations. In developed countries, mega-projects are prohibited from harming environmental quality by law. Funding is often predicated on complying with sustainable environmental criteria such as clean air and water. Hence, environmental analyses are normally executed in the early stages of project planning and, should they show acceptable results, this factor ceases to affect the decision process. In many cases, however, environmental issues become the subject of disputes that, as shown earlier, prompt delays, cost overruns and sometimes project cancelation.

At this junction, when recalling the original question at the heart of this book—"Why are unworthy projects implemented?"—we need to consider what we are to make of all the responses provided here. Given the effects described and the inherent planning, the technical, economic, social and other complexities of mega-projects, one may conclude that nothing much can be done to alter the project choice process. We might expect that secured funding will always represent the necessary and sufficient conditions for project selection. Given the rivalry among agencies and stakeholders, the projects selected will undoubtedly represent negotiated compromises irrespective of their transportation-economic value. We can thus expect this reality to promote construction of *shovel-ready* projects, meaning projects that have gained expressed or tacit consensus, whose planning and engineering details have already been worked out (more or less), and have access to funding that can be spent immediately. Cost and demand estimates, whether biased or not, are consequently presumed to have a minor if any impact on project's choice. Given this scenario, cost overruns and demand under-utilization will remain *symptoms* of project unworthiness rather than factors guiding decision-making.

But should this depiction be regarded as a *fait accompli*, so solidly entrenched that no changes can be introduced? In a world where political agendas and a spate of influential organizations and stakeholders take part in decision-making, even if covertly, can steps be taken to ameliorate execution of unworthy transportation mega-projects? I shall take up this question in Sect. 11.7, below.

11.3 Decision-Making Entities

Those interested in contradicting the thesis advanced in this book might very well argue that it is a specific decision-maker who ultimately makes the final decision, that her assessment is directly responsible for the choice of inferior and unworthy projects. The rationale underlying this argument is that in many cases, project implementation requires the final approval of an identifiable individual, such as a mayor, governor or department minister, each of whom has particular objectives and works under specific constraints.[4] Although the identity of these factors may remain ambiguous or unknown to the public, we cannot assume that the decisions to implement or eliminate projects are made irrationally or haphazardly.

If we accept the tenets of the individual decision-maker approach, any empirical assessment of real-world practice would require a different research strategy than the one adopted in this book. First and foremost, we would need to identify the specific *decision-maker*, her objectives and situational constraints, her attitudes toward uncertainty and risk and, it follows, how she arrived at her final choice. Given the vast literature on decision-making (and its limitations) spawned in recent years, I merely highlight some of the key questions that pertain to the main issues of transportation mega-project choice.

I begin, however, with a qualification: While recognizing the potential merit of the identifiable decision-maker approach, I regard it as complementary to the theoretical framework and arguments advanced in this book. I use the word *complementary* in the sense that I conceive the explanatory factors analyzed in previous chapters as forming the fundamental set of constraints—the *feasibility set*—within which decision-makers must operate when reaching decisions. Given this stipulation, I begin by asking the following: In the realm of transportation mega-projects, what constitutes the *decision* to be made relative to its content and the locus of responsibility?

11.3.1 Nature of the Decision

As already noted, the availability of funding often becomes a necessary *and* sufficient condition for a project's acceptance and consequent realization. So, which of the two conditions—to fund or to implement—should be regarded the crucial decision? In what follows, I consider the union of these two acts as *the* decision. As the data show, they are often so interwoven within the project authorization process that it is largely impossible to specify which came first or which is more pivotal.

As demonstrated in the previous chapters, while transportation agency decision-makers are normally more involved in maintenance or expansion of existing infrastructure, in the world of mega-projects, the decision to invest in new systems is made predominately by national, state or regional decision-makers. Implementation decisions demand confrontation with a broader set of issues than those faced with respect to strict project worthiness. It includes guaranteeing a continuous flow of funding, overcoming opposition and garnering support.

Analysis of the dataset described in Chap. 4 shows that most project decision-making is conducted on the national level (70%), followed by the regional level (40%), transport agencies (23.3%), the local level (21.6%) and lastly, in terms of percentages, the international level (15%).[5] While these figures are based on data from a broad sample of countries having diverse decision-making frameworks, mega-project investment decisions across the globe tend to be subject to national-level decision-making and sources of funding.[6]

It is also important to remember that each level of government has its own motivations for the investment decisions it makes. I begin with the national level. First of all, it makes more sense for a national government to invest in very large transportation infrastructure projects when we consider the scale, network and environmental effects. Second, infrastructure may contribute to state and national competitiveness.[7] Third, national governments are, at times, more interested in providing equal access to transportation for socio-political rather than for transport-economic reasons. The extensive rail networks servicing rural areas in Europe or China attest to the verity of this observation. Fourth, national governments may be guided by international political-economic criteria and interests. Examples of such endeavors are the major European integration projects such as the Øresund Bridge linking Sweden and Denmark, or the German post-re-unification rail projects.

11.4 A Rational Choice?

In Fig. 4.1 (Chap. 4) the rubric *decision-making* is presented as a black-box into which the factors discussed in this book enter and an implementable project exits. While unable to pin down just how a decision was made in any particular case, the decision-maker approach requires that *decision-makers* make their choices in a rational manner.[8] The question I raise here is whether this assumption is realistic, at least in the sphere of transportation mega-projects.

11.4.1 Types of Decision-Making

Decision-making, in any sphere, cannot be reduced to one uniform or universal process. We can distinguish between several types of decision-making: (a) *dictatorial*, where self-interested individuals (say, top administrators) make decisions (e.g., how to split an endowment) while subordinate entities (whether lower-level agencies or professionals) adhere to that decision,[9] and (b) *circumstantial*, which implies escalation of prior commitments. In economic terms, continued investment in a project, even if leading to cost overruns, often results from large monetary or political sunk costs, as in the case of New York's Second Avenue Subway. Another type is (c) *predisposed* decision-making, where policy-makers make judgments on the basis of preconceptions embedded in the policy lexicon.[10] Here the role of project history may enter (see Chap. 6), implying that the historical perception of a project as *the* solution to transportation, economic, social and political needs remains intact even if it no longer responds to present-day needs. The phrase "Don't confuse me with the facts" captures this attitude when it comes to ascertain a project's continued appropriateness. The Tel Aviv Subway project, whose route alignment and station locations were designed years ago without revision to present needs, is an apt example. The last type is (d) *simplistic*, implying that decision-makers remain strong in their belief that complex issues can be solved by easy solutions. Shovel-ready investments are common manifestations of this approach.

11.4.2 Decision-Maker's Objectives

Assuming classic rationality, what possible objectives may a decision-maker entertain in the context of transportation mega-projects? Below I list the most-common key objectives, which may nonetheless be accompanied in a range of goals, covert as well as overt.

1. Political

(a) Garner advantages in the form of project costs that can be translated into political benefits, such as job creation
(b) Power: expansion of one's sphere of influence
(c) Control: ability to freely grant contracts and fill administrative positions

2. Economic

(a) Growth: job creation, real-estate development, tax revenues
(b) Enhance competitiveness on national and/or regional/state level

3. Legacy

(a) Ensure the decision-maker's place in history

These objectives are best attained through short-term projects, where benefits accrue in the foreseeable future and political and economic gains are quickly realized. If correct, this approach explains the tendency to favor ready-to-go type projects, irrespective of other preferable yet longer-term alternatives. As a corollary, the net transportation-economic value of short-term projects is generally downgraded in relevance, if considered at all. However, such projects do have the benefit of mitigating potential opposition by stakeholders and interest groups.

When applying rationality geared toward optimization, the decision-maker tries to maximize her objectives within the set of constraints identified in this book. For example, the accumulation of political power is often constrained by the power of other institutional stakeholders and the rivalry spawned by potential shifts in its allocation.

11.5 Biases in Decision-Making

In the last several decades, there has been an explosion of studies analyzing the behavioral biases affecting decision-making. Given space limitations, I merely mention here the core choice biases.[11] My guiding assumption is that similar behavioral biases afflict decision-makers facing mega-investment decisions as well.

I begin with the bias of exaggerated *optimism*, which causes a decision-maker to believe that she is subject to negative outcomes at lower levels of risk than are other individuals. Lovallo and Kahneman (2003) convincingly demonstrate how executives tend to believe that they are less exposed to losses than are their peers. Decision-makers suffering from this bias play down the risk of encountering significant delays and running over-budget. The dataset used in this book provides ample examples of projects chosen by overly optimistic decision-makers.

A second type of bias, known as *reference class*, comes into play when selecting the cases considered comparable to a particular project for the purpose of estimating the probability of a negative or positive event occurring. For example, Berechman and Chen (2011) computed the probability distribution of cost overruns based on several databases, each containing a large number of observations. However, unlike Berechman and Chen, decision-makers tend to use a small number of projects, generally those with which they may be familiar, to construct their reference set. By limiting the number of observations and the statistical validity of the results, these decision-makers often open themselves to the colossal cost overruns and demand under-utilization characterizing a significant proportion of transportation mega-projects.

Prospect theory is the third type of decision-making bias (Kahneman and Tversky 1979a). Put succinctly, when making decisions, people tend to base the potential value of a project's losses and gains on selected heuristics (experience-based problem-solving techniques) rather than on a systematic analysis of actual results. As our dataset demonstrates, decision-makers, by and large, tend to rely on heuristic assessment of a project's value, selected according to their experience and beliefs. This supports (or perhaps rationalizes) their penchant to avoid conducting a comprehensive and systematic CBA that might more accurately assess a transportation mega-project's relative benefits (gains) and costs (risks).

To summarize, if we accept the rational decision-maker premise to explain the choice of unworthy transportation mega-projects, we reach two key conclusions. First, the objectives of public sector decision-makers are mainly political in nature. Under such conditions, measurement of a project's value by referring to common transportation-economic criteria is liable to reveal that the project is inferior and unworthy. Second, a public sector decision-maker, like most decision-makers in every sphere, is subject to cognitive decision biases, a situation that can result in selecting undeserving investments.

11.5.1 Deliberate Deception and Manipulation

A different explanation to why inadequate projects are selected rests on the deliberate efforts of powerful individuals or advocacy coalitions to conceal the true values of a project's parameters. The most common instances involve politicians and other stakeholders intentionally under-estimating a project's costs and over-estimating its benefits in order to obtain federal funding (Flyvbjerg et al. 2009).

This can be accomplished in a variety of ways, ranging from the use of high- or low-end values of benefits and costs (e.g., modal split values or input prices), to the use of so-called policy variables such as the value of time assigned to various trip types, to the utilization of alleged high-level positive secondary benefits (jobs, real-estate development). We should also bear in mind that project evaluation is commonly performed by external consultants, who have vested interests in satisfying their clients, which they may do by accepting inflated projections and performing a CBA accordingly.

11.6 Group Decision-Making

In the previous sub-section I discussed the model of a single decision-maker who makes the final choice about approving or rejecting a mega-project. But what if the decision is to be made by a group of decision-makers, such as the board of a transportation agency? If the group is homogenous with respect to objectives as well as preferences over policy outcomes and risk, then the analysis of investment choices will be tantamount to equating the group's goals and constraints with the single decision-maker case. But what if this group is heterogeneous in their decision-related attributes? In this case, following Arrow's impossibility theorem (Arrow 1951), we would have a collective decision-making scenario that may not yield a single decision.

While Arrow's conclusion might be interpreted as *chaotic* in that it leads to no solution, in reality we observe that decisions, albeit non-optimal or inferior ones, are nonetheless made and implemented by groups. Two explanations of this phenomenon are possible. The first is known as *collective decision-making*, whereas the second is *dictatorial decision-making*, or as the *first among equals* (e.g., the mayor)[12] or as a *solo decision* made by a dominant decision-maker, irrespective of other group members' objectives and preferences.[13] It is often difficult to distinguish between these types of individuals since decision-makers generally prefer to obtain the approval of their peers and subordinates even though their lack of support would not have altered her decision.

Assuming collective decision-making, why is it that Arrow's theorem rarely holds? One plausible explanation is that group members do tend to share some common beliefs, thus restraining the degree of their heterogeneity. If this is indeed the case, we need to inquire into what these common attributes are. In the list below, I suggest some of the more crucial shared attributes.

1. Common framing of the problem or issue
2. Similar preferences, which can be translated into an identifiable common objective (e.g., under-ground metro over above-ground rail solutions)
3. Agreement regarding limits to tangible (e.g., funds) as well as intangible (e.g., political support) resources
4. Shared views of external dynamics, namely the pace of change and the path leading from *here* to *there*
5. Personality, especially the ability of the group's members to withstand pressure when imposing their agenda
6. Common assumptions regarding policy outcomes and their credibility
7. Openness to the information provided by technical analysts together with the ability to comprehend and interpret that information while recognizing its limitations
8. Common attitudes toward risk

If these attributes are indeed shared by all or most members of the group, group decision-making can indeed explain mega-project choice. And yet, when considering the issues and evidence presented in previous chapters, the likelihood of such an event—shared attributes—is rather scant. Alternatively, with respect to routine agency-initiated projects, such as maintenance and facility upgrading, group decision-making is more likely to occur.

11.7 What Can Be Done to Improve Mega-Project Choice?

This book has presented a bleak picture regarding the likelihood of selecting a worthy transportation mega-project in which to invest. My purpose for writing this book was not, however, to increase the pessimism surrounding project selection but to suggest some steps to be taken to ameliorate the unhappy outcomes of choosing unworthy projects. I begin by sketching what appear to be the constants characterizing the decision-making environment. I therefore consider it unlikely that political and funding realities will change, that inter-agency rivalry in metropolitan areas is here to stay, and that built-in estimation biases will remain part of any technical analysis. Against this background, some of the measures I suggest below require minor policy changes whereas others require significant transformations.

11.7.1 Statutory Project Evaluation

Comprehensive project evaluation is to become a formal and enforceable prerequisite for project approval and implementation. This condition demands that a comprehensive CBA be carried out as close as possible to the decision-making moment. It also requires that the quality of the analysis be evaluated by an external panel of independent experts. Most importantly, this stipulation must ensure that no project would be eligible for funding in the absence of a bona fide, approved evaluation.

11.7.2 Accountability

Forecasters and project analysts are to be made accountable for the data, methods and models they use, as well as for the accuracy of the published results.

11.7.3 Mandatory Risk Analysis

In general, a high Net Present Value (NPV) or a favorable Benefit-to-Cost (B/C) ratio do not guarantee a project's worthiness as both dimensions can be associated with high risk. Hence, a risk analysis, performed within the context of a comprehensive CBA, is mandatory if we are to improve project appraisal and choice. Given the lengthy planning time, mega-projects inherently reflect known and established technologies in the spheres of construction, travel modes, communication, search techniques (Global Positioning System [GPS]) and users' activity locations. A mandatory risk analysis is thus requisite for any consideration of the adjustments to be made to a plan's potentially outdated travel technologies and urban forms.[14]

11.7.4 Transparency

In the process of constructing the main database referred to in this book, it became apparent that crucial information about the projects had remained concealed from public eyes. In some instances, this occurred simply because a CBA had not been done while in others it reflected the CBA's unfavorable results. Introduction of transparency measures, such as mandatory uploading of all the project's relevant documents on the Internet, is expected to expose just how well the investment meets the relevant criteria and whether the decision-making leading to its acceptance was properly conducted.[15]

11.7.5 Centralization of Authority

The objective behind this measure is to create one agency that will evaluate and oversee all mega-projects in the same region or state, especially when funding comes from federal coffers. Not only will such a measure help take advantage of scale economies in planning and construction as well as avoid duplicity and waste, it will also ensure uniformity and consistency in project evaluation. That such a step is feasible was demonstrated by the UK when its Cabinet and Treasury joined forces in 2011 to establish a Major Projects Authority, with an enforceable mandate received directly from the prime minister to oversee and guide the management of all large-scale projects funded or implemented by the central government.[16]

11.7.6 Adequate Public Participation

Without significant public participation during assessment of a project's physical characteristics, such as location (mainly roads, rail tracks and stations), anticipated environmental nuisances such as noise and loss of green space, the likelihood of selecting unworthy public projects will remain constant. When citizens are uninformed and not engaged, public decision-making can become quixotic and arbitrary.[17] Furthermore, when people make decisions based on insufficient deliberation, they are more-easily influenced by superficial presentations, deceptive wording and irrelevant details.[18]

I do not mean to imply that the above list of measures is either exhaustive or readily implementable. Rather, the list is suggestive, meant to show what can be done to reduce the number of unworthy projects implemented. Considering the magnitude of resources invested in transportation mega-projects on the one hand, and the real needs such investments should fill on the other, the opportunity costs of building unworthy and poorly performing projects are indeed quite immense and must be taken into account.

Notes

1. Hirschman (1976) rationalized this phenomenon and called it the *Hidden Hand*. Flyvbjerg (2009) opposes this view and calls implementation of unworthy projects the *Survival of the Unfittest*.
2. See, for example, Flyvbjerg (2014), who regards the confluence of what he calls the *four sublimes* as key explanatory factors. These include the technological delight derived by planners and engineers from building large-scale innovative projects; political enhancement accruing to politicians who invite the projects meant to serve as their monuments; economic bliss in the form of financial gains to various stakeholders; and esthetic pleasure, derived by project designers.
3. "News that the Transbay Terminal is something like $300 million over budget should not come as a shock to anyone. We always knew the initial estimate was way under the real cost. Just like we never had a real cost for the [San Francisco] Central Subway, or the [San Francisco–Oakland] Bay Bridge or any other massive construction project. So get off it. In the world of civic projects, the first budget is really just a down payment. If people knew the real cost from the start, nothing would ever be approved. The idea is to get going. Start digging a hole and make it so big, there's no alternative to coming up with the money to fill it in." Willie Brown,

Assembly Speaker and Mayor of San Francisco, discussing a large cost overrun on the San Francisco Transbay Terminal mega-project in his *San Francisco Chronicle* column (July 27, 2013), quoted by Flyvbjerg (2014).

4. An example, already mentioned, of this reality is the Access to the Region's Core (ARC) rail project between New Jersey and New York's Penn Station, which included a tunnel to be built under the Hudson River. The budget was estimated to be $8.7 billion. Construction began in mid-2009 but the project was canceled in October 2010 by New Jersey's Governor Chris Christie, who cited cost overruns and the State's lack of funds.
5. There is some overlap between decision-making levels; hence, these figures do not add up to 100%.
6. Generally speaking, national-level decision-makers play more dominant roles in European countries, whereas sub-national levels predominate in project decisions within federal states. In the USA, transportation decision-making is characterized by fragmentation and devolution.
7. One example is the Alameda Corridor (Chap. 7), whose promoters successfully demonstrated to members of Congress the project's economic benefits accrued to the national economy as well as to the their districts.
8. In the sphere of economics, the concept of rationality has evolved over time from the optimal use of resources to maximization of a well-defined objective such as utility function subject to constraints, to compliance with a set of formal rules, such as consistency, completeness and transitivity of preferences, which define a rational choice.
9. Exemplified by the ARC rail project, cited in Note 4, this chapter.
10. The famed historian Barbara Tuchman once stated that, "When information is related to policy-makers, they respond in terms of what is already inside their heads and consequently make policy less to fit facts than to notions and intentions formed out of the mental baggage that has accumulated in their mind since childhood" (Tuchman 1981).
11. For more on these biases the reader is referred to the following: Kahneman and Tversky (1979a, b), Flyvbjerg et al. (2009), Kahneman (2011) and Viscusi and Gayer (2015).
12. It is believed that extension of the Number 7 subway in New York City (from 8th to 11th Avenue at 34th street) was decided by the city's sitting mayor at the time (Michael Blumberg). The city government began issuing bonds to fund the 1 mile, $2 billion project in November 2006.
13. Building a railroad to Eilat, Israel's southernmost city, involving about 260 km of electrified double-track rail, estimated at $8–10 billion, is a very complicated project to implement due to a range of engineering, economic, environmental and political factors. Over the last several decades, numerous expert committees and civil society groups (e.g., environmentalists) have concluded that the project is totally unworthy and even harmful. Nonetheless, Israel Katz, the current Minister of Transportation, backed

by Prime Minster Netanyahu and cabinet approval, has decided to take active measures toward the project's implementation (*Haaretz*, September 21, 2014).

14. For example, various forms of computer applications are becoming available that allow, in real-time, shared-ride travel. These are expected to gradually assume a significant proportion of metropolitan transit travel.
15. In the Netherlands, the Parliamentary Committee on Infrastructure Projects held extensive public hearings to identify measures to reduce the misinformation about proposed major infrastructure projects (Dutch Commission on Infrastructure Projects 2004).
16. An additional benefit emanating from such an authority is the curbing of optimism bias. To illustrate, the UK's Treasury now requires that all government ministries develop and implement procedures to curb such bias with respect to mega-projects (Flyvbjerg 2006). One such measure is the prohibition against funding projects that do not take optimism bias into account (UK Department for Transport 2006).
17. The He et al. (2016) study of public participation with respect to high-speed rail projects in China shows how the lack of adequate public involvement resulted in welfare losses and planning errors.
18. Manipulative framing is a major tool used by politicians to influence decisions (Robert Shiller, Economic View, *New York Times*, September 2, 2012).

References

Arrow, K. 1951. *Social Choice and Individual Values*. New York: Wiley.

Berechman, J., and L. Chen. 2011. Incorporating Risk of Cost Overruns in Transportation Capital Project Decision Making. *Journal of Transport Economics and Policy* 45 (1): 83–104.

Dutch Commission on Infrastructure Projects. 2004.

Flyvbjerg, B. 2006. Design by Deception: The Politics of Megaproject Approval. In *Urban Planning Today*, ed. William S. Saunders, 131–148. Minneapolis: University of Minnesota Press.

———. 2009. Survival of the Unfittest: Why the Worse Infrastructure Gets Built, and What We Can Do About It. *Oxford Review of Economics Policy* 25 (3): 344–367.

———. 2014. What You Should Know About Megaprojects and Why: An Overview. *Project Management* 45 (2): 6–19.

Flyvbjerg, B., B. Garbuio, and D. Lovallo. 2009. Delusion and Deception in Large Infrastructure Projects: Two Models for Explaining and Preventing Executive Disaster. *California Management Review* 51 (2): 170–193.

Haaretz. 2014. Israel Approves Controversial Rail Route to Eilat. September 21. http://www.haaretz.com/news/national/1.550777.

He, G., A. Mol, and Y. Lu. 2016. Public Protest Against the Beijing-Shenyang High Speed Rail in China. *Transportation Research D* 43: 1–16.

Hirschman, A.O. 1976. *Development Projects Observed*. Washington, DC: The Brooking Institution Press.

Kahneman, D. 2011. *Thinking, Fast and Slow*. New York: Farrar, Straus and Giroux.

Kahneman, D., and A. Tversky. 1979a. Prospect Theory: An Analysis of Decisions Under Risk. *Econometrica* 47: 313–327.

———. 1979b. Intuitive Prediction: Biases and Corrective Procedures. In *Studies in the Management Sciences: Forecasting*, ed. S. Makridakis and S.C. Wheelwright, vol. 12, 313–327. Amsterdam: North Holland.

Lovallo, D., and D. Kahneman. 2003. Delusions of Success: How Optimism Undermines Executives' Decisions. *Harvard Business Review* 81: 56–63.

Tuchman, B. 1981. *Practicing History*, 287–293. New York: Alfred Knoff.

UK Department for Transport. 2006. *The Estimation and Treatment of Scheme Costs: Transport Analysis Guidance*. TAG Unit 3.5.9. http://www.dft.gov.uk/webtag/documents/expert/unit3.5.9.php.

Viscusi, W.K., and T. Gayer. 2015. Behavioral Public Choice: The Behavioral Paradox of Government Policy. *Harvard Journal of Law and Public Policy* 38: 973–1007.

Author Index[1]

[1] Note: Page numbers followed by 'n' refer to notes.

J. Berechman, *The Infrastructure We Ride On*,
https://doi.org/10.1007/978-3-319-74606-7

Subject Index[1]

[1] Note: Page numbers followed by 'n' refer to notes.

J. Berechman, *The Infrastructure We Ride On*,
https://doi.org/10.1007/978-3-319-74606-7

The manufacturer's authorised representative in the EU is Springer Nature Customer Service Centre GmbH, Europaplatz 3, 69115 Heidelberg, Germany. If you have any concerns regarding our products, please contact ProductSafety@springernature.com

Printed and bound by CPI Group (UK) Ltd, Croydon, CR0 4YY
30/09/2026
02225660-0003